Paul

His Story

Jerome Murphy-O'Connor

OXFORD UNIVERSITY PRESS · OXFORD

OXFORD

UNIVERSITY PRESS

Great Clarendon Street, Oxford OX2 6DP

Oxford University Press is a department of the University of Oxford.
It furthers the University's objective of excellence in research, scholarship,
and education by publishing worldwide in

Oxford New York

Auckland Cape Town Dar es Salaam Hong Kong Karachi
Kuala Lumpur Madrid Melbourne Mexico City Nairobi
New Delhi Shanghai Taipei Toronto

With offices in

Argentina Austria Brazil Chile Czech Republic France Greece
Guatemala Hungary Italy Japan Poland Portugal Singapore
South Korea Switzerland Thailand Turkey Ukraine Vietnam

Oxford is a registered trade mark of Oxford University Press
in the UK and in certain other countries

Published in the United States
by Oxford University Press Inc., New York

British Library Cataloguing in Publication Data
Data available

Library of Congress Cataloging in Publication Data
Data available

Typeset by Newgen Imaging Systems (P) Ltd., Chennai, India
Printed in Great Britain
on acid-free paper by
Ashford Colour Press Limited, Gosport, Hampshire

ISBN 0–19–926653–0   978–0–19–926653–1
ISBN 0–19–928384–2 (Pbk.)   978–0–19–928384–2 (Pbk.)

1 3 5 7 9 10 8 6 4 2

For

DAVID and CATHERINE MANNING
Who Asked for the Story

and

DECLAN and EMER MEAGHER
Who Ensured that I Survived to Write It

Preface

THE writing of this book was a wonderful adventure in attempting to transform a life into a story. There are many lives of Paul of Tarsus, but all of them are content to highlight the points that can be established with a degree of probability. The focus is on the arguments that sustain the conclusions, and the 'facts' that come to light are presented as trophies in splendid isolation. The very nature of the process ensures that Paul can never emerge as a vital personality. Certain things are discovered about him, but he is not *seen* as a distinctive individual. In most instances he comes across essentially as a disembodied mind from which pour theological ideas.

In *Paul: A Critical Life* (Oxford: Clarendon Press, 1996), I wrote just such a book. What made it different from the others was the weight I gave to the letters as the prime source of biographical material. The result was the outline of a life, which not only differed at crucial points from that elaborated by Luke in the Acts of the Apostles, but was much more detailed. All the points established there are taken for granted here without further documentation: namely, the chronology of Paul's life, his relations with his foundations, the problems he faced in various situations, the composite character of certain letters, etc.

I now see these 'facts' as the parts of a skeleton. It is well preserved. The skull and all the bones are there. They have been measured and defined. They are strong and weight-bearing. But they do not move. In this book I want to make these bones live by clothing them with flesh, and infusing them with the breath of life. Paul has to become the hero of a story.

Thus I reconstruct his life in sufficient detail to give it consistency and colour, and recount the events in chronological order. A strong narrative line is the only way to give a sense of Paul as a person. Inevitably, much is hypothetical and imaginative. In every case, however, the underlying hypothesis is the most probable one, and my imagination is controlled by contemporary sources and monuments, and by my own experiences in the places that Paul visited.

Unlike Luke, I put no speeches in Paul's mouth, but I do concern myself with what Paul might have thought and felt. The control here is simple common sense. He must have worked things out before he made decisions. Thus I have him sift possibilities, often in the context of a journey towards a new situation. He could be impetuous and rush into disastrous errors in strategy or tactics. In such cases I try to explain why things went wrong, and how he worked to avoid the same mistakes in the future.

I assume also that Paul was normal in his response to external stimuli. Thus, since I was moved by the extraordinary beauty of Mount Casius at dawn, I presume that Paul's heart also lifted at the sight as he tramped south out of Antioch-on-the-Orontes. I would have been astounded at the main street in Pessinus, which was built in a river bed and by design filled with water in heavy rain, so I imagine that Paul often scratched his head in amazement during the winter he spent with the Galatians. It was not the way they did things back home in Antioch! The Celts were really very odd.

One feature of this book is the emphasis I give to times and distances. These are scaled from the *Barrington Atlas of the Greek and Roman World* (Princeton: Princeton University Press, 2000), to which I give references wherever possible. Its scale is so large, and the maps so beautifully drawn and coloured, that one can virtually see the terrain through which Paul is travelling. My purpose is to remind the reader that everything took a lot longer in Paul's day. We need to slow down radically if we are to appreciate the rhythm of his life. We tend to imagine that travel and communications were just somewhat slower than today. In fact, there was a huge quantitative difference, which had a great impact on the quality of communication.

Only when we realize that Paul, or one of his letter-carriers, was lucky to average 20 miles (32 km) a day—a figure which takes into account sickness, injury, bad weather, rumours of bandits or wolves on the road, or the need to wait for a caravan that would provide some measure of security—can we understand 'the daily pressure on me of my anxiety for all the churches' (2 Cor. 11: 28). Letters took weeks, if not months, to reach their destination. Paul was out of touch with his converts most of the time, even when they were in greatest need of him. To say that frustration and apprehension ate at his soul is legitimate interpretation, not gratuitous imagining. And when information did arrive, his feelings inevitably coloured his response.

This is but one illustration of how I exploit details in his letters in order to reveal what was going on inside Paul. His emotions were very close to the surface. The swiftness of the mood swings in chapter 4 of 1 Corinthians is extraordinary. Reasonable moderation (vv. 1–6) gives way to savage sarcasm (vv. 7–10), which is replaced by brave self-pity (vv. 11–13), which becomes anxious affection (vv. 14–17), and explodes into heated warnings (vv. 18–21). There are many such clues to Paul's feelings. Yet they have never been systematically followed up. We get to know Paul's character, however, by discovering what made him exhilarated or depressed, concerned or indifferent, carefree or frightened. His emotions were as much part of his personality as his intelligence, and the two were in continuous interaction. He was anything but the passionless thinker that mainstream scholarship has made him out to be.

In order to avoid slipping into the genre of the historical novel, I have not created highly *specific* situations or imagined dialogue. I do not have Paul start up, his face alight with anticipation, at the knock on the door that might herald the long-delayed arrival of Timothy from Thessalonica. Nor do I put words in the mouths of Peter and Paul when they talked about Jesus in Jerusalem, or when they violently debated the rights and wrongs of eating with Gentiles at Antioch. To go into such specific detail, I feel, would be illegitimate use of historical imagination in this sort of book, because no control is possible.

The *typical* is another matter entirely. One first-century boat, road or inn was very much like another, and we have a mass of contemporary data on which to base a vivid picture of a voyage, a journey or a night at an inn. In such instances, the imagination is under tight control. It is inventive only to the extent that it generalizes and colours individual historical experiences.

There are a number of reasons for the complete absence of footnotes. The most obvious one is that I am telling a story, not writing a treatise. I have much more experience of the latter than the former, and I feared that my intention would be corrupted if I adopted a familiar literary form. Footnotes not only subconsciously affect the writing of the text; they send the wrong signal to readers who have been promised a story. They hint at a detached internal dialogue with colleagues or awkward data, whereas story-tellers should be absorbed in their characters. The opportunity for distraction is not appreciated by those who want to be caught up into the story. However, for those who desperately want to know the justification for the principal options, I have included a series of endnotes.

Throughout my academic career I have worked on many aspects of Paul's life and theology, but the attempt to distill that refined knowledge into a story brought me to insights that I had never anticipated. Paul is now more real to me as a person, and more intelligible as a theologian. I can only wish the same for my readers.

Jerome Murphy-O'Connor, OP.

1 January 2003

Contents

Contents

Contents

List of Figures

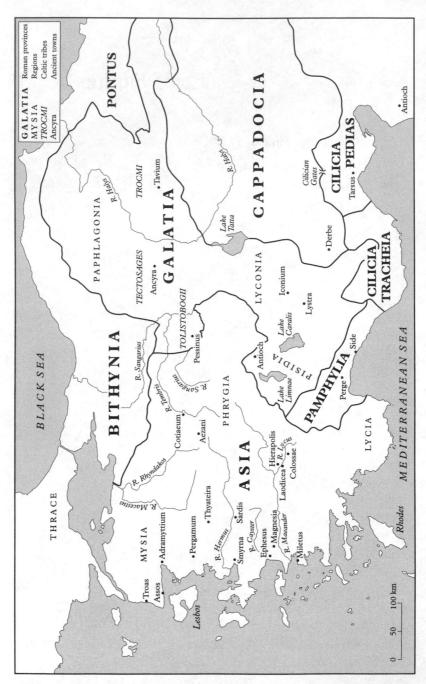

FIG. 1 Asia Minor at the Time of Paul (*Source: Tübinger Atlas des Vorderen Orients, BV7, copyright Dr Ludnig Reichert Verlag, Weisbader.*)

The Early Years   1

PAUL was proud of his heritage. He boasts of it twice. He wrote to the Philippians, 'If anyone thinks he has reason for confidence in the flesh, I have more:

circumcised on the eighth day
of the people of Israel
of the tribe of Benjamin
a Hebrew born of Hebrews
as to the law a Pharisee' (3: 4–5).

In 2 Corinthians he contrasts himself with his opponents. 'But whatever anyone dares to boast of—I am speaking as a fool—I also dare to boast of that.

Are they Hebrews? So am I!
Are they Israelites? So am I!
Are they the seed of Abraham? So am I!' (11: 21–2).

In both of these texts Paul claims to be not merely an 'Israelite' but a 'Hebrew'. The two words overlap to a considerable extent, and both were widely used at the time of Paul to identify a Jew. But when they are used together, as here, it must be because one is considered to add a further specification to the other.

In opposition to 'Israelite', which has only the one obvious meaning, 'Hebrew' is often used in the New Testament to mean the language spoken by Jews in Palestine. Luke, for example, depicts Paul as speaking to the Jerusalem crowd 'in the Hebrew language' (Acts 22: 2), while

John gives us a series of Hebrew place-names in Jerusalem. Hebrew, however, was little spoken, and at least one word that John identifies as Hebrew is in fact Aramaic (John 19: 13), which was the dominant language in Palestine in the first century. Clearly 'Hebrew' was commonly used to mean Aramaic, an extremely close cognate language.

Paul, therefore, is claiming with pride to be an Aramaic-speaking Jew who had inherited the language from his parents. The immediate inference is that the family was of Palestinian origin, because Jews who lived outside the Holy Land had no need of Aramaic. They used whatever local dialect was necessary for daily contact, and spoke Greek in order to communicate with a wider world. The Hebrew Bible had to be translated into Greek for Jews of the Diaspora.

Galilee

Paul was a Galilean by birth.[1] His parents lived in Gischala (modern Jish), a village in the mountains of Upper Galilee that was famed for the quality of its olive oil. Paul would have been about two years old in 4 BC when the tranquil life of his parents was brutally disrupted.

King Herod the Great died that year, and the country exploded. His people had hated him, and when he passed beyond their reach, they turned against his sons. These, however, had the backing of Rome, and to impose peace, Varus, the governor of Syria, twice brought his legions into Palestine. On his second expedition he destroyed Sepphoris, the capital of Galilee.

It was standard Roman practice to make the vanquished pay for their defeat. This could have been done in various ways, but they opted for the simplest and most efficient one. They took prisoners, not just combatants, but also from the general population, and sold them abroad as slaves. Paul's parents were unlucky, and were taken by one of the Roman search parties that fanned out across Galilee when the uprising had been crushed.

Before returning to their base at Antioch-on-the-Orontes (modern Antakya in southern Turkey), the legions would have sold their captives to the omnipresent slave-traders who shipped slaves all over the Mediterranean. After all, they were just another commodity, like wine and fish paste, to be brought to where demand was greatest. In the huge island market of Delos 10,000 slaves were traded in a single day. Paul's parents and their baby probably sailed out of Ptolemais (modern Akko in northern Israel). As they watched the green mountains fade in the distance, they could hardly know that they were destined to end up in the shadow of much higher mountains, the Taurus range in south-eastern Turkey.

Tarsus

Their new home was Tarsus, the capital of the Roman province of Cilicia Pedias.[2] Located 10 miles inland on the River Cydnus, it had a history stretching back 4,000 years. It lay on one of the great trade routes of the ancient world linking Syria and points further east with Asia Minor and the Aegean. The surrounding well-watered fertile plain grew cereals and grapes and, above all, flax, which provided the raw material for the major industry of the region, the production of linen. More characteristic was the felt cloth made from the wool of the black goats that roamed the fringes of the Taurus. It was so specific that it took its name *cilicium* from the region.

Since the native inhabitants did not exploit to the full the economic potential of Tarsus, Greek and Jewish colonists were brought in by the Seleucids of Syria in the second century BC, when they gave Tarsus the status of a Greek city-state. This mixture of East and West was to remain one of the abiding characteristics of the city. It was so impressed by Julius Caesar, who visited in 47 BC, that the city changed its name to Juliopolis, yet women continued to wear the all-enveloping oriental chador well into the second century AD.

Absorbed into the Roman system when Pompey reorganized Asia Minor in 63 BC, it was governed by officials of the caliber of the great orator Cicero (51–50 BC). Mark Antony rewarded its loyalty to the memory of Julius Caesar after his assassination in 44 BC by granting it freedom and immunity from imperial taxation. This rare privilege

3

for a city that was not a Roman colony was confirmed by Octavian, the future emperor Augustus, after his defeat of Mark Antony at the battle of Actium in 31 BC.

Such consistent Roman interest in Tarsus certainly implies that Roman citizenship was conferred at least on the leading personalities. As their families grew, the number of Roman citizens increased proportionally. This is important in that it offers the simplest explanation of Paul's inherited Roman citizenship (Acts 22: 27–8). Paul's parents would have been bought by a Roman citizen in Tarsus, and would have automatically acquired Roman citizenship when he set them free.

There is no way of knowing how old Paul was when this happened. In fact, we have no certain knowledge of his childhood. Two things, however, can be inferred. First, his parents must have been in easy circumstances when he reached his teens, because he exhibits a snobbish leisured class attitude towards manual labour. He regards it as 'slavish' (1 Cor. 9: 19) and 'demeaning' (2 Cor. 11: 7). Those bred to be artisans spoke of their craft with pride, and often had it inscribed on their tombstones.

Second, Paul's letters show that he had an excellent education, both religious and secular. This was an expensive privilege, and was not available to the vast majority of Jews. Someone, presumably his parents, had to pay for it, and study demands leisure. Paul clearly did not have to go to work either as a child or as a young man.

Education

As regards Paul's religious education, he knew the Greek translation of the Hebrew Scriptures very well.[3] He quotes it almost ninety times, and there are many other allusions and echoes in his letters. The way in which he handles the sacred writings of his people betrays the profound familiarity that results from frequent contact. It must have been a feature of his home life that was reinforced by attendance at the synagogue. He remembered the texts because he was convinced that the Scriptures were speaking to him personally. They were a voice, not of the past, but of the present. This revelation of God's care evoked a love which enabled Paul to use the Scriptures with a freedom that is often inexplicable to us. Even though he subsequently abandoned the Law of Moses as a rule of life, he never lost the sense of the Scriptures as God's communication with his people.

The quality of Paul's secular education is manifest not only in his command of Greek, but in the way in which he organized the content of his letters. He was not a stylist, but he wrote a vigorous Greek that betrayed his emotions as it conveyed his thoughts. His mastery of the figures of style, and the rhetorical structure of his letters, can only have been the fruit of serious study and long practice. His grasp of the principles of persuasive presentation was so sure that he could even parody them.

One example will have to suffice. When speaking in one's own defence, the standard technique was to enumerate one's achievements in ascending order so as to climax with the greatest success. When Paul is defending himself against the criticisms of his enemies at Corinth, he turns this technique on its head. He lists his failures, culminating in his most humiliating experience. He was dropped over the walls of Damascus like a little baby in a basket (2 Cor. 11: 32–3)! No one who had merely picked up the rudiments of rhetoric in a casual way would have attempted this artistic *tour de force*. He was a trained expert in the field that led to social promotion in the Graeco-Roman world. Moreover, the sophisticated philosophical ideas encountered in Paul's treatment of the resurrection in 1 Corinthians 15 could not have been learned in casual conversations. He must have received some philosophical training.

If home and synagogue explain Paul's religious education, where did he get his secular education? The simplest answer is that he went to the University of Tarsus. As befitted a city with a great thirst for education, in the first century this great institution of learning ranked beside those of Athens and Alexandria, the pre-eminent graduate schools of antiquity. Its schools of rhetoric were especially well known. Many of those who studied in Tarsus went abroad in search of further knowledge, and made their careers in other lands. A prime example was Athenodorus of Tarsus, who became an eminent Stoic philosopher and a friend of the great defence lawyer Cicero and of Strabo the geographer. He served the emperor

Augustus in Rome as a court philosopher, and was sent by him to govern Tarsus after the fall of Mark Antony.

Inevitably, the University of Tarsus became a bastion of Stoicism, and Paul could hardly have escaped its influence even if he did not study it. Certainly traces of it surface in his letters. The basic tenets of the system were simple.[4] Whatever happens does so in accordance with divine reason. Wisdom is the acceptance of this truth, and virtue consists in striving to live in harmony with divine reason. The wise, therefore, simply acquiesce in whatever happens to them. All external circumstances are indifferent and irrelevant. In consequence, it is a lack of virtue to protest against pain, poverty, injustice, death. None the less, human action is rooted in freedom, and one is responsible for one's deeds. Since everyone possesses a spark of the divine reason, distinctions between Greek and barbarian, master and slave, are meaningless. All belong to a universal brotherhood.

These were heady ideas for idealistic young men, but Paul could not subscribe to them completely. As a Jew he believed that he belonged to a unique people, set apart from all others. The Law of Moses under which he lived reinforced that fundamental belief by effectively separating Jews from Gentiles through the application of the dietary laws. These made social intercourse between Jews and Gentiles impossible, unless the latter accepted the severe conditions laid down by the former as to what could and could not be eaten.

Paul, like any Jew who attempted to live in both the Jewish and the Gentile worlds, experienced continuous tension between conflicting demands. It would be surprising if he had not developed a rather ambivalent attitude to the Law of Moses. On the one hand, it cut him off from full participation in the activities of his fellow students. He could not even share a drink of wine with pagan friends unless he brought the bottle. But on the other hand, the Law was a source of pride that grounded his identity. It was what held Jews together in an alien world. Compromise was not possible. He could not opt to observe merely a selection of the 613 precepts of the Law. It was all or nothing. Paul had to immerse himself in the Jewish world, or else abandon it completely and live like a pagan. He opted for the first, and headed for Jerusalem.

Going up to Jerusalem

Since the four-year course in rhetoric normally terminated when the student was 19 or 20, Paul would have been just out of his teens when he set out for Jerusalem, probably around AD 15. He did not know it, but this was to be the first of many journeys.

In principle he had two options. He could travel by land or by sea. To take passage on one of the many trading ships that worked their way up and down the coast would have been the most comfortable and the most secure. His feet would not get tired, and he would be out of reach of brigands. This option cannot be excluded, but what we know of Paul's ardent temperament makes it improbable. He would have wanted to arrive in Jerusalem under the most ideal conditions—that is, as a Passover pilgrim. And pilgrims walked.

We should imagine a rather nervously excited young man joining a group of Jewish pilgrims from Cilicia, which had a home synagogue in Jerusalem (Acts 6: 9). Jerusalem was just over 500 miles (800 km) away, and he could look forward to about six weeks on the road.[5] Passover can fall anywhere between the middle of March and the end of April. An early date would have imposed extra hardship on the pilgrims, because February is the middle of the rainy season. Travel would have been uncomfortable, but far from impossible. The road across the plain of Cilicia might have been muddy, but the altitude of the one pass through the Amanus mountains, the Syrian Gates, was only 500 feet (154 m).

Once out of the pass, Antioch-on-the-Orontes was only a good day's march away. It was the capital of Roman Syria, and one of the most splendid cities of the East. There was no time to admire it, however; the faces of the pilgrims were set towards Jerusalem. Paul could not have envisaged that a quarter of a century into the future it would be his home base for a number of years.

The pilgrims' journey over the mountains to the south of Antioch was lightened by the pleasure given by the splendid breast-shape of Mount Casius (modern Jebel al-Aqra, 5,616 ft; 1,728 m) out to the west. Its extraordinary aura had made it a sacred mountain for both Phoenicians and Greeks. From the time the pilgrims reached the

7

coast at Laodicea (modern Latakia), they had only to follow the highway down the narrow coastal plain with the continuous sound of the sea on their right.

Their hearts swelled with pride as they followed the arches of the aqueduct to the north gate of Caesarea Maritima. Then only 25 years old, it was the supreme secular building achievement of Herod the Great. Its grid pattern of wide streets and its gleaming monuments (theatre, stadium, temple) were familiar to them from the Graeco-Roman cities they knew. But here they were the creation of a *Jewish king*, who in addition had built a harbour second to none. Did Paul recall that Herod's death was the occasion of his parents being forced into exile?

From Caesarea it was an easy two-day walk to Jerusalem. The most likely road was also the most ancient. The ascent of Beth Horon was the route followed by Joshua over a thousand years earlier when he chased the coalition of the five kings from Gibeon (Joshua 10). Coming down from the north, pilgrims on this route would have been only a couple of miles from the city when they first saw it. Poetically, Jerusalem is a city set on a mountain. In reality, it is surrounded by higher hills.

The pilgrims would have immediately identified the Temple on the eastern side of the city. The smoke rising from the altar of sacrifice would have directed their attention to the characteristic shape of the holy of holies, just visible to the left of the brooding mass of the Antonia fortress. If they wondered about the building with three immense towers on the opposite side of the city, they would soon have learnt that it was the palace built by Herod the Great, but now the seat of the Roman governor when he came up from Caesarea.

The instinct of the pilgrims would have been to go immediately to the Temple, but it was forbidden to enter there with a staff, rucksack, sandals or the dust of a journey. They had first to find accommodation where they could leave their gear and tidy up. That would have been no easy task at Passover, when pilgrims from all over the world outnumbered the inhabitants of Jerusalem by as much as three to one. Only the rich could afford lodgings in the city. Poorer pilgrims had to camp out to the north of the city or on the slopes of the

Mount of Olives if they failed to find space in nearby villages such as Bethany or Bethphage.

A City Set on a Mountain

The Jerusalem that Paul was to get to know very well was effectively a creation of Herod the Great.[6] He had to fight to establish the authority of the kingship that the Romans had conferred upon him in 40 BC. Jerusalem did not submit easily, and during the early summer of 37 BC the catapults of his Roman allies pounded the city unmercifully for fifty-five continuous days. When the army finally broke through, Herod found a wasteland of ruined buildings and a decimated population. His fierce energy and incisive sense of organization ensured that the miserable situation did not last long.

Fully aware that he had very few friends, Herod's primary concern was his own security. His first monumental building was the fortress Antonia, named for his friend Mark Antony, at the north-west corner of the Temple. It had four towers, that on the south-east corner being 30 feet higher than the others. At his first sight Paul could not have known that he would one day be an unwilling guest there at the behest of the Roman garrison (Acts 21: 31–5).

No sooner was the Antonia nearing completion than Herod initiated an even more grandiose project: a new palace at the highest point of the city, to the west. What impressed onlookers were the three great towers named Miriamme for Herod's murdered wife, Hippicus for his friend, and Phasael for his brother. Originally the tower was 150 feet (46 m) high, taller than the Lighthouse of Alexandria, which was one of the seven wonders of the ancient world.

Such investment in construction brought prosperity to the city. To ensure that his supporters had the means to enjoy themselves, Herod built a theatre just outside the city to the south and a hippodrome or amphitheatre whose location is unknown. The games they hosted had all the trappings of pagan festivals and, in consequence, gave great offense to pious Jews.

9

The Temple

The latter, however, were not a constituency that Herod could afford to ignore. To placate them, he rebuilt the much-repaired Temple of Solomon. He enlarged the original sacred area on three sides, thereby creating the biggest religious complex in the Graeco-Roman world. Since he had to build out over three slopes, this involved gigantic retaining walls to hold the fill within. Covered galleries ran around three sides. Running along the south side was the Royal Portico, where most of the commercial business of the city took place.

In the middle of the vast esplanade the limits of the original square Temple were marked by a waist-high wall, at each of whose gates was a notice forbidding entrance under pain of death to all non-Jews. Pagans had access only to the Court of the Gentiles, the northern and southern parts of which were linked by a narrow passage along the west side.

All the specifically religious buildings were within the square. Entered from the east, there were successive courtyards of increasing holiness, of women, of Israel, of priests, then within a building the sanctuary, and finally the holy of holies. The façade of the sanctuary was covered with gold. Instead of a door there was a curtain embroidered with blue, scarlet and purple.

Members of the pious aristocracy, perhaps some of them chief priests, built expensive houses in the vicinity of the royal palace and on the western escarpment of the valley running through the centre of the city. The lower ranks of the priesthood were certainly not so luxuriously housed, and could only admire with envy. The vast majority of the houses were small, in some cases only one side of a courtyard.

Water is crucial to the survival of any city. Each house in Jerusalem had its cistern to collect rain-water. The Pool of Siloam fed by the Gihon Spring was at the lowest point of the city, and would have been a last resort, because from it water had to be carried up a steep hill. The greater part of the water supply came from two aqueducts that started at Solomon's Pools just south of Bethlehem.

The low-level aqueduct fed the Temple and the lower city, while the high-level aqueduct supplied the palace and the upper city.

Every edifice great and small was constructed of Jerusalem limestone, which in reflecting light enhanced it. The golden radiance was subtly modulated by the movement of the sun. The shining brilliance of the walled city contrasted vividly with the barren landscape in which tombs were the most prominent feature. The fruitful trees on the Mount of Olives just emphasized their absence elsewhere.

Aspects of Jerusalem would have been very familiar to Paul. He had seen modern buildings and Roman garrisons in Tarsus and in Antioch. There they may have seemed natural, but here they were an alien presence, a reminder of Jewish subjection. Yet they did not detract from the overwhelming authority of the Temple. The magnificence that Herod had given it proclaimed unambiguously that it was the House of the Lord, the symbolic home of the one living and true God. It was this that determined the ethos of the city. It gave Jerusalem a sense of unity unparalleled in other cities, with the possible exception of Rome, where the emperor was above all rivalries. This did not mean, however, that all Jerusalemites agreed on how God was to be served. If Paul wanted to be fully integrated, he had to make choices.

A Pharisee in the Holy City

Only when the pilgrims had dispersed at the end of Passover, and Jerusalem had returned to its normal routine, would Paul have had time to consider his future. He tells us that he became a Pharisee (Phil. 3: 5).

Luke makes this seem very natural, because he has Paul say, 'I am a Pharisee, a son of Pharisees' (Acts 23: 6). In other words, he merely accepted without conscious decision the religious option of his parents. It is most improbable that Luke is right. The Pharisees had no permanent presence in Galilee, so his parents could not have joined them in Gischala. If some Pharisees went to Galilee, as the Gospels suggest, it was for brief visits to check the tithing and quality of food produce being shipped to Jerusalem. Neither could Paul's parents have become members in Tarsus. There were no Pharisees in the Diaspora. Only in Jerusalem could Paul have encountered Pharisees.

What attracted him to this group? If Paul's motive in coming to Jerusalem was to live in an authentically Jewish world, then Pharisaism was virtually the only option. He could not have become a priest, because he was of the tribe of Benjamin (Phil. 3: 4). The priesthood was hereditary, and he would have had to have been born into the tribe of Levi. The Sadducees were another possibility, but these were drawn from the priestly nobility and the rich patrician families, and stood apart from the general population, in whom they had little interest. Both the groups from which its members were drawn were unreceptive to newcomers. An extremely wealthy and influential Jew from the Diaspora might have broken into this closed circle. An unknown one in his early twenties had no chance.

The Pharisees, on the contrary, were happy to accept recruits. They had a reforming agenda for Judaism in so far as they wanted to forge a new social and religious identity for Jews in a developing and changing world. They had no power to impose their vision, so they strove continuously to influence the governing class by providing political support, and to win the respect of the lower classes by clarifying the requirements of the Law in matters of daily domestic life. Over two-thirds of their surviving teachings concern the dietary laws, ritual purity for meals, and the quality and tithing of agricultural produce.

Paul's time in Jerusalem coincided with the prime of the great Pharisaic teacher Gamaliel I, who was famous for his wise tolerance (Acts 5: 34). An enthusiastic recruit like Paul would have eagerly sought his guidance (Acts 22: 3), because he could not but take seriously the Pharisaic axiom that 'an ignorant man cannot be holy'. Meticulous observance of the commandments demanded detailed knowledge not only of the written Law but also of its traditional interpretation, which came to be known as the oral Law.[7]

Life-style

This had two practical consequences for Paul's life-style as a young Pharisee. Consensus regarding what should be done was hammered out in common study and discussion, so we can infer that he spent considerable time with his fellow disciples. This tendency for Pharisees to concentrate in groups was reinforced by the common-sense recognition that life was simplified if one ate with people who respected the same exigent standards of ritual purity. They could be fully themselves only with like-minded people. Table fellowship was the high point of their life as a group.

It takes little imagination to visualize the hothouse atmosphere of such groups, and the competitive and exhibitionistic drives that it stimulated. The utter weariness of Simeon, the son of Gamaliel I, graphically evokes the feverish atmosphere of incessant debate: 'All my days I have grown up among the Sages and I have found nothing better for a person than silence. The expounding of the Law is not the chief thing, but the doing of it, and he that multiplies words occasions sin' (*Tractate Aboth* 1: 17 in the Mishnah).

Paul was not immune. In fact he was willingly complicit. Writing many years later, and looking back at a time in his life that he had completely repudiated, he still could not keep a note of smug self-satisfaction out of his words. 'I was advancing in Judaism beyond many Jews of my own age, so extremely zealous was I for the tradition of my fathers' (Gal. 1: 14). 'The tradition of my fathers' carries clear Pharisaic overtones of the oral Law, while the combative tone and competitive spirit are characteristic of membership in an élite group.

Paul was proud to have belonged to such a minority, but he did not exaggerate. He did not claim to be the best Pharisee absolutely, but only the top of his age-group. None the less, this was a signficant achievement, because Paul was an assimilated Diaspora Jew who had come to Pharisaism late. He would have been in his twenties when he started, whereas others, like Simeon ben Gamaliel, would have been indoctrinated since early childhood.

The energy and total dedication implied in Paul's claim to have caught up successfully meant that he devoted little or no time to earning a living. Ben Sira begins to develop his contrast between the craftsman and the scholar with the words, 'The wisdom of the scribe depends on leisure; only the one who has little business can become wise' (Sir. 38: 24), and goes on to exclude from access to wisdom 'every artisan and master craftsman who labours by night as well as by day' (Sir. 38: 27). Any occupation was distraction from the study of the Law.

Poverty

How, then, did Paul survive? It is not impossible that he was funded by his family. If they had had the resources to give him an expensive education in Tarsus, they could have continued to support him in Jerusalem. It would have been a source of pride to his parents that he had returned to the land from which they had been forcibly deported.

But Paul spent almost twenty years as a Pharisee in Jerusalem before becoming a Christian. Did his parents remain prosperous into a ripe old age? Even if they did not, there was a mechanism in place to take up the slack.[8] It was not the most efficient, but it was far better than nothing. Alms giving was considered particularly meritorious when done in the Holy City, and visitors to Jerusalem were expected to bring funds to distribute as charity. For many scholars this supplement to the tangible gratitude of their students made the difference between life and death. And they had a better claim than the beggars who contributed nothing.

Was Paul speaking from the experience of lean days as a Pharisee when he wrote to the Corinthians, 'If we have sown spiritual good among you, is it too much if we reap your material benefits?' (1 Cor. 9: 11)? The energy he invested many years later in the collection for the poor of Jerusalem (2 Cor. 8–9) was certainly inspired by his firsthand knowledge of the precarious condition of many in Jerusalem. Things got steadily worse for Christians. They were progressively cut off from Jewish charity, as the gap between the two groups widened, and support from their fellow believers abroad became imperative if they were to survive.

Despite their poverty, no Pharisee refused marriage as a means of economizing. For Law-observant Jews celibacy was not an option. 'Be fruitful and multiply' (Gen. 1: 28) was a commandment, and all understood marriage to be a matter of obligation.[9] To defer marriage

14

beyond the age of 20 was strongly discouraged. The speculative opinion of the great Jewish philosopher Philo of Alexandria that 40 was the ideal age for a wise man to marry was unlikely to have had any influence. As an immigrant from the Diaspora who desperately wanted to be accepted, there can be little doubt that Paul cheerfully bowed to the expectation that young men would marry in their twenties. He could not have spoken so complacently of his success in Galatians 1: 14 had he been in flagrant disobedience to a fundamental social obligation. His bride would almost certainly have come from a Pharisaic family, which makes it improbable that she brought him a large dowry.

If Paul had a wife, he probably had children. Why does he never mention either? We have absolutely no data on which to base an answer to such a personal question. I personally suspect that they perished in an accident so traumatic that he sealed off their memory for ever. It was too painful to be revisited, and too sacred to be disclosed to others. In any case, Paul never remarried (1 Cor. 7: 8).

Did Paul meet Jesus in Jerusalem?

If Paul came to Jerusalem in AD 15, and accepted Jesus of Nazareth as the Messiah sometime around AD 33, he must have been in the city when Jesus visited during his public ministry, and when he was crucified there in AD 30. Yet he never even hints that he had the slightest contact with the historical Jesus.

There is no reason why one life should have impinged on the other. During these years Paul was totally dedicated to his studies. Why should he waste time seeking out, and listening to, someone whom he had three good reasons to dismiss, in the event that he had in fact heard of Jesus? He was from Galilee. He had no qualifications to teach. And he appeared to think that he was the Messiah.

It is a Christian fallacy to imagine that the whole of Jerusalem turned out to watch the crucifixion of Jesus. No one would have had the time. Friday, 7 April AD 30, was the Day of Preparation for the Feast of Passover, which began at sunset. That year it coincided with a Sabbath, which meant that no work could be done after sunset.

15

During the day the women had to ensure that not a scrap of leaven was left in any garment or in any room. The streets were full of men carrying lambs. Some 18,000 lambs were needed for the crowds of pilgrims that augmented the population of Jerusalem. At Passover laymen could slaughter the animals themselves but, because they were sacrificial victims, it had to be done in the Temple. Thus those heading towards the Temple were burdened with struggling animals, and were pushing against those emerging with slaughtered carcasses. A single door gave access to the place of slaughtering, which had only 5,000 square yards (4,255 sq. m) of usable space, which, moreover, was broken up by the great altar and the laver! Queuing discipline has never been a feature of the Middle Eastern personality.

The chaos was such on the Day of Preparation that no one who was not obliged in one way or another went out into the streets. The little procession of Roman soldiers escorting a criminal on his way to execution was not something to be followed in anticipation of excitement. It was simply another frustrating barrier to free circulation on a day when blockages were the rule.

Paul first thought seriously about Jesus only after he had confronted Christianity.

Confrontation with Christianity

The disciples' encounter with the Risen Lord was in effect a reconversion experience which infused them with new courage and energy. They now knew with utter conviction who Jesus was, and that what he had said was true. There were no further doubts or denials. Empowered by the Holy Spirit, they went out and boldly proclaimed that Jesus was the promised Messiah, the final agent of God in history. Their enthusiasm was contagious, and they made converts.

As the numbers in the Jesus movement grew, it inevitably attracted the attention of the Pharisees, who saw it as a competitor for popular support. Any thought of a response, however, was nipped in the bud by Paul's teacher, Gamaliel I, who said, 'In the present case I tell you, keep away from these men, and let them alone. For if this plan or this undertaking is of men, it will fail. But if it is of God, you will not be able to overthrow them. You might even be found opposing God' (Acts 5: 38–9). The Pharisees in general, therefore, adopted a wait-and-see attitude.

Paul refused the party line. He did not accept that time would tell. He saw more clearly than his contemporaries what the Jesus movement implied. The Pharisees, following Gamaliel, thought of nascent Christianity as simply the newest of the Messianic movements that had occasionally troubled Jewish history. If not given importance by opposition, the odds were that it would fade away. For their part, Christians in Jerusalem thought of themselves as normal Jews. The fact that they had accepted Jesus as the Messiah and celebrated a memorial meal in thanksgiving did not stop them from frequenting the Temple. They might have felt superior to other Jews, but not radically different.

For Paul both of these approaches were merely examples of sloppy thinking. In the interest of their own comfort Pharisees and Christians wanted to believe that it was a both-and situation. With the gift for going straight to the heart of a problem that eventually became his trademark, Paul saw that it was an either-or situation that permitted no tolerance.[10] There would be winners and losers, but no fence on which anyone could sit.

Either the Law or the Messiah

Like all Jews, Paul the Pharisee lived in a spiritual world in which present and future were clearly distinguished. The present was dominated by the Law of Moses. This phase of salvation history was characterized by meticulous obedience to the commandments of the Law. It had no place for the Messiah. He was a figure of the future. One day he would simply arrive in the community of salvation, as defined and guaranteed by the Law, and inaugurate a new age in which there would be no necessity for the Law.

In insisting that Jesus was the Messiah, Christians did not fully realize what they were doing to Jewish tradition. They were claiming

17

that the two phases of salvation history, which should be successive, were in fact overlapping. The Messiah had appeared in the period of the Law. This is why they felt that they could accept Jesus and still continue to obey the Law. For Paul, on the contrary, this was radically subversive. By insisting on belief in Jesus as necessary for salvation, Christians were effectively saying that the Law did not guarantee salvation. By accepting 'sinners' whom the Law rejected, they were saying that the decisions of the Law had been superseded.

Paul alone had the perspicacity to see that the *coexistence* of the Law and the Messiah made them deadly rivals. Jews did not need *two* saviours. They were either saved through the Law or they were saved by the Messiah. Those who opted for Jesus the Messiah in fact rejected the Law. Equally, those who were committed to the Law had to reject the identification of Jesus as the Messiah.

There was no doubt on which side Paul stood. He was totally immersed in the Law, and there had been no revelation, either public or private, that the Law had been abrogated. Moreover, the activities of Jesus did not remotely resemble those of the Messiah that the Pharisees expected. These are revealed in the *Psalms of Solomon*, a Pharisaic work of the first century BC.

Psalms 17 and 18 look forward to the advent of a king, who will be the son of David, and the Annointed Lord, or Annointed of the Lord. He will rid the nation of its enemies, and restore Jerusalem, making it holy as of old. His weapon will be his word. As a righteous king, taught by God and pure from sin, he will be judge and shepherd. By destroying sinners and driving out Gentiles, he will gather together a holy people in whom unrighteousness will have no place. The Messianic community will be sinless.

When measured against this template, Jesus could not possibly be the Messiah. His followers, in consequence, were wrong, and needed to be corrected. This duty Paul took upon himself as proof of his zeal for the Law (Phil. 3: 6). It was a way of setting himself apart from others who had not had the insight to see the threat to the Law that Christians represented. His activity proclaimed how seriously he, in contrast to others, took his Pharisaic responsibilities. To what extent this also represented an acceptable outlet for Paul's repressed anger at the loss of his wife and children must remain a matter of conjecture.

Nothing in his letters suggests that Paul had any official standing in his treatment of Christians. It was a personal choice. He was satisfying only himself. Hence, in opposition to what Luke says, he could not have used arrest, torture or imprisonment as means of forcing Christians to recognize that they had been misled. All that he could have done was to hound and harass them, and in general make their lives a misery. The consistent intensity of his desire to destroy them (Gal. 1: 13) meant that Christians could never relax or feel secure. Every time they went to the synagogue, they laid themselves open to an abrasive challenge from Paul. He could invite them, for example, to recite a traditional Jewish prayer that implied that the Messiah had not yet come. If they did, he could sneeringly point out the contradiction. If they refused, he could revile them as false Jews. Even though no physical force was involved, the pressure he brought to bear on Christians was considerable.

There was another side to Paul's 'them or us' attitude towards Christians, which was to have important consequences. On the surface his position was, 'We are right and they are wrong', but the framework of this option was his refusal of the possibility of *two* saviours. Only one was necessary, either the Law or Jesus. Thus, the day he was convinced that Jesus was in fact the Messiah, he was mentally prepared to abandon the Law immediately and completely.

Conversion and Its Consequences

THE simplest explanation of Paul's presence near Damascus when he encountered the Risen Lord is that he was on his way back to Tarsus for a visit. For security, it was imperative to travel with a caravan, and there was regular traffic between Jerusalem and Damascus, the great trading crossroads of Syria. From there he could be sure of regular caravans to Antioch-on-the-Orontes and further west.

The route to Damascus brought Paul the ambitious scholar into areas that he had not seen before.[1] Even for a sedentary Pharisee the first day's march would not have been too difficult. It was all downhill through the Judaean desert to the oasis of Jericho. The next four days in the heat in the Jordan valley, which in the south is 1,200 ft (369 m) below sea-level, were another matter. It was certainly with great relief that Paul saw the Sea of Galilee in its deep cup. The sound of the little waves at least gave an impression of coolness.

At that point the caravan was about half-way to Damascus. The route then switched to the east bank of the Jordan, and skirted the vast Huleh swamp with its myriads of wildlife. The stiff uphill climb to the plateau of the Golan passed Caesarea Philippi, of which Peter would speak to Paul in the not too distant future. Even if he had exceptional eyesight, Paul could not have picked out Gischala, his ancestral home on the far side of the Jordan rift, but he could certainly have seen Mount Meron, on whose slope the village lay.

The massive bulk of Mount Hermon (9,000 ft; 2,769 m) kept the travellers company on their left until they dropped down into the fertile plain of the Hauran. As the peak faded behind them, the great oasis gradually came into clearer view. The Barada River poured out of the gorge between the Hermon and Anti-Lebanon ranges and, east of Damascus, fanned out to block the ever advancing sands as they swept out of the Arabian desert.

Recognizing the Unrecognizable

Where exactly in the Hauran Paul had the experience that changed his life is unknown. There were few, if any landmarks, and none familiar to him. Moreover, the encounter with Jesus made such an impact that Paul literally did not know where he was.

Only in the most general way does Paul reveal what happened. One thing he tells us is that his experience was identical with that of Peter and the others to whom Jesus appeared after the resurrection (1 Cor. 15: 5–8). When read carefully, these apparition stories in the Gospels reveal a common pattern: (1) Jesus is dead, and all hope has been lost; (2) Jesus intervenes; (3) Jesus offers a sign of his identity; and (4) the disciple(s) recognize(s) Jesus.

A little reflection reveals how true to life these narratives are, be it a question of a single individual such as Mary Magdalene (John 20: 11–16); a couple, the two disciples on their way to Emmaus (Luke 24: 13–42); or a group, the Eleven (John 20: 19–20). Even though Jesus had proclaimed that he would rise from the dead, what predominated in the minds of his disciples was that he had died an agonizing death on the cross. He was dead, and that was the end. Inevitably, the reaction to Jesus' appearance is shocked incredulity. The disciples cannot believe their eyes. Reality penetrates their consciousness only when Jesus offers proof of his identity; he shows them his hands and his feet (Luke 24: 39), or he blesses and breaks bread for them (Luke 24: 30). Finally the disciples admit the impossible. The Crucified stands before them as the Risen Lord.

In order to follow up Paul's hint, it is within this framework that we must interpret his experience. These narratives, however, are recognition stories. Disciples who had known Jesus during his earthly life come to know him again in a different way. This forces us to ask: what did Paul know about Jesus prior to the moment of the encounter near Damascus?

A Pharisee's Knowledge of Jesus

Paul's admission that 'we have known Christ in a fleshly way' (2 Cor. 5: 16) unambiguously shows that he once thought about Christ in a way of which he is now ashamed. He can only be referring to his pre-conversion knowledge of Jesus. It is inconceivable that Paul should have persecuted Christians without learning something about the founder of the movement. Thus, we can safely assume that he knew at least as much as a self-confessed fellow Pharisee of the first century, the Jewish historian Josephus. The latter says (1) that Jesus had been a teacher to whom wonders were ascribed; (2) that he had been crucified by the Romans under Pontius Pilate on charges laid by the Jewish authorities; and (3) that his growing number of followers thought of him as the Messiah (*Antiquities of the Jews* 18. 63–4).

It is unlikely that Paul would have been content with such bare bones. His animosity towards Christians, particularly when coupled with his specifically Pharisaic interests, would have driven him to flesh them out.

Given their concern to transform the Jewish people through instruction in the written and oral Law, the Pharisees would have been extremely sensitive to the fact that Jesus had disciples whom he taught. Any success by other teachers threatened their hoped-for monopoly. Through infiltration or, less dramatically, through questioning of verbosely enthusiastic supporters of Jesus, Pharisees could have learnt that Jesus downgraded the importance of the Mosaic Law. Even the simplest of his followers must have recognized the implications of assertions such as, 'It was said to those of old [in the Law] . . . but I say to you . . .' (Matt. 5: 21), particularly when coupled with a claim that Jesus was the touchstone of salvation (Matt. 10: 32–3).

In other words, it would appear to a curious Pharisee that Jesus thought of himself as the Messiah empowered to articulate God's will definitively. The Law was no longer the sole or the final authority. In this Paul would have found confirmation for the assessment that had been the basis of his persecution of Christians: namely, that any proclamation that the Messiah had already come was a radical threat to the Law which had become his life.

Finally, there was one aspect of the gossip about Jesus that would have been of particular interest to Pharisees. In opposition to the Sadducees, who denied any afterlife, the Pharisees believed in the resurrection of the body. Fundamental to the preaching of the first Christians was the proclamation that God had raised Jesus from the dead. The Resurrection was the great sign which validated the mission of Jesus and guaranteed his teaching. No Christian could avoid speaking of it, and, once heard, the claim would have rankled in the mind of a Pharisee.

It goes without saying that Paul the Pharisee did not believe a word of what he heard about Jesus. His resurrection must have been some sort of a trick, because God could never reward anyone who had set himself above the Law as Jesus had.

Encounter with the Risen Lord

Given this attitude on the part of Paul, it is certain that he was in no way disposed to expect anything to happen on his journey to Damascus. His mental attitude paralleled that of Jesus' followers, for whom the crucifixion was the end of hope. Jesus, Paul was convinced, had died a death that befitted his presumption, and all that remained was to return his misguided supporters to the fold of authentic Judaism.

Paul explicitly reports that Jesus took the initiative, 'Last of all, as to one untimely born, he appeared also to me' (1 Cor. 15: 8), which permitted Paul in another context to ask rhetorically, 'Have I not seen Jesus our Lord?' (1 Cor. 9: 1).[2]

But how did Paul know that it was Jesus? Unlike Mary Magdalene, Peter and other disciples, he had not been acquainted with Jesus during his lifetime. We can only assume that, from what he knew about Jesus, Paul had somehow built up a mental image to

23

which the Risen Lord corresponded. The stress under which Paul was operating would have heightened his susceptibility to anyone and everything associated with the focus of his emotion.

However it happened, the one thing that we can be absolutely sure of was that as a result of the experience Paul knew with the inescapable conviction of direct experience that the Jesus who had been executed by Pontius Pilate was alive. The resurrection of Jesus that Paul had contemptuously dismissed as fraud proved to be a fact, as undeniable as the nose on his face. Jesus continued to exist on another plane of being. This recognition is all that is necessary to Paul's conversion, because it completely transformed his value system.

The brutality of the 180-degree turn-around is evoked by Paul when he says, 'I was apprehended by Christ Jesus' (Phil. 3: 12). With irresistible power Jesus arrested him, and set him on a completely different path. It would be difficult, if not impossible, to find a more graphic illustration of what an act of lordship means. Paul's first conviction regarding the true identity of Jesus, therefore, must have been that he was 'Lord'. Once Paul had accepted Jesus as Lord, he had to acknowledge that he was 'Christ' (the Annointed One). Jesus was not just any 'Lord' but the Jewish Messiah for whom Paul had hoped. Moreover, if Jesus was the Messiah, he was the 'Son of God', because the two notions were intimately associated in Judaism.

Thus right from the beginning of his life as a Christian, 'Jesus', 'Christ', 'Lord' and 'Son' would have been intimately associated in Paul's mind, because they were rooted in his experience of the power of Jesus.

The next step followed naturally, because Paul had anticipated it mentally, and was prepared for it. If Jesus was the Messiah, then the time of the Law was over. What the Law laid down as the prerequisites for salvation no longer had any validity. Gentiles, therefore, in terms of their hope of salvation were no longer in any way different to Jews. It was not obedience to the Law that mattered, but acceptance of Jesus. The Messiah was not just for the Jews. He was Lord of the whole world.

In Paul's case this rational deduction was reinforced by his personal experience. He had opposed Jesus in the name of the Law, yet grace had been given to him. His acceptance of Jesus was in no way dependent on the Law. It followed that grace was also accessible to the pagans whom the Law had excluded.

These two aspects fused in Paul's mind. '[H]e who had set me apart from my mother's womb, and had called me through his grace, was pleased to reveal his Son to me, in order that I might preach him among the nations' (Gal. 1: 15–16). As Paul saw it, his submission to Christ was at the same time acceptance of a duty to proclaim him as Lord to the pagan world.

Mission in Arabia

Still in shock after his encounter with Jesus, Paul somehow got to Damascus, and made contact with the Christian community there. It is not impossible that they had heard of his persecuting activities in Jerusalem, but this quickly became irrelevant when they recognized that he confessed Jesus as Christ and Lord precisely as they did. For Paul it would have been a homecoming to be with others who had had the same experience of the Risen Lord. He did not enjoy this comfort for long. He himself tells us that his first decision after his conversion was to go into 'Arabia' (Gal. 1: 17).

For ancient geographers 'Arabia' was what we today know as Saudi Arabia, the huge land mass between the Red Sea and the Persian Gulf. A first-century Jew from Jerusalem, however, in practice would have applied 'Arabia' to a much more restricted part of that vast area: namely, the modern kingdom of Jordan plus both sides of the Gulf of Aqaba. This was the territory of the Nabataeans, whose king, Aretas IV, ruled from Petra.[3]

The early thirties AD was not a good time for a Jew to venture into the northern part of 'Arabia'. Herod Antipas, a son of Herod the Great who had inherited the kingdom of Galilee, also ruled Peraea, which shared a border with 'Arabia'. Relations between Jews and Nabataeans had always been rather tense, but Antipas brought them to boiling-point by repudiating his wife, a daughter of Aretas IV. This insult was not something that Aretas could tolerate. He went to war

25

and soundly trashed the army of Antipas before returning to his own territory. Antipas complained bitterly to Rome.

Aretas knew from personal experience that any changes on the eastern frontier of the Roman Empire, and in particular violent ones, were totally unacceptable to the emperor Tiberius. Thus, he and his people waited with increasing trepidation for the Roman reaction. The emperor had just to give an order to the governor of Syria, who had four legions at his disposal. As Aretas waited tensely for something to happen, his attitude towards Jews was anything but benign. They, in the person of their king, were responsible for the desperate anxiety that weighed upon him. A Roman reprisal, which he could never hold off, would be just the latest in a series of disasters that the Jews had brought upon his people. His subjects shared his apprehension and anger.

By the time Paul arrived sometime around AD 34 the tension had been mounting for over three years. It was not a propitious moment to begin preaching what the Nabataeans could only understand as a new variety of Judaism. To those who were the objects of his ministry, it appeared to be a Jewish attempt to infiltrate, divide and weaken them. What they perceived as an invitation to betrayal would have prompted an immediate and violent reaction. There was real danger that Paul would be lynched. Somehow he escaped. But he was remembered as dangerous, and three years later the Nabataean authorities prepared to call him to account.

If this assessment of the situation is correct, it is most unlikely that Paul penetrated very deeply into 'Arabia'. He may not even have reached Bosra, which is close to the southern border of modern Syria. There were three Nabataean cities—Phillopolis, Kanatha and Suweida—closer to Damascus. It is also probable that Paul did not stay very long. Once he had opened his mouth, he would have been suspect. I would give him a week at the most. His silence as to the duration of his visit confirms that it was very short, since he lists his two weeks in Jerusalem and three years in Damascus (Gal. 1: 18). The sole importance of his imprudent venture is that it indicates that from the beginning he was convinced that his mission was to Gentiles.

Three Years in Damascus

If Paul went back to Damascus with his tail between his legs, it may have been some small consolation that he could lick his wounds in a beautiful city whose scale was similar to that of Jerusalem.[4]

The Roman citadel in the north-west corner anchored a three-mile (5 km) wall pierced by eight gates, which enclosed a roughly rectangular area (east–west 1.35 km) virtually identical in size to that surrounded by the walls of Jerusalem. One feature, however, clearly differentiated the two cities. The north side of Damascus was protected by the Barada River, the source of the fertility of the oasis. Water was brought into the city by at least two main channels, including an aqueduct from the Barada.

The streets of the city crossed in a grid pattern, creating rectangular building blocks of unequal sides. The principal east–west street cut through the middle of the city linking two gates. With its covered colonnaded sidewalks it was 28 yards (26 m) wide. The topography forced it to make two slight deviations, both marked by an arch placed at a major intersection. At this period streets did not have names, which made finding anyone in a city very difficult. So when Luke speaks of Paul lodging in Damascus in a house on 'the street called Straight' (Acts 9: 11), it might reflect a Damascene joke. By definition, all the streets in the grid pattern were straight. The principal thoroughfare, however, was crooked! Hence, the mocking name.

The dominant monument of the city was the sanctuary of Jupiter. The huge open space surrounding the temple building was majestic in its proportions, but Jews would have taken secret satisfaction in the fact that it was slightly smaller than the Temple in Jerusalem built by Herod the Great. Damascene Jews, however, would not have been as proud of Herod's contributions to their city: namely, a gymnasium and a theatre. Both were most offensive to pious Jews. With some reason they felt that Herod could have built something more useful to his own people.

Damascus had a big Jewish population, but there was no doubt that it was a pagan city. As a founding member of the League of Ten Cities designed to propagate Greek culture, its culture was strongly

Hellenized. Its coins, for example, exclusively carried the images of Greek gods and goddesses. It owed its prominence and wealth to its position at one of the great crossroads of the ancient world. The trade routes from Anatolia and Mesopotamia joined there before splitting again to go down the plateau to Arabia and out to the Mediterranean coast and south to Egypt. If its merchants went as far as the island Delos in the Aegean Sea in the second century BC, we can be quite sure that merchants of other nations had permanent bases in Damascus. They swelled the normal pagan majority in the city. Thus, during his three years in Damascus (Gal. 1: 18), Paul would have had no difficulty in fulfilling his missionary vocation. There were Gentiles in abundance to be called to Christ.

Learning a Trade

In Damascus Paul did not only give, he received. If he was a preacher, he was also a learner. There was much about Christianity that he had to absorb, and he had to master a skill that would make him self-sufficient. Only financial independence could guarantee his mobility as a missionary.

What we have seen of Paul's life in Damascus and Jerusalem makes it clear that he did not work for his living. In both places he was a full-time student supported by charity. As a missionary, however, he says on a number of occasions that he worked with his hands (1 Thess. 2: 9; 2 Thess. 3: 7–9; 1 Cor. 4: 12). Thus, at some point he must have learnt a trade. To claim that he did so in Damascus goes beyond the evidence, but during those three years Paul must have given considerable thought to his missionary strategy, particularly in the aftermath of the fiasco in Arabia.

Paul had a number of options. He could acquire a patron who would support him. This, however, would put him at the mercy of his master, to whose whims he would have to tailor his teaching. Moreover, he would be stuck in one place. An alternative was to beg as he travelled. The objection to this was not the precariousness of the livelihood, but the fact that the cities of the Graeco-Roman world were infested by charlatans who made a good living out of pious promises supported by fake miracles. If he took this option, Paul would simply be lost in the throng.

Despite his inherited bias, Paul must have worked out relatively quickly that there was no alternative to paying his own way. He would have to earn as he travelled. This meant that he had to become a skilled craftsman. He had to serve an apprenticeship.

What trade would best serve his purposes? His object was not to become rich, but to survive on his own terms. Paul no doubt approached the issue with the acute intelligence that he later applied to the resolution of theological problems. The skill to be acquired would have to be in demand throughout the Graeco-Roman world, on land and sea, in towns and villages, as well as in great cities, and on the roads that linked them. It had to be a trade that would bring him into contact with all sections of the population. The tools had to be easily portable. The craft had to be quiet and sedentary, so that he could preach as he worked.

As far as Paul was concerned, the trade that met all these criteria was that of tent-maker (Acts 18: 3). To us this seems a rather bizarre choice. Paul exercised his ministry in an urban environment, and what need have city dwellers of tents? From a first-century perspective, however, it was a very clever decision.[5]

The skill involved was minimal, so was quickly learned. It was essentially the ability to cut and shape lengths of leather and canvas, and then to sew them together with a neat turned-over seam. The tools were simple and light. Paul needed a half-moon knife to cut heavy leather or canvas, an awl to make the holes to take the waxed thread, and curved needles. The lot fitted neatly into a small wallet. Exercise of this trade developed muscular shoulders and strong calloused hands. The stitch was set by a sudden outward jerk of both hands into which the thread bit. Little wonder that Paul could write only with awkward large letters (Gal. 6: 11)—a sign that he had plenty of work.

Work for a Tent-maker

In cities several types of awning were in demand. They all involved sewing strips of canvas of various weights together. Those in sailcloth shading the theatre and forum could be moved backwards and forwards on guy wires. The courtyards of private houses had to be protected from the summer sun. Inscribed awnings both advertised and shaded shop fronts. Those who went to the beach used linen pavilions to provide shade without impeding the cooling breezes.

The market for tents in the strict sense was also far from negligible. Inns needed them to accommodate overflow customers, which occurred on the occasion of great festivals. Shrewd travellers took the precaution of providing themselves with tents in case an accident should prevent them from reaching an inn at night. If they planned to travel any distance by boat, tents were indispensable. There were no ferries, and cargo boats had no cabins. Without tents deck passengers could not protect themselves from sun or spray, and had nowhere to sleep when the ship docked at nightfall.

Every town with a temple had its festival, when traders erected their leather or canvas booths around the sanctuary. Cities fortunate enough to host the major pan-Hellenic festivals had work year round for tent-makers. The competitions went on for the better part of a week, and the great numbers of visitors from all over the Greek world had to be housed in tents, as had the shopkeepers who catered to their needs. At Corinth, for example, the Isthmian Games were celebrated every second year in April or May. New tents were always needed to replace old ones, and ongoing maintenance was imperative.

Minor repairs were also a valuable source of income. Paul could repair the canvas roof of a wagon or the harness of the draught animals. A torn sail could become as new in his hands. He had the ability to put a stitch or two in any of the multifarious articles of leather used by travellers: sandals, gaiters, belts, cloaks, wallets and gourds. He would have been welcomed in any short-handed workshop.

Paul had chosen to arm himself with a skill that virtually guaranteed him jobs on every road he walked and on every sea he sailed. His choice, however, had one disadvantage. It stigmatized him as belonging to the labouring class, which was despised by the leisured class from which he had to recruit one or two believers in each city if he was to find a house large enough to assemble his converts. The natural place to meet them was as clients of the workshop that hired him. That provided an opportunity to talk business, but it must have been something in Paul's personality that drew them back to speak of Jesus Christ.

A Hurried Departure

Paul's tranquil, busy life in Damascus came to an abrupt end in the autumn of AD 37. The emperor Tiberius had died on 16 March of that year, and was succeeded by Gaius, nicknamed Caligula ('Little Boots'), who immediately changed his predecessor's policy regarding the eastern frontier of the empire. Tiberius had put his trust in well-organized Roman provinces rather than client kingdoms, unless the latter were governed by kings as utterly committed to Rome as Herod the Great. Gaius, on the contrary, cared little for reliability, and carved kingdoms for his friends out of bits of the frontier.

Gaius owed a debt of gratitude to the Nabataeans, who had once supported his father, Germanicus, against Gnaeus Calpurnius Piso, the all-powerful governor of Syria. Gaius, then age 7, was present when his father died in Antioch in AD 19 claiming that he had been poisoned by Piso. If there was any city the Nabataeans lusted after, it was Damascus, which was a key staging point on their important trade routes. Its transfer to their hands created an unanticipated danger for Paul. 'At Damascus the governor under King Aretas guarded the city of the Damascenes in order to arrest me, but I was let down in a basket through a window in the wall and escaped his hands' (2 Cor. 11: 32–3).

This is a very curious incident. The lapse of time had made it clear that Rome had no intention of bringing Aretas to book for going to war against Herod Antipas. More importantly, Tiberius had died, and the new emperor Gaius was their friend. All the anxieties that had led the Nabataeans to see Paul as a Jewish *agent provocateur* had dissipated. There was no reason for the representative of Aretas to move against Paul. One is forced to wonder if Paul did not exaggerate the danger. It is well within the bounds of probability that he merely presumed that he was still a wanted man in Arabia, and took precautions to ensure that he could preach another day elsewhere. In that case, the greatest danger of his dramatic escape was that the rope might break!

Peter and Jesus

Having left Damascus, never to return, Paul headed back to Jerusalem. Given the importance he attached to his mission to the Gentiles, one would have expected him to head north-west into virgin territory, the great pagan cities on the Mediterranean coast. To have done the opposite implies the compulsion of an overriding reason. He had something very important to do in Jerusalem.

For reasons that will become apparent when we deal with his letter to the Galatians, Paul uses a deliberately ambiguous verb to explain his motive for going to Jerusalem. He hoped that his readers would understand it in the sense of 'to get acquainted with Cephas', but he really intended the meaning as 'to get information from Cephas' (Gal. 1: 18). What did he need to talk to him about? It is absurd to imagine that Paul spent his two weeks with Peter discussing the weather, the health of the latter's mother-in-law, or his nostalgia for fishing on the Sea of Galilee. Only one basic question burned in Paul's mind: what was Jesus really like?

During his time in Damascus Paul undoubtedly heard stories about Jesus from the Christians there. But they had only second-hand knowledge, and could not answer the searching questions that Paul wanted to ask. He must have been consumed with envy of those who had been Jesus' companions during his earthly life. I would not be surprised if he did not bitterly regret the waste of the years when he could have listened to Jesus' preaching in Jerusalem. But it was too late for that.

Peter was the ideal person to take up the slack. He had been an eyewitness of Jesus' words and deeds since they were both disciples of John the Baptist. At this point in AD 37 Peter had been preaching Jesus for some seven years. Through repetition his story had inevitably acquired a fixed form, in which the sayings and miracles that Peter considered the most important were highlighted. This was obviously grist for Paul's mill. More importantly, Peter could answer any questions about Jesus that Paul wanted to ask.

The Personality of Jesus

From these sources Paul built up a very detailed picture of the personality of Jesus. It became a fundamental part of his oral preaching (2 Cor. 11: 4), and the basis of his ethical teaching (Gal. 6: 2). The comportment of Jesus was so clear to Paul that it could be imitated (1 Cor. 11: 1) to the point where he in his own life-style consciously mirrored 'the life of Jesus' (2 Cor. 4: 10).

Unfortunately, Paul does not reproduce in his letters the vivid portrait of Jesus that he painted orally (Gal. 3: 1). All that we get is a short list of 'facts'. Jesus was born into a Jewish family (Gal. 4: 4) of Davidic descent (Rom. 1: 3). He had several married brothers (1 Cor. 9: 5), one of whom was called James (Gal. 1: 19). On the night he was betrayed, he celebrated a final meal of bread and wine with his followers, and directed that it become a commemorative ritual (1 Cor. 11: 23–5). These, however, were but the tip of the iceberg. We are fortunate that Paul occasionally fills out the picture by offering tantalizing glimpses of two character traits that particularly impressed him.

The first was Jesus' total dedication to his mission. Paul admires his 'steadfastness' (2 Thess. 3: 5) and his 'fidelity' (Gal. 2: 16, 22). Despite the growing hostility that surrounded him, Jesus never wavered; his life was 'an enduring Yes' in realizing the promises of his Father (2 Cor. 1: 19). Jesus' complete reliability was 'the truth of Christ' (2 Cor. 11: 10). He was the 'pattern' of his own teaching (Rom. 6: 17).

Such single-mindedness can often breed a selfish coldness, but this is not what Paul saw in the way that Jesus interacted with those around him, and this is the second trait. Jesus' manner was characterized by 'gentleness and kindness' (2 Cor. 10: 1), and in his dealings with others he displayed 'tenderness' (Phil 1: 8). Their needs took precedence, for 'he did not please himself' (Rom. 15: 3). On the contrary, he gave himself totally to others in love (2 Cor. 5: 14; Gal. 2: 20).

Paul quotes Jesus only three times (1 Cor. 7: 10–11, 9: 14, 11: 23–5), but allusions to, and echoes of, his teaching abound in the letters. We would like him to have given us more explicit citations, because his letters are at least a generation earlier than the final editions of the Synoptic Gospels. This is because we think as historians. Paul, however, was operating as a pastor, who knew that echoes and allusions had a powerful bonding effect on those who grasped the hints. They constituted a shared secret language inaccessible to outsiders. It is hard to say exactly to what extent this was conscious pastoral technique on the part of Paul, because the teaching of Jesus informed his thought to the point where any attempt to distinguish source and personal elaboration would be both meaningless and impossible.[6]

A Messiah who should not have Died

It is difficult to think that Peter did not sympathize with Paul's insatiable thirst for knowledge about Jesus. No doubt Paul's inquiries brought to the surface of his mind incidents and impressions that he had forgotten. To this extent they delighted in a common quest. There was one important issue, however, on which they might have differed.

It was characteristic of Paul's preaching that he focused on the fact that Jesus had died by crucifixion.[7] He made his hearers believe that they were present at the cross. No mere rhetorical tricks could achieve such an effect. Paul had to have the imagination to re-create the event for himself, and relive the appropriate emotions, before he could achieve the verbal vividness that he claims in Galatians 3: 1. Paul's compulsion to replicate the crucifixion is explicable only if it made a huge impact on him.

There is no hint that it had the same effect on Peter. The preaching of the early church, of which he must be considered one of the principal authors, highlighted the fact of the death of Jesus, and its salvific meaning, but remained resolutely silent on how Jesus had died (e.g. 1 Cor. 15: 3–5). Such reticence is entirely understandable.

It was difficult enough to preach a Messiah who had died without apparently achieving anything. To preach a Messiah who had been crucified as a traitor was virtually asking for a refusal.

Why, then, did Paul make the crucifixion of Jesus, of which he had heard as a Pharisee, the centre-piece of his preaching, when none of his contemporaries did? Just as Paul the Pharisee had seen to the heart of the fundamental opposition between Christianity and Judaism, while Christians did not, so here too Paul's penetrating intelligence detected a problem that others did not perceive. If Jesus was the Messiah, he should not have died!

Let us begin by recalling Paul's Pharisaic background, and in particular the portrait of the Messiah drawn in *Psalms of Solomon* 17. It tells us that the Messiah will be 'pure from sin' (v. 36), and that his people will be holy (vv. 26, 32, 43). In thus stressing the sanctity of the Messianic people, it reflects the mainstream Jewish vision of the end time. It is the teaching of the great prophets that 'all your people shall be just' (Isa. 60: 21); 'they shall all live and never again sin' (*1 Enoch* 5: 8). Common sense dictates that, as the leader of a holy people, the Messiah cannot be a sinner. His absolute righteousness is taken completely for granted.

This intuition had one supremely important consequence. All Jews believed that the Messiah would not die. The advent of the Messiah was seen as the glorious climax to history beyond which no one thought to venture. Inevitably the Messiah was thought of in terms of eternity. Why should he die? This common-sense insight was reinforced for many Jews by the teaching of the Scriptures that death was not integral to the structure of the human being, but a penalty imposed for sin. The Book of Wisdom can serve as representative of a series of texts reaching back to Genesis and forward to the second century AD: 'God created humanity in a state of incorruptibility. In the image of his own eternity he made it. But through the devil's envy death entered the world' (Wis. 2: 23–4).

Paul's dilemma should now be clear. The Messiah whom he had recognized on the Damascus road had been put to death on a cross. Paul was confronted with a sinless Messiah who was also a dead Messiah. Perhaps other Christians had seen the paradox. If so, they chose to ignore it. The absolute streak in Paul's character meant that he could not live with the tension between the incompatible elements. It had to be resolved, but not by the calculated ambiguity of compartmentalization, nor by abandonment of one or other truth.

Crucifixion as Self-sacrifice

Eventually Paul perceived that there was only one possible solution. If someone on whom death had no claim had actually died, then that person must have *chosen to die*. All other human beings can only accept death; it will take them whether they like it or not. Jesus did not suffer that restriction. His death was the result of a personal decision. For Paul, in consequence, Jesus is 'the one having *given himself* for our sins' (Gal. 1: 4). He is 'the Son of God who ... *gave himself* for me' (Gal. 2: 20).

Once Paul had accepted that the death of Jesus was an act of *self-sacrifice*, a dead sinless Messiah ceased to be a problem. Its modality then became the central issue: why did Jesus choose the most horrible way to die, the agonizing suffering of crucifixion? It goes without saying that in posing such a question Paul was working backwards. Jesus did not have to die. But if he did die, and in a particular way, then he must have chosen that form of death.

Paul was given a clue to the answer by the teaching of Peter and others, which he had inherited. They stressed that 'Christ died for our sins' (1 Cor. 15: 3), and 'our Lord Jesus Christ died for us' (1 Thess. 5: 9). In other words, humanity benefited from Christ's death. In his search for a motive for Christ's decision, Paul turned this the other way round. By dying, Christ intended those benefits for humanity. His motive, therefore, in choosing to be crucified was to do good to others who were both unaware and uninterested. In Paul's eyes such altruism was explicable only as an act of love. 'He *loved* me, that is, *he gave himself* for me' (Gal. 2: 20).

This insight so overwhelmed Paul that henceforth he could not think of the death of Christ without wanting others to appreciate the extraordinary depth and power of the love it revealed. He could not merely speak of that love. He had to show it in action. In practice this meant forcing his hearers and readers to confront the crucifixion. Hence his vow, 'I decided to know nothing among you except Jesus Christ and him crucified' (1 Cor. 2: 2)—hence his correctives to traditional teaching. In his letters he quotes two liturgical hymns. One says, 'He humbled himself becoming obedient unto death', and Paul adds, 'even death on a cross' (Phil. 2: 8). The other hymn speaks of God 'reconciling all things to himself through Christ', which Paul interprets as meaning 'making peace by the blood of his cross' (Col. 1: 20).

It now becomes understandable why his death is the only 'event' in the life of Jesus to which Paul returns again and again in his letters. It was important for Paul that his converts knew what Jesus had said and done, and so he told them in his oral preaching (2 Cor. 11: 4), but in the last analysis that was not what made Jesus unique. Other teachers offered profound theological and ethical insights. Others had the reputation of being miracle workers. For Paul the fact that Jesus had a choice whether to die or not set him apart from all others for whom death was inevitable. Thus Jesus' death became the key to the meaning of his life. It revealed to Paul that what makes a person genuinely human is the self-sacrificing love shown by Christ. This, above all, is what he wanted his readers to take to heart.

Apprenticeship in Antioch 3

AFTER the stimulus of his two weeks with Peter, Paul must have left Jerusalem burning with fervour. The Jesus to whom he had committed his life was now infinitely more real. We should have expected Paul to rush into an intense missionary campaign. If so, it took place in Syria and Cilicia (Gal. 1: 21), but it has left no trace, and Paul effectively disappears for three years. We pick up his story again around AD 40, when Barnabas recruited him to work in Antioch-on-the-Orontes (Acts 11: 25–6).

The church in Antioch (modern Antakya in Turkey) was founded in the same ill-defined way as that in Damascus. This appears to have occurred in AD 39–40. The enthusiastic preaching of the new converts that the Messiah had arrived in the person of Jesus of Nazareth evoked profound resentment in the Jewish community, which was already under extreme pressure.

In the spring of AD 40 the emperor Gaius had ordered the governor of Syria, P. Petronius, to transform the Temple in Jerusalem into an imperial shrine by erecting a gigantic statue of the emperor as Jupiter in the holy of holies. Fully aware of the bloody backlash that this sacrilege would provoke among all Jews, Petronius temporized until sometime during the summer Gaius was persuaded to change his mind.

During these tense months the Jews in Antioch were preparing to sacrifice themselves in what they knew would be a vain attempt to stop the legions of Petronius marching on Jerusalem. Some hotheads in the community cracked under the strain, and used the

Christian preaching as a pretext to whip up opposition to Rome. In the process they alienated their pagan neighbours, who rose against the Jews and killed many. When Petronius succeeded in stopping the violence, he looked for the instigators. Realizing that they were likely to be blamed, the founders of the church fled, leaving behind converts saddled with the name 'Christians', which identified them in the popular mind as trouble-makers. This, at least, is the way the name is used by the Roman historians Suetonius and Tacitus.[1]

News of this disaster for the infant church in the most important city of the region quickly reached Jerusalem, which responded by sending Joseph, a Jewish Cypriot convert (Acts 4: 36–7), to stabilize the demoralized community. His nickname, Barnabas, meaning 'son of consolation' (Acts 11: 22), might explain why he was chosen for the task, or may reflect the memory of what he achieved at Antioch.

Once he had settled the community, Barnabas went to Tarsus to recruit Paul. It is not difficult to work out how he knew Paul or where he was. The memory of the persecuting Pharisee, Saul of Tarsus, would have been vivid in Jerusalem, and his name betrayed his place of origin. The implications of Paul's apparently secret visit to Peter would eventually have seeped out into the community (Gal. 1: 23).

Barnabas' purpose is equally obvious. The presence of Paul among the distressed believers of Antioch would verify the power of grace promised in the Gospel. It would be a tremendous boost for the community to have a converted persecutor among its members. God did work miracles. There was hope for the future. Antioch was to be Paul's home base for the next decade.

The Third City of the Empire

Damascus was a very old but still gracious lady long before Antioch was even born. Its founder, in about 300 BC, was Seleucus, who had fought his way to India as one of Alexander the Great's generals. He discovered a magnificent site for a port city where the valley of the

River Orontes opened out to the Mediterranean. For its prosperity and security, however, he had to control the inland end of the valley, where trade routes criss-crossed the wide fertile plain of Amuk, with its lake abounding in fish.[2]

Seleucus built this inland city on a flat plain bounded on the west by the Orontes and on the east by foothills of Mount Silpius (1,600 ft; 492 m). Walls limited a grid pattern of streets, which created rectangular blocks. The original agora was on the bank of the river, which carried significant commercial traffic. An aqueduct coming from the garden suburb of Daphne some 5 miles (8 km) to the south carried abundant sweet water to the city.

The beauty and prosperity of Antioch continuously attracted new inhabitants, but its growth was carefully controlled. Under the Seleucids, as extra housing became necessary, new quarters were added in turn, each with its own wall. The first two were north of the original city and on an island in the Orontes. The third, called Epiphania, was between the original city and Mount Silpius. Despite their walls, these new quarters continued the grid pattern of Seleucus' foundation.

Once Antioch was made the capital of the Roman province of Syria by Pompey in 64 BC, emperors, kings and simple millionaires vied for the honour of augmenting its splendour. By the time of Paul it had been transformed into the most Roman of all the cities of the East. In importance it ranked just below Rome and Alexandria. Inevitably the population increased. Agrippa, the son-in-law of the emperor Augustus, added a new quarter, probably north of Epiphania, and two public baths. He also expanded the capacity of the theatre; it had to be further enlarged shortly after. To entertain a growing population, Agrippa also brought the hippodrome back into use. In the first century AD the inhabitants numbered at least 100,000. A wide variety of temples met their religious needs.

The pride of the Antioch that Paul knew was due in part to Herod the Great, whose buildings he had admired in Jerusalem. A clever, anonymous planner had seen that what the expanding city needed in order to bind the various quarters together was a wide avenue of magnificent proportions. There was room for it between the original city and Epiphania, and it could easily be driven further north.

Once the proposal had been floated, donors quickly appeared. Herod provided the marble paving for the entire length (2 miles; 3.2 km) of the 31 feet (9.6 m)-wide street. The future emperor Tiberius is given credit for the 32.5 feet (10 m)-wide portico that lined it on both sides, and for the domed *tetrapyla* at each main cross street. The planner was too clever to make the street perfectly straight. Columns getting smaller as they faded into the distance would have been boring. He gave it a focal point, an oval piazza with a statue of Tiberius on a column, and there shifted the direction slightly.

Paul may have seen this glorious street, the first of its kind, in its pristine brilliance, but twice during the time he lived in Antioch it was damaged by an earthquake, first in the reign of Gaius (AD 37–41) and again in the reign of Claudius (AD 41–54) while it was still under repair. It would have been difficult, however, to tarnish its immense dignity, and we should assume that Paul viewed it with the pride of an adopted son.

A Mixed Community

One of the aspects of Antioch that proved attractive to Paul was its tolerance. Of course, there were occasional 'incidents', but in general the cosmopolitan inhabitants got on well together. This was particularly obvious in the Christian community, where converts from Judaism and paganism exhibited unusual integration.

There is no way of estimating the number of Christians in Antioch, but all the hints we have suggest a large and vital community. Thus the minimum cannot have been less than the fifty believers postulated for Corinth. This number would have created a practical problem for Paul and Barnabas.

Unlike the Jews, who had their synagogues, Christians at this point had no right to a public meeting-place. They had to make do with the hospitality offered by the more affluent members of the community. There is no evidence that any of these belonged to the patrician class which owned vast mansions. Upper middle class is about as high on the social scale as first-century Christians went. A house belonging to such a person could not have contained fifty people in comfort. Any assembly of the whole church would have meant undignified crowding. Hence, we must assume that at Antioch, as elsewhere, the Christian community was made up of a number of sub-units, the house-churches.[3]

Such an arrangement had the advantage of offering converts a choice. While in theory they were joining a single community, in practice they had to opt for one particular house-church among a number. Many, highly diverse factors no doubt influenced selection, but it would be rather unrealistic to assume that individual house-churches had both Jewish and Gentile members. That would simply have made life too complicated. The trend must have been towards the creation of separate Gentile and Jewish house-churches, which were grouped together under the umbrella of 'The Church of Antioch'. Unless the umbrella was to be a complete fiction, however, there had to be strong and regular links between the various house-churches.

Table Fellowship

The most important of such links was table fellowship. In the ancient Near East a formal meal was the prime social event. To share food was to initiate or reinforce a social bonding which implied permanent commitment and deep ethical obligation. In the eyes of their contemporaries at Antioch, there would have been no genuine community among Christians unless, in addition to the ritual of the Eucharist, they gathered around a common table.

Nowhere was the significance of a meal more accentuated than in Judaism.[4] All Jews would not have been as scrupulous as the Pharisees. It is equally certain, however, that the vast majority would have observed the fundamental distinction between clean and unclean food, and would have insisted on the former being entirely drained of blood (cf. Acts 10: 14). It was a matter of principle for which their ancestors had died (1 Macc. 1: 62–3), and it was one of the most obvious identity markers of the Jewish religion. 'Separate yourselves from the nations, that is, eat not with them' (*Jubilees* 22. 16). Recognition of the bonding effect of shared meals is the reason for this prohibition.

How, then, did the Jewish and Gentile house-churches of Antioch maintain any semblance of unity? We can immediately exclude the idea that the Jews created no difficulties for Gentiles by ignoring their own laws, or that the Gentiles created no problems for Jews by adopting a Pharisaic level of dietary observance. The most probable scenario lies somewhere in the middle.

When Gentile believers dined with Jews, they accepted the food offered them, even though kosher meat might not have been to their taste. When Jews dined in a Gentile house, they trusted their fellow believers to offer them Jewish food and drink. From a Jewish perspective such trust was an extraordinary concession. Most if not all the meat available outside Jerusalem would have been part of a pagan sacrifice, and the common assumption among Jews was that Gentiles out of sheer malice would pollute Jewish food and drink if they got the slightest chance.

The plausibility of this compromise is enhanced by the number of Gentiles who were attracted to Judaism at Antioch but without becoming converts. If, as seems probable, the majority of Gentile converts to Christianity at Antioch were drawn from these 'God-fearers', it would have been very easy for them to make the relatively minor concession which made table fellowship with their Jewish fellow believers possible. In practice, all they needed to do was to buy at a Jewish shop when they had Jewish guests. It would be more expensive, as specialized products always are, but the legal purity of what they bought was guaranteed, and their guests would be at ease.

Another Shift Regarding the Law

Instead of responding with unqualified admiration to the immense goodwill on both sides that made this sort of arrangement possible, Paul's reaction was ambivalent. On the one hand, he recognized that Antiochean Christians were living the basic commandment to love their neighbours. On the other hand, ever since his encounter with

43

Jesus he had been convinced that the Law, which the Jewish converts obeyed, no longer had any binding authority. In his eyes the problem was a false one, and the energy that went into solving it was wasted.

None the less, Paul accepted the situation, thereby revealing that he had once again changed his mind about the Law. As a student in Tarsus, the Law was a source of both pride and embarrassment. As a Pharisee in Jerusalem, his commitment to the Law was total. As a follower of Jesus, he was convinced that the Law was completely irrelevant in terms of salvation. Now in Antioch he tolerated the Law, seeing it as providing Jewish converts with the traditional signs of their ethnic identity. As far as he was concerned, however, these were of no more importance than the garments and/or headgear that marked out other segments of the population as being of different ethnic origins.

Subsequently, Paul was to become aware that to give the Law even such a minimal toe-hold in a Christian community was to invite disaster. His final position on the Law was to be that Jewish converts to Christianity should not be permitted to obey it (Acts 21: 21). This realization, however, was still many years in the future.

Missions from Antioch

Given the charity that animated the internal relations of the church at Antioch, it was to be expected that it should be missionary. The natural outcome of its members' sharing with one another was that they should want to share the good news of the gospel with outsiders.

Paul's first missionary journey under the auspices of Antioch is narrated only by Luke (Acts 13–14), who presents Paul and Barnabas going first to Cyprus, and thence into the southern part of central Asia Minor. A close analysis of this account brings to light so many improbabilities that it becomes impossible to accord it any real confidence.[5] One can only speculate as to what Luke's sources might have been, and then on the use he made of them. It seems likely, however, that Luke had vague information about two missionary expeditions, one to Cyprus and the other to the southern part of the interior of Asia Minor. Both of these are in themselves probable, especially in relation to Antioch-on-the-Orontes.

Antioch had strong relations with Cyprus. They were natural trading partners, and sea communications between the two were facilitated by high mountains which acted as landmarks for the navigators: the Troodos mountains (4,000 ft; 1,230 m) in Cyprus and Mount Casius (5,616 ft; 1,728 m) just south of Seleucia Pieria, the port of Antioch.[6] In fact, Cyprus is visible from Mount Casius. Such practical and mundane links were undergirded by mythological associations. According to legend, the first settlers in the area of Antioch were from Cyprus. Moreover, some of their gods followed them. Realizing that their priests would block the transfer of their statues, the gods inspired Antiochean craftsmen to make copies so perfect that they were easily substituted for the originals, which were then carried away openly to Antioch! Finally, Acts 11: 19–20 reflects a tradition that Christians from Cyprus were the first to have preached in Antioch.

It is most unlikely, however, that Paul would have been interested in a mission to Cyprus. His rule was to preach exclusively in virgin territory (Rom. 15: 20), and not only had the seed of the gospel already been sown in Cyprus, but it was effectively in his own backyard. Asia Minor, on the contrary, would have been a most attractive proposition for someone with Paul's ambition to spread the gospel to the ends of the earth. In order to understand the possibilities that crowded his mind, it is necessary to know a little about the road system in Asia Minor.[7]

Roman Roads in Asia Minor

The most important road in Asia Minor was the trade route between the Aegean coast and the Euphrates River. Its origins are lost in the mists of remote antiquity. At the end of the second century BC the Greek geographer Arthemidorus of Ephesus recorded the trace of the entire route through to India, with the distances between the important towns. When this description was taken over by the

Roman geographer Strabo a hundred years later, he called the route the 'Common Highway' (*Geography* 14. 2. 29) because everyone used it.[8]

The Romans acquired the western half of the route when they inherited the kingdom of Attalus III of Pergamum at his death in 133 BC, and transformed it into the province of Asia. One of the great achievements of the governor Manius Aquillius (129–126 BC) was to have paved the 180-mile (288-km) stretch between Ephesus and Apamea (modern Dinar). This section followed the north bank of the River Meander, crossing to the south bank near Antioch-on-the-Meander. On its way to the plateau of Anatolia, it passed through Laodicea in the valley of the Lycus River, where in future years there would be Pauline churches. From Apamea it made a big curve around the north-western tip of the Sultan Dagh mountain, which it kept on its right until it rounded the south-eastern end and came to Iconium (modern Konya). Presumably one or other of the successors of Manius Aquillius had continued the paving project from Apamea. From Iconium the 'Common Highway' passed too far to the north to be of interest to anyone in Antioch-on-the-Orontes.

The second route was the Via Sebaste, which was completed in 6 BC by the governor of Galatia, Cornutus Arruntius Aquila, to link the Roman colonies behind the Taurus mountains on the Anatolian plateau.[9] Paved all the way from Comama/Colonia Iulia Augusta Prima Fida to Lystra, this road stayed to the east of Apamea and curved around the north end of Lake Egridir to Antioch-in-Pisidia. Thence it kept the Sultan Dagh on its left, until at Pappa/Tiberiopolis it cut through a pass directly east to Iconium, and then due south to Lystra. Two side-roads linked the Via Sebaste with the 'Common Highway', one just south of Lake Burdur, the other going to Apamea. This had practical consequences for the 'Common Highway'. It was effectively abandoned between Apamea and Iconium, because the Via Sebaste cut the distance between the two cities from 180 miles (288 km) to 155 miles (248 km). The difference is a day's march (25 miles; 40 km), an important factor for anyone travelling on foot.

Mission with Barnabas

Knowledge of these routes would have been available in Antioch-on-the-Orontes to anyone with the curiosity to talk to the caravan masters coming through from the west. The believers of vision who were the missionary strategists of Antioch saw that they could use this road system to bring Christianity right to the western limit of Asia Minor. The longer a line of communication, however, the more important it is to guarantee its centre. From this perspective Antioch-in-Pisidia and Iconium took on a new importance in the eyes of the planners in Antioch. These cities were the centre. It was essential to capture them for Christ before pushing further west.

Thus one day in early summer—in those days travel on the Anatolian plateau in winter was extremely difficult, if not impossible—Barnabas and Paul set off from Antioch. The route with which they were most familiar led due north from Tarsus through the extremely narrow pass in the Taurus mountains known as the Cilician Gates.[10] North of Podanos, a river opened a pass to the west. Keeping along the southern edge of the plain of Lycaonia, the route brought them to Derbe, Lystra and eventually to Iconium and Antioch-in-Pisidia. The whole journey was roughly 515 miles (824 km). These were not the only cities or towns en route. Presumably the names that did survive in Luke's source were the only places in which Barnabas and Paul succeeded in establishing churches.

How long did this mission take? If the missionaries averaged 20 miles (32 km) a day, they could have reached Antioch-in-Pisidia from Antioch-on-the-Orontes in twenty-six days. Hence, the round trip would have taken two months. This figure, of course, is entirely theoretical. It makes no allowance for blisters, illness, excessive heat, accidents or the need to work to pay one's way. It ignores whether the route was uphill or downhill. Moreover, it is impossible to estimate the time Barnabas and Paul spent in each place they preached. Their ministry was not easy. In the last letter that Paul wrote, he recalls what he had to suffer 'at Antioch, at Iconium and at Lystra' (2 Tim. 3: 11). How long did the missionaries struggle in a place before giving up and moving on? If they were successful, how long did they spend instructing their converts? Did one or other move around making repeat visits to their foundations in order to stabilize them? One should think of a minimum of two years (at least), and perhaps a more realistic maximum of four years, before Barnabas and Paul returned to Antioch-on-the-Orontes.

Despite this investment of time and energy, it would appear that Paul took no further interest in the welfare of the churches in Antioch-in-Pisidia, Iconium, Lystra and Derbe. Such 'neglect' stands in sharp contrast to the careful maintenance that Paul lavished on the churches of which he was the sole founder; for example, he went back to Corinth twice, and wrote five letters to the Corinthians. The only possible inference is that Paul was convinced that someone else had the responsibility for these churches, and that he was faithfully exercising it.

Who was he? Our meagre sources permit only one answer: Barnabas. Just as he had been the one who brought Paul to Antioch-on-the-Orontes, so he took the lead in establishing Antioch's missionary springboard in southern Anatolia. Paul willingly and ably co-operated with him, but did not carry the final responsibility. Paul's role in this first missionary expedition was similar to that of his assistant Timothy when Paul operated independently of Barnabas.

A Traveller in a Strange Land

At this point in his life, Paul had walked well over 2,000 miles (3,200 km). He was a seasoned traveller, but of his experiences he gives only the most summary account some years later: 'During my frequent journeys I have been exposed to dangers from rivers, dangers from brigands, dangers from my own people, dangers from Gentiles, dangers in the town and in the country, dangers at sea, dangers at the hands of false brothers' (2 Cor. 11: 26). The conditions of travel in the world of his day are well documented, and permit us to amplify his hints.[11] The point is not merely of historical interest. The integration of his experience into a world-view had a significant impact on his theology.

The surprising feature of 2 Corinthians 11: 26 is the emphasis, not on difficulty, but on 'danger'. The element of risk, not struggle, is evidently uppermost in his mind. There would have been little peril from rivers on the great Roman arterial roads furnished with bridges. Secondary roads were another matter. In the east they were built for the long dry season, when stream beds had little or no water. In the spring the runoff of the winter rains turned crossings into dangerous fords whose violence can still be experienced on the banks of the Dead Sea and in the Arava valley.

Dangers on the Road

Such danger, however real, was sporadic. Robbers were a much more consistent threat. Even in Italy, as a consequence of the anarchy of the civil wars, brigandage was endemic, and travellers faced the additional risk of being shanghaied as slaves by owners of land bordering the roads. The emperor Augustus reacted by stationing troops on the roads, and by delegating Tiberius to inspect the slave prisons to ensure that no freemen were being held. When the latter became emperor, he had to concentrate garrisons even closer together in order to make the roads safe. Yet, at the end of the first century AD, Pliny the Younger could write of the disappearance without trace of a Roman knight and of a centurion and their parties on main roads in Umbria as if it were a not-unheard-of occurrence.

If such was the case at the centre of the empire, one can infer with a high degree of probability that conditions were much worse in distant provinces. The Roman legions stationed in Syria, Asia and Macedonia did not double as police forces in anything like the modern sense. Detachments might be sent to deal with a particularly troublesome robber band, yet even then not as a matter of policy, but in response to pressure from an influential person. In senatorial provinces the proconsul normally had at his disposal some auxiliary units, which accompanied him as he travelled throughout his territory. In principle a proconsul was expected to hold court in various cities within his charge during his year of office, but the size of provinces and the length of proceedings ensured that even an energetic and competent administrator (a rare species) could intervene only sporadically and in the more important centres, where, we can safely assume, access was monopolized by prominent figures. The poor had no recourse, and the vast majority of small towns and villages never saw a Roman official. Apuleius catches the reality of the situation in the warning that a friend gives Lucius in Hypata (modern Ipati) in Thessaly:

Don't stay too long at the party. Come back as soon as you can, for in the early hours Hypata is terrorized by a gang of young thugs who think it amusing to murder whoever happens to be passing by, and to leave the streets strewn with corpses. They are members of the first families in town, and the Roman barracks are so far away that nothing can be done to end the nuisance. (*Metamorphoses* 2. 18, trans. Graves, adapted)

Security in the countryside was much worse. Poverty forced many into brigandage. Any robber anywhere could be sure that all travellers had money on them; they had to pay their way, and no credit cards or cheque books were available. Those obliged to travel alone did so with fear and trembling, certainly in lonely wooded stretches of the road, where in Greece wild animals were as much a danger as bandits. Apuleius mentions bears and wild boar, both of which attack without warning, but reserves his goriest language for wolves.

The authorities requested us not to continue our journey that night or even the following morning, because the district was overrun by packs of enormous wolves, grown so bold that they even turned highwaymen and pulled down travellers on the roads or stormed farm-buildings, showing as little respect for the armed occupants as for their defenceless flocks. We were warned that the road we wished to take was strewn with half-eaten corpses and clean-picked skeletons and that we ought to proceed with all possible caution, travelling only in broad daylight—the higher the sun the milder the wolves—and in a compact body, not straggling along anyhow. (*Metamorphoses* 8. 15, trans. Graves)

Travellers voyaged in groups whenever possible, and, given the double danger, it seems reasonable to assume that many were armed, at least with staves. This meant that they could be seen as a threat by any village they approached. The consequences were predictable.

When we reached a small village, the inhabitants very naturally mistook us for a brigade of bandits. They were in such alarm that they unchained a pack of large mastiffs which they kept as watch-dogs, very savage beasts, worse than any wolf or bear, and set them at us with shouts, halloos and discordant cries. (*Metamorphoses* 8. 17; cf. 9. 36; trans. Graves)

The villagers had to rely on themselves for protection. If self-help was not sufficient, only neighbours could be relied on for aid. Slaves could loot the house of their dead owners, and escape retribution by moving to another town. Inevitably all strangers came under suspicion, whose degree was the inverse of the size of the place. This was not xenophobia but the fruit of hard experience.

A moment's absence from a cottage carried the risk of pilferage, and those who tried to defend their poor possessions endangered their lives. Though protected by walls, stout gates and numerous slaves, who could be armed in an emergency, large houses were not immune. Thieves used all sorts of tricks to infiltrate the premises, both to spy out where valuables were stored and to open doors for accomplices. The alternative was a silent forced entry. When they thought they could get away with it, brigands in a frontal attack simply broke down the main gate, and held off the inhabitants with swords while looting the house.

Inns were even less secure. On the Roman roads across Asia Minor they were spaced a day's journey apart—25 Roman or 22 English miles (35 km)—with a small establishment (*mutatio*) where dispatch-riders could change horses roughly half-way between two inns. The rooms of an inn were grouped around three or four sides of a courtyard, with public rooms on the ground floor and sleeping accommodation above. Those with money to spend could buy privacy, but those with slender purses had to share a room with strangers—how many depended on the number of beds the landlord could cram in, or on his or her attitude to guests sleeping on the floor. Unless they wanted to cart their baggage with them, guests had to leave it unguarded while they visited the baths and a restaurant.

The ease of theft needs no emphasis. Roman legislation made innkeepers responsible for the acts of their employees, but not all guests were honest, and in a crowded room at night one had only to stretch out a hand to appropriate something from another's baggage. If an inn was isolated and the bandits numerous, they did not hesitate to attack it.

Each town, of course, had its magistrates, who were responsible for public order, and who carried out their duty through servants of the court. Only the wealthy, however, could be elected to municipal offices. In smaller towns, therefore, office circulated among the few dominant families, who effectively ran such towns in their own interests. Inevitably those subject to their whims watched their performance carefully, with a hint of barely repressed violence. The wealthy could rob or murder with impunity, but if they went too far on occasion, there could be a vicious backlash. Popular opinion could force the magistrates to take action if, for example, there was a spate of thefts. But the officers of the court, instead of seeking the real culprit, would naturally tend to take the easy course of accusing an outsider without local connections.

The Origin of Paul's Concept of Sin

This brief and generalized description is valid for that part of the Graeco-Roman world in which Paul was active: namely, the provinces of Syria, Asia, Macedonia and Achaia. It takes little imagination to visualize the tension set up within him by such an environment. His conversion had made him a follower of Jesus, who had given his life for the salvation of humanity. That totally other-directed mode of existence became Paul's ideal. His goal was to make it transparent in and through his own comportment, 'always carrying in the body the dying of Jesus so that the life of Jesus may be manifested in our bodies' (2 Cor. 4: 10).

Yet every road he travelled forced him to worry about his personal safety. Every inn he visited obliged him to consider others as potential thieves, at least in so far as he had to take measures to protect the precious tools on which his livelihood depended. Circumstances conspired to push the self to the centre of his consciousness, whereas he wanted to be totally focused on the other. His life became a perpetual struggle against the insidious miasma of egocentricity.

It is in this tension that we find the roots of Paul's concept of Sin. When he says 'all, both Jews and Greeks, are under (the power of) Sin' (Rom. 3: 9), he is obviously speaking of something other than personal sinful acts; hence my use of the capital letter. Manifestly Sin in these texts is a symbol or a myth expressive of a world in which individuals were forced to be other than they desired to be. The authentic self was alienated (Rom. 7: 20). From his own experience as a travelling missionary, Paul learned that people were not selfish because they chose to be. They were forced to put number one first in order to survive. Their pattern of behaviour was dictated by irresistible societal pressures. They were controlled by a force greater than any individual, the value system which had developed within their society. The power of this system became clear to Paul in the difficulty he experienced in being true to himself as the model of Jesus Christ (1 Cor. 11: 1). Hence his anguished cry, 'Who is not weak, and I am not weak? Who is made to fall, and I do not burn with anger?' (2 Cor. 11: 29).

In addition to this insight into the factors that made it impossible for people to live up to their aspirations— 'I can will what is right but I cannot do it' (Rom. 7: 18)—Paul learnt another important lesson while on the road. He discovered that co-operation was indispensable to survival. Only a strong, well-organized caravan could move safely through bandit territory or through an area in which wild animals were on the rampage. Reciprocal protection ('All for one, and one for all') meant that no one in a group of friends was forced to be egocentric. Instead of looking out for oneself, one looked out for one another. In an inn Paul would not have to worry about the security of his tools while he went for a meal or a bath if Timothy was there to take care of them.

By bringing these two insights together in the light of the self-sacrificing love that the crucifixion of Christ has revealed as constituent of genuine humanity, Paul was led eventually to see that something much more fundamental than co-operation was necessary for spiritual survival against the power of Sin. The radical divisions of society could be repaired only by the shared existence of community.

A Journey into Europe 4

AFTER their return from Anatolia to their base in Antioch-on-the-Orontes, a rift developed between Paul and Barnabas. The reason that Luke gives is hardly credible (Acts 15: 36–41), but it does seem to have been some sort of personality clash. Certainly there was no divergence either on doctrine or on missionary practice. On the contrary, five or so years later Paul and Barnabas stand shoulder to shoulder for Antioch-on-the-Orontes against the interference of Jerusalem (Gal. 2: 1). Whatever the cause, the partners went their separate ways.

Luke narrates Paul's second missionary expedition in Acts 16–18. This time, however, the successive stages of the journey—that is, the place-names—can be confirmed from Paul's own letters. The broad outline, in consequence, is certain. The details given by Luke are another matter. The closer the link between the details and the outline, the greater the confidence they can be accorded. Other aspects, notably the sermons that Luke puts into Paul's mouth and the dialogues that he reports, are the conventional devices of contemporary historians to put flesh on a skeleton version of events, and so should be taken as reflecting Luke's purpose rather than historical reality.[1]

As we might have expected, Paul, accompanied by Silas/Silvanus, headed straight for the forward base that had been established in the triangle formed by Antioch-in-Pisidia, Iconium and Lystra. In either Derbe or Lystra Paul had the good fortune to recruit Timothy, who was to become his life-long friend and closest collaborator (Acts 16: 3).

Timothy's mother, Eunice, and grandmother, Lois, appear to have accepted Christianity (2 Tim. 1: 5), perhaps on Paul's first visit, before Timothy was converted by Paul (1 Cor. 4: 17). Luke claims that his mother was Jewish, but this is not confirmed by the two names. Neither is specifically Jewish (no more than is Timothy), and both are extremely rare even among pagans. Perhaps it was their uniqueness that fixed them in Paul's mind to the point that he remembered them to the end of his life. No doubt, his close bond with Timothy also helped.

Paul cannot speak of his assistant without an affectionate or complimentary phrase. Timothy is 'like-souled' (Phil. 2: 19). Paul unconsciously reveals the depth of the relationship in one of his letters to the Corinthians. He had sent Timothy to Corinth to report on the situation there. All of a sudden, when writing 1 Corinthians 4: 14–21, Paul realized the implications of what he had done, and his imagination ran wild. He had dropped Timothy into a snake pit! If the intellectuals at Corinth had treated Paul with contempt, what would they do to Timothy, who was younger and much less experienced? They would eat him alive. Timothy would be no match for their skill in debate. At best he would be humiliated; at worst his self-confidence might be destroyed. Paul's blood boiled at the threat to his young assistant, and he lashed out with a savage warning that, if push came to shove, he himself would come to Corinth to sort things out. 'What do you wish? Shall I come to you with a rod or with love in a spirit of gentleness?' (1 Cor. 4: 21).

We will find Paul using Timothy for other important missions, and the latter appears as the co-author of six letters. His beneficent influence on Paul in terms of pastoral strategy emerges most clearly from a comparison of 2 Corinthians with 1 Corinthians, which was written while Timothy was away. Sadly, Timothy did not turn out well when he was given independent authority as the head of the church of Ephesus. He had been a perfect number two, but he did not have it in him to be a leader. It must have been with a heavy heart that Paul, now an old man, summoned him to Rome to resume their old relationship of chief and assistant (2 Tim. 4: 9).

An Unexpected Visit to the Celts

Paul's intention on leaving Antioch-in-Pisidia was to head west down the 'Common Highway' to Ephesus, the capital of the Roman province of Asia. This was the natural second step in the missionary strategy of the planners in Antioch-on-the-Orontes. Something, however, happened to block him. Luke provides only a pious explanation. The missionaries were 'forbidden by the Holy Spirit to preach the word in Asia' (Acts 16: 6). No doubt everything that Paul did was guided by Providence, but one would like to know exactly by what set of circumstances the divine decision was conveyed to Paul.

If Asia had been put out of Paul's reach, the logical thing to do would have been to take the Via Sebaste south. It would have brought him out of the Roman province of Galatia, in which there may have been criticism of his activities, and into the province of Pamphylia. Luke does not explain why this obvious option was refused. Instead he merely tells us that Paul decided to head north to the province of Bithynia. Just beyond Antioch-in-Pisidia and the Sultan Dagh, the province of Asia bulged out to the east.[2] In order to stay as close as possible to the eastern frontier of the province, Paul must have taken the Ancyra road from Antioch-in-Pisidia, which angled north-east to Germa, where he could have turned north-west to Dorylaion, and thence into Bithynia.[3]

This project was also aborted. With his customary helpfulness Luke simply says that 'the spirit of Jesus did not allow them' (Acts 16: 7). This time, fortunately, Paul himself provides an explanation as to how Providence operated. He fell ill.

On the basis of Paul's reference to 'a thorn in the flesh' (2 Cor. 12: 7), many scholars have concluded that he had some sort of congenital disease, be it psychic or physical.[4] None of the suggestions resists close examination, and when one thinks of the thousands of miles that he had already covered in so many different areas, it is clear that Paul enjoyed good health and a robust constitution. Hence, on this occasion we should think of a sudden attack whose nature cannot be determined.

Since the effect of his illness was the evangelization of the Galatians, Paul must have crossed the River Sangarios (modern Sakaria) when he was stricken, because at this point the river is the southern border of ethnic Galatian territory and that part of the Roman province of Galatia.[5] The only Galatian town after the river crossing was Pessinus (modern Balahissar), so it must have been to some of its inhabitants that Paul later wrote with deep feeling, 'you know that it was because of a bodily ailment that I preached the gospel to you at first. And though my condition was a trial to you, you did not scorn or despise me, but received me as an angel of God, as Jesus Christ.... I bear you witness that, if possible, you would have plucked out your eyes and given them to me' (Gal. 4: 13–15). Paul's recognition of the generosity of his hosts betrays the seriousness of his illness. He had been a grave burden to them. They had to invest time and energy to nurse him back to health.

The Tolistobogii

Located in the foothills of Mount Dindymos (modern Günjüsü Dagh), Pessinus was the capital of the Tolistobogii, the westernmost of the three Celtic tribes that made up ethnic Galatia. Classical authors use 'Celts' and 'Galatians' interchangeably.[6] Their ancestors had come from the region of the Pyrenees in the third century BC, and after a vicious war against Rome in 189 BC, they settled peacefully around Ancyra (modern Ankara). Livy's description of the behaviour of the Galatians in this war shows that they did not really differ from the Celts of Gaul, as evoked in much more detail by Didorus Siculus (80–20 BC):

The Gauls are tall of body, with rippling muscles, and white of skin, and their hair is blond, and not only naturally so, but they also make it their practice by artificial means to increase the distinguishing colour which nature has given it.... Some of them shave the beard, but others let it grow a little; and the nobles shave their cheeks, but they let the moustache grow until it covers the mouth. Consequently, when they are eating, their moustaches become entangled in the food, and when they are drinking, the beverage passes, as it were, through a kind of strainer....

They invite strangers to their feasts, and do not inquire until after the meal who they are and of what things they stand in need. And it is their custom, even during the course of the meal, to seize upon any trivial matter as an occasion for keen disputation, and then to challenge one another to single combat without any regard for their lives. . . .

The clothing they wear is striking—shirts which have been dyed and embroidered in varied colours, and breeches, which they call in their tongue *bracae*, and they wear striped coats, fastened by a buckle on the shoulder, heavy for winter wear and light for summer, in which are set checks, close together and of varied hues [= tweed]. . . .

The Gauls are terrifying in aspect and their voices are deep and altogether harsh; when they meet together they converse with few words and in riddles, hinting darkly at things for the most part, and using one word when they mean another; and they like to talk in superlatives, to the end they may extol themselves and depreciate all others. They are also boasters and threateners and are fond of pompous language, and yet they have sharp wits and are not without cleverness at learning. Among them are found lyric poets whom they call Bards. (*The Library of History* 5. 28–31; trans. Oldfather)

The common view of Paul's contemporaries was that the Galatians were large, unpredictable simpletons, instinctively generous, ferocious and highly dangerous when angry, but without stamina and easy to trick. These qualities had never been eradicated. The Galatians had not been Hellenized, and the Romans had imposed their administrative system directly on Celtic tribal structures. Celtic was still being spoken in that region in the fifth century AD. Of course, the Galatians who lived in the few cities would have acquired some Greek, which was the second language. Otherwise Paul could not have communicated with them.

An Alien World

None the less Paul found himself in a completely alien world. Once he was able to walk around the city, he would have noticed that Pessinus shared one feature with Antioch-on-the-Orontes. Both were built at the foot of a mountain and, in consequence, had a severe problem with rain-water pouring down the slopes. At Antioch the Roman

58

engineers adopted the obvious solution. They cleared and reinforced the stream beds that ran through the city, and bridged them where roads crossed. The solution at Pessinus would have accentuated its strangeness in the eyes of Paul. The bed of the river Gallos was paved, and colonnades were erected on the banks. In times of heavy rain it served as the evacuation channel. For the rest of the year it was the main street![7]

The contrast between the tall, red-haired, fair-complexioned individuals who walked the streets of Pessinus and the Semitic types to whom he was accustomed would have reinforced Paul's sense of being out of place. He would never have chosen to minister in Galatia. Language and a sparse, spread-out population made it an unpromising mission field. He was incapable, however, of wasting the opportunity.

Paul's initial preaching took the form of conversations with those who had given him hospitality. They were pagans, and in all probability had never met a Jew. Northern Galatia was one of the few places in the Graeco-Roman world that did not have a Jewish population. How Paul got his message across remains a mystery, because there would have been little or no common ground on which to build. I can only think that it was the compelling force of his personality as he spoke with burning fervour about Jesus as the saviour of the world.

In any case, he made so deep an impression on the Galatians that six years or so later they were not easily won over by emissaries from Antioch-on-the-Orontes who attempted to convince them that Paul's version of the gospel had been wrong. The pressure the latter brought to bear was certainly heavy, and the Galatians may have wavered, but that could be Paul's uncharitable interpretation of the fact that his converts had given a hearing to his adversaries. As we shall see, Paul was possessive about his converts, and had few scruples about the way he attacked those who disagreed with him. Such opposition, however, lay some years in the future.

The rootedness of the Galatians in the Pauline gospel is inexplicable unless Paul spent considerable time with them. He could not have arrived in north Galatia before the end of the summer of AD 46, and we do not know how long his convalescence lasted. No matter how short it was, his hosts would have raised strong objections to his moving on before the beginning of the summer of AD 47. They knew much better than he the risks of winter travel in the high country. The weather was so severe that those without imperative reasons did not stir from their villages between the beginning of October and the end of May.

By that time, however, Paul would have realized the advantages of a longer stay in Pessinus. Not only was it the most important commercial centre in the area, which drew in merchants, but it hosted the temple of the Mother of the Gods, which was a potent attraction for pilgrims. Although her cult had spread far and wide by Paul's day, Pessinus was the home of Agdistis/Cybele, the supreme deity of Phrygia, who had been adopted by the Galatians. This was the one area of the ancient world in which a goddess reigned unchallenged. Attis, the male god associated with her, was merely her inferior companion and servant. This, of course, affected the status of women in Phrygia. It undoubtedly reinforced Paul's recognition of Christian women as full equals.

Being a double source of attraction, Pessinus in the summer of AD 47 would have been a bustling place with many new faces for Paul to buttonhole, and perhaps clients who sought his leather-working skill. If he ministered there for any considerable time, which seems very likely, he was condemned to stay there for the winter of AD 47–8, because he would have had to set off early in order to be off the Anatolian plateau before another winter set in.

By the beginning of the summer of AD 48 Paul had done what he could for the communities he had founded in Galatia. He had given them roughly the amount of time he would spend on his other foundations, and there was work to be done elsewhere. Despite such staunch commitment, Paul's heart must have been heavy as he said farewell to those who had been so generous to him in his hour of need. It is most unlikely that he had any plans to return. At this stage of his career he believed that his mission was to found churches. Nurturing them once they were out of swaddling clothes was the responsibility of the Holy Spirit. He would soon realize that things were not quite that simple.

To the West and Europe

We know from Paul's own letters that after evangelizing Galatia he went on to found churches in the Roman province of Macedonia in northern Greece. Unfortunately he does not tell us how he got there. Luke's simple words, 'passing through Mysia they came down to Troas' (Acts 16: 8), contain ample room for elaborate hypotheses. When taken at face value, however, they suggest that Paul adopted a variation on his original plan.

If he could not go through the province of Asia to Ephesus, Paul's situation so far north in Pessinus suggested that it would be easy to do the next best thing. Even though Mysia was technically the northern part of the province of Asia, the greater part of it belonged to the separate administrative unit of Hellespontus ruled by a procurator. Paul gambled that he would have a better chance in a different juris-diction. In that case, he was intentionally heading for Troas, the city that Julius Caesar once considered a suitable capital for an empire that had expanded so far eastward.

The options open to Paul going from Pessinus to the Aegean coast can be visualized as a figure eight lying on its side. Cotiaeum is the city at which the circles touch. The northern curve from Pessinus through Dorylaeum would have been the shorter. At Cotiaeum the traveller had a choice between following the valley of the River Rhynaldakos up to the north-west, or a southern curve following first the valley of the River Asteles up to its source, and then over the watershed at Synaos and down to the head-waters of the River Mekestos, which made a big curve to the north. In this instance the southern route would have been preferable. Both routes met again at Hadrianoutherai, from which a good road ran to the port city of Adramyttium, whence he followed the coast around to Troas.[8]

The whole journey was a minimum of 400 miles (640 km). In the-ory it could be done in three weeks, but the brutal heat of the Anatolian summer would have taken its toll quickly in the very diffi-cult terrain, which, moreover, was infested with brigands. It is more likely that it took Paul and his companions, Timothy and Silas, a maximum of two months. Unless he failed everywhere he opened his mouth, Paul did not preach as he travelled. His goal was to reach Troas, and he permitted no distractions.

If these calculations are correct, Paul would have reached Troas in the middle of the summer of AD 48—say the end of July. Troas, according to the geographer Strabo, was 'one of the most notable cities in the world' (*Geography* 13. 1. 26). A massive 5-mile (8-km) wall encircled a population of between 30,000 and 40,000. Its strategic location as the transit point for trade between Europe and Asia made it very prosperous. Travel was easy in all directions, both by land and by sea.[9]

An Invitation to Macedonia

These advantages were precisely the features that Paul was later to seek out deliberately when he established his personal missionary strategy. Yet, apparently he made no effort to found a community at Troas. It was only much later that he preached there (2 Cor. 2: 12–13). Fortunately we do not have to speculate on Paul's motivation. At this point Luke quotes one of his sources, which stems from an eyewitness. Note the shift from 'they' in the previous verses to 'we': 'A vision appeared to Paul in the night. A man of Macedonia was standing beseeching him and saying, "Come over to Macedonia and help us!". And when he had seen the vision, immediately we sought to go into Macedonia, concluding that God had called us to preach the gospel to them' (Acts 16: 9–10).

This 'we-source' continues with a description of Philippi that is so detailed and accurate that scholars have suggested that the author was 'the man from Macedonia', and more specifically a citizen of Philippi. Let us assume, then, that he was somehow converted by Paul in Troas, and pressed him very strongly to preach the gospel in Philippi, where he could afford Paul at least an initial foothold. The ensuing turmoil in Paul's mind did not last very long.

Paul's mandate from Antioch-on-the-Orontes was to plant the faith in western Asia Minor. If he succeeded, he would be the pioneer apostle of that region rich in possibilities for spiritual growth. Philippi, however, belonged to another continent. Paul's studies at

Tarsus had certainly made him familiar with the three great territorial divisions of the ancient world. Europe and Asia faced each other across the Bosphorus, and off to the south lay Libya (= Africa). The challenge of being the first to establish Christianity in Europe proved irresistible to Paul. It was easy for him to convince himself of the providential character of the opportunity. Moreover, he could always return to Troas at another time, and perhaps even to Ephesus. Paul was not to know that missionaries from Jerusalem had already penetrated Rome, the very heart of Europe.

The First Sea Journey

At the head of the most extensive road system in northern Asia Minor, Troas had frequent sailings to Neapolis (modern Kevalla), an eastern terminal of the Via Egnatia, the great paved highway running across northern Greece to the Adriatic coast. Built around 130 BC by Cn. Egnatius, the proconsul of Macedonia, it was Rome's main route to the east. Paul and his companions would have had no trouble in finding a ship to take them to Neapolis, which was the nearest port to Philippi.

For all of them it was their first experience of a sea voyage, and they must have approached it with some trepidation. They certainly had a lot to learn.[10] Since passengers were only an incidental benefit to the owner, who none the less screwed the maximum out of them, the ship provided neither food nor services. The passengers had to furnish their own provisions for the unpredictable duration of the voyage. No one cooked for them, but they could use the hearth in the galley after the crew had been fed. But there was no guarantee of hot food. The fire might be doused by a stray wave. In rough conditions the crew threw the hot coals overboard. Were they to spill, the wooden boat would go up in flames.

But there was also a positive side for Paul. He was in a position to provide the tent that made life on deck bearable. It protected them from sun, spray and rain. He could also contribute to his passage by mending the tents of others, or doing any repairs to sails or other equipment that were beyond the ability of the crew.

While they waited for the necessary conjunction of cargo, favourable winds and auspicious omens, no doubt gloating acquaintances informed them of the dangers. There were none, however, on this voyage to spoil Paul's initiation. On other occasions he was not so lucky: 'Three times I have been shipwrecked; a night and a day I have been adrift at sea' (2 Cor. 11: 25). These words were written some ten years later. We do not know where or when these events took place, but the laconic summary betrays Paul's stoic courage.

If he was adrift at sea, the boat must have gone down far from land, either because it caught fire or because the seams opened. He was lucky that a current brought him to shore. Even if other ships were in the vicinity, they would not have the control to run down and pick him up. Or the interest. Life was cheap. Paul may have felt that the hand of God had protected him when he first survived the battering of heavy surf as he was washed on to a stony beach, but that thought is unlikely to have calmed him the next time, or the time after that, when he was tipped into the water in the midst of a storm as the boat holed itself on a rock.

Any one of these experiences would have made most people swear off the sea for ever. If Paul persevered, it was because he thought it was necessary. Either a sea voyage was the only way to get from A to B (as in the present case), or it was the quickest. He believed that there was little time before the return of Christ in glory, and it was his duty to reach as many people as possible with the gospel before then. If he suffered in the process, or was merely scared out of his wits, that simply had to be accepted.

Luke gives the impression that this first sea voyage passed without incident: 'Setting sail from Troas, we made a direct voyage to Samothrace and the next day to Neapolis' (Acts 16: 11). The travellers spent the night on the island of Samothrace. This was typical, and another reason why tents were necessary.

A glance at a map illustrates why ships of the period did not sail at night or in the winter.[11] In order to get to Samothrace from Troas, the captain (1) had to leave the island of Tenedos to port, (2) had to avoid the series of tiny islands dead ahead, (3) had to be aware that the hugh volume of water pouring out of the Hellespont (modern

Dardanelles) would push him towards the island of Lemnos as he struggled to round the island of Imbros (modern Gokce) on the west. In such a crowded sea it was infinitely safer to sail only in daylight, when one could move confidently from one landmark to another. In winter visibility could be drastically reduced by fog, driving rain or lowering skies. This increased the danger to the point where maritime insurance was not available from October to April.

From Samothrace the travellers passed north of the island of Thasos, and safely reached the harbour of Neapolis by the eve of the second day. Paul's captain was not only a skilled navigator, but he had read the weather with extreme accuracy. To make runs of some 60 nautical miles (112 km) on two consecutive days means that they averaged 5 knots,[12] which in turn implies that they had the wind astern or on the quarter, the most favourable winds possible for their destination and the type of boat. Such winds, however, were most unusual in that area, where the prevailing wind was from the northern quadrant. Much later Paul made the same voyage, but in reverse—that is, from Neapolis to Troas (Acts 20: 6)—but it took five days. They barely made an excruciatingly slow 1 knot against head winds, and had several uncomfortable nights at sea.

Partnership at Philippi

As Paul walked the 10 miles (16 km) from Neapolis to Philippi, the milestones would have reminded him that he was returning to the familiar territory of a Roman colony. The bilingual milestones near the port gave way to exclusively Latin ones as he approached the city. Presumably the propaganda of 'the man from Macedonia' had led him to expect something similar to Troas. If so, Paul would have been disappointed. Philippi was so small that one could walk across it in 10 minutes.[13]

The 2-mile (3.4-km) city wall enclosed an area of only 167 acres (68 hectares), in which lived a mixed population of between 5,000 and 10,000 made up of Thracians, Greeks, Macedonians and Romans. The latter, of course, were in control. Veterans of the legions had been settled on land around the city first by Mark

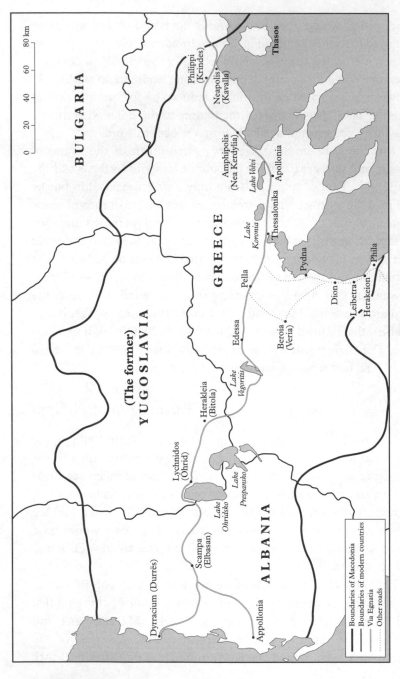

Fig. 2 The Roman Province of Macedonia and the Via Egnatia (*Source*: F. Papazoglou, *ANRW* II 7/1, copyright Walter de Gruyter GmbH & Co. KG.)

66

Antony in 42 BC, and again by Augustus in 31 BC. As the dominant class, they made Latin the official language, but Greek continued to be spoken by the indigenous population. The complexity of the linguistic situation is illustrated by Latin inscriptions written in Greek characters, and inscriptions in which Latin and Greek characters are used promiscously.

Even though he did not live there for very long, Paul found that he was not immune to the influence of Latin. His Greek style was affected. Instead of addressing the Philippian believers in authentic Greek as *Philippeis* or *Philippênoi*, he instead used *Philippêsioi*, which is derived from the Latin *Philippenses* (Phil. 4: 15). The fact that Paul wrote to the Philippians in Greek indicates that the vast majority of his converts did not belong to the Latin-speaking element in the population. This is confirmed by the few names of members of the community that he mentions. Clement (4: 3) is Roman, but Euodia, Syntyche (4: 2) and Epaphroditus (2: 25) are Greek, and none is Jewish.

The majority of the Gentile converts in Antioch-on-the-Orontes, Paul's home base, would have been 'God-fearers': that is, pagans who were attracted by the monotheistic austerity of Judaism, and who, by attendance at the synagogue, would have come to know the Scriptures. This was the common ground on which Paul and Barnabas based their missionary appeal. Paul must have known that there were Jews in Macedonia, and Philippi with its prime economic position on the Via Egnatia would have seemed a likely place to have attracted a Jewish community. Thus on Paul's first Saturday in Philippi he went to look for the synagogue, because that was where 'God-fearers' would congregate.

To his surprise, there was no synagogue in the city. Nor was there a house in which Jews congregated. All that he could discover was that Jewish women gathered for prayer near the river outside the Marsh Gate (Acts 16: 13). One might suspect that they were married to pagans who permitted them to practise their religion. Like Philippina domestic servants today, they congregated where they could.

The one convert that Paul made on this occasion was a female 'God-fearer' from Thyatira in western Asia Minor called Lydia

(Acts 16: 14). She was a wealthy business woman with her own house and servants, who acted as the agent in Philippi for the purple-dyed goods of her hometown.[14] The dye in question was not derived from the murex sea snail—that was an imperial monopoly—but from the madder root, which produced a turkey-red colour. Though much cheaper than imperial purple, her goods were still luxury items.

Women Ministers

With the decisiveness of a forceful personality, Lydia persuaded Paul to make her house his base while in Philippi (Acts 16: 15). We should presume, in consequence, that her house became the place where Christians at first assembled. Thus, she may well have taken part in the evangelization of Philippi. Certainly other women did. Paul singles out two, Euodia and Syntyche, as having 'striven side by side with me in the gospel, together with Clement and the rest of my co-workers, whose names are in the book of life' (Phil. 4: 3).

The verb used by Paul to describe the activity of the two ladies has given us 'athlete' and 'athletics'. It highlights the energy and commitment that they invested in the spread of the gospel. They preached it in precisely the same way that Paul, Clement and others did. No distinction is made between the contributions of men and those of women. They were all 'co-workers'.

Was Philippi the first place in which Paul encountered dynamic women who co-operated in the spread of the gospel? Certainly, it is the first place we hear about, and there is no hint that there was any problem that had to be solved. Apparently, Paul took it completely for granted that, as Christians, women were fully equal to men. After all, they were followers of Christ, just as he was. And that said everything. The idea that they might be less capable than men never entered his mind. As far as he was concerned, there was no need to justify or explain to other Christians such a radical repudiation of the patriarchal ethos of the world in which he ministered. It should have been obvious to believers that they had entered a new world.

Once Paul had recognized the effectiveness of the ministry of Euodia and Syntyche, and possibly other women, he certainly encouraged them. Their success proved that they were graced by the Spirit. But, if women were the equal of men in founding the church at Philippi, it must be assumed that they continued to enjoy that equality in internal church affairs. Not surprisingly, therefore, Euodia and Syntyche became heads of house-churches. This is why Paul, contrary to his normal practice, draws public attention to the need for reconciliation between these two ladies (Phil. 4: 2). The dispute must have gone beyond the personal, and polarized the community. Clearly the women were leaders with a significant number of followers.

Paul would never admit to having a favourite among his foundations, but the community at Philippi clearly had a special place in his heart. It is understandable that he should cherish a particular affection for the first church that he had founded on the continent of Europe, but it went far beyond that. Philippi came closest to Paul's ideal of what a church should be. Collectively its members 'shone as lights in the world, holding forth the word of life' (Phil. 2: 15–16). Transformed by grace, they demonstrated the presence of God's power. Without words they proclaimed the gospel. They were the irrefutable proof of the truth of Paul's saving message. Understandably, he thanks them for their 'partnership in the gospel from the first day [in Europe] until now' (Phil. 1: 5).

The quality of community life at Philippi and the depth of their relationship with Paul implies that he ministered for the better part of a year at Philippi—that is, from late summer AD 48 to roughly the same time the following year. If he intended to stay longer, which seems unlikely, the decision was taken out of his hands.

Expelled

Paul and his companions were charged before the magistrates in the forum: 'These men are disturbing the city; they are Jews and are advocating customs that are not lawful for us as Romans to adopt or observe' (Acts 16: 20–1).[15] Paul's ministry among pagans at Philippi had been successful enough to make some people uneasy. The magistrates had responsibility for maintaining public order. By expelling

Jews from Rome in AD 19, because they were proselytizing, the emperor Tiberius had sent a signal to other magistrates that such behaviour should not be tolerated. The example of the capital would have carried particular weight in a Roman colony. Without any inquiry, therefore, the magistrates had Paul and his companions stripped and caned by the lictors, before throwing them into prison for the night (Acts 16: 22–4). In the morning they were ordered to leave town as undesirables.

At that point Paul protested that their rights as Roman citizens had not been respected (Acts 16: 37). This frightened the magistrates. Paul might have the ear of the governor of Macedonia, who was based at Thessalonica and close enough to be a threat. Not surprisingly, the magistrates apologized, but none the less only mitigated their order. They 'requested' Paul and his companions to leave town (Acts 16: 39).

Philippi, therefore, was one of the three places where Paul was 'beaten with rods' (2 Cor. 11: 25), and where he was 'shamefully treated' (1 Thess. 2: 2). Paul, of course, could have avoided all this by invoking his citizenship much earlier. But by acting as he did, he put the magistrates in the wrong, secured *de facto* recognition of his ministry, and guaranteed a certain measure of protection for his converts. Paul did not make his mark on the Graeco-Roman world by turning the other cheek on all occasions!

Missionary Strategy

Even without Luke's notice, 'when they had passed through Amphipolis and Apollonia, they came to Thessalonica' (Acts 17: 1), we could have been sure that Paul went west along the Via Egnatia after his expulsion from Philippi. Not only had his first foundation been successful, which presaged well for the future in Europe, but why should he turn back to Asia Minor, whose centre had already been captured for Christianity? Whatever the plans of his superiors in Antioch-on-the-Orontes, it was now the obligation of the churches in Galatia and around Antioch-in-Pisidia to radiate out to the coasts of the Black Sea, the Aegean and the Mediterranean. The West called him. The great highway reeling out before him was the direct route to Rome, and who knows what dreams that inspired.[16]

The stages on the Via Egnatia between Philippi and Thessalonica given by Luke are those recorded in the itineraries of the third and fourth centuries AD, which in addition note the distances. It was 29 miles (47 km) to Amphipolis, a further 28 miles (45 km) to Apollonia, and a final 34 miles (55 km) to Thessalonica. Even though the road was flat all the way, with the exception of the last few miles into Thessalonica, these distances are unusually long. Imperial dispatch-riders had to change horses twice in each segment, rather than the usual once.

Since Paul was certainly out of training for long-distance walking, I suspect that he made his first day a short one. As its name indicates, the village of Ad Duodecimum was just 12 Roman miles (11 English miles; 18 km) from Philippi. The next day, stiff as he was, he had to face the 18 miles (29 km) to Amphipolis, a beautiful walled city on a high outcrop in a loop of the River Strymon.

The fact that Paul did not minister at Amphipolis, even though it was twice as big as Philippi, suggests that he was following a definite plan. His uninterrupted journey from Pessinus to Troas was dictated by his residual fidelity to the strategic plan of his superiors in Antioch-on-the-Orontes. Troas was the next best thing to Ephesus, but there he had been distracted by the summons to Europe. In Philippi, Paul had time to reflect. His ministry there was the result of a providential call. Where was he to go next? Should he wait for a divine sign, or should he use his common sense? Not surprisingly, he opted for the latter.

Given the limited time available (Paul expected that Christ would return shortly in glory) and the vastness of the world, it was clear to Paul that he could not afford to fritter away his energies by stopping at any town or village just because it happened to lie on his path, or by accepting any invitation that happened to be offered. He needed places that, in addition to absorbing his message, had the capacity to radiate it out. His focus had to be on places that multiplied his efforts. In practice this meant cities with a mobile population, where returning visitors could bring the gospel to places that he himself

71

could not reach. Thus Paul trudged a further three or four days from Amphipolis to the nearest city that met this criterion: namely, Thessalonica (modern Salonika), capital of the Roman province of Macedonia.[17]

Labour in Thessalonica

Paul's sojourn in Thessalonica brought home to him how lucky he had been in Philippi. There, at the very beginning, he had found a wealthy patron, Lydia, who provided him with accommodation, and facilitated his ministry by furnishing him with access to the middle class. Freedom to draw on their resources relieved him of the need to earn his living. He could give himself entirely to preaching the gospel. And there were people with the leisure to listen.

Things were very different in Thessalonica. Paul twice reminds his converts there how long and hard he had to work: 'we worked night and day that we might not burden any of you' (1 Thess. 2: 9); 'we did not eat anyone's bread without paying, but with labour and toil we worked night and day that we might not burden any of you' (2 Thess. 3: 8). The normal artisan laboured only from sunrise to sunset. If Paul had to work at night, it was because he had difficulty in making ends meet. He could not afford the warm clothing that would make the winter chill of northern Greece bearable (2 Cor. 11: 27).[18]

The further implication is that his converts, all of whom were pagans (1 Thess. 1: 9), were not able to help him financially. They too belonged to the working class, and had to slave twelve hours a day seven days a week to make a living (1 Thess. 4: 11; 2 Thess. 3: 12). There is not the slightest hint of any wealthy patron at Thessalonica. There was no one to host the community, with the result that all were expected to make a contribution to the common meal (2 Thess. 3: 10). Thessalonian Christians met in tenements, not in villas.

No Longer a Salon but a Workshop

Correspondingly, the workshop, not the salon, was the scene of Paul's ministry at Thessalonica. It is not known who employed him, or how big the establishment was. It is clear, however, that there must have been a considerable demand for tents and other leather articles in a city which had so many travelling merchants. Not only did Thessalonica enjoy the advantages of being the main station on the Via Egnatia, but it had an excellent sheltered port, and an important trade route ran north up the valley of the River Axios to the Danube basin.

The workshop provided Paul with an address, a stable base and a web of ready-made contacts deriving from his employer, the clients and his fellow workers. All three groups had families and friends, and there must have been continuous interchange on a variety of different levels, all of which Paul could put to use ('working we proclaimed', 1 Thess. 2: 9). Such a workshop would be in a busy street or market, another world which made further demands on Paul's energies.

As Paul's ministry began to bear fruit, inevitably there were demands on his time that cut into his working hours, and therefore into his earnings, since undoubtedly he was doing piece-work rather than drawing a salary. How did he survive? He was saved by the generosity of the Philippians who sent him money (Phil. 4: 16). Did a visitor from Philippi recognize Paul's precarious situation? Or did Paul beg for support, knowing full well that his converts at Philippi had the resources to help him? The latter is perhaps more likely. He was convinced that those who gave spiritually deserved to receive materially (1 Cor. 9: 11), and he speaks of aid from Philippi as 'robbery' (2 Cor. 11: 8). Perhaps because they were business people themselves, or because their women leaders had greater concern for the poor, the Philippians had the wit to see that the more successful Paul was in his ministry, the less capable he would be of supporting himself. Thus they continued to fund him at Thessalonica, where he received a second subsidy. This would suggest a ministry in Thessalonica at least as long as that in Philippi—that is, from the summer of AD 49 to early spring of AD 50.

For Paul, to preach was as essential as breathing. No matter how exhausted he was, he would make time. But why would anyone in the working class bother to listen? Why did they pause for a moment in their exhausting lives? At this precise moment in Thessalonica, Paul's message filled a spiritual vacuum.[19]

The Cabirus Catch

The Cabirus legend tells of a young man, murdered by his two brothers, who was expected to return to aid the powerless and the city of Thessalonica. His symbol was the hammer, and his blessings were invoked for the successful accomplishment of manual labour. He was the god to whom the Greek working class looked for security, freedom and fulfilment. For some unknown reason, in the Augustan age Cabirus was taken up by the ruling elite and incorporated into the official cult. This left the artisans and workers of Thessalonica without a benefactor. They naturally assumed that Cabirus, like other gods, was more responsive to the appeals and gifts of the wealthy. The sense of alienation was intensified by the fact that the members of the Roman ruling élite were perceived as outsiders. Not only did they deny to the indigenous population the democratic equality which Greeks felt to be their birthright, but they monopolized the sources of profit, and now they had taken away the one traditional divine friend of the poor.

Given these circumstances, it is easy to see how attractive Paul's preaching would be to the dispossessed. It reproduced the broad lines of a theology which they had thought lost. Paul proclaimed a murdered young man, who had in fact risen from the dead, and who, in consequence, had the power to confer all benefactions in the present. Moreover, he would assume all his followers into a very different world.

It is not difficult to surmise that the hint of a new 'god', who would radically transform the situation of the underprivileged, would have been perceived by the municipal authorities as subversive. Were the movement to take root and grow, it would threaten the fabric of society. However ridiculous the crucified Jesus of Nazareth might appear as a 'god' to sophisticated Romans or Greeks, the ruling class was politically astute enough to recognize the danger of an uncontrollable 'god' outside the structures of civic religion. He could

74

serve as a rallying-point for a proletariat which by definition was unsatisfied, and therefore unstable. His message could be the magnifying glass to give inflammatory focus to frustrated ambitions. Under his inspiration, stirrings of unease could become revolutionary action.

Eventually the word filtered down to the Christian community that the authorities were considering taking action. Paul and his companions went into hiding, and were spirited out of the city, which at that stage was apparently unwalled. Paul's first instinct was simply to continue west along the Via Egnatia, just as he had done after similar trouble in Philippi. A little reflection, however, brought it home to Paul that such a course would make it very easy for the authorities to find him. Thus there may be a historical reminiscence behind Luke's assertion (Acts 17: 10) that Paul got off the Via Egnatia just after it crossed the River Axios and went south-west to Beroea (modern Veroia).

It soon became clear, however, that there was no real security as long as Paul stayed in Macedonia. He had come to the attention of the authorities in both Philippi and Thessalonica. Opposition was only going to spread and harden. This put paid to any plans that Paul might have had to carry his gospel west along the Via Egnatia. What mattered now was to get out of Macedonia as quickly as possible. A boat going south along the coast to the adjoining Roman province of Achaia was the best solution. An abrupt move to a different jurisdiction wiped the slate clean.[20]

As Paul sailed out from Methone or Pydna, his gaze was held by the snow-capped peaks of Mount Olympus, the highest mountain in Greece (9,573 ft; 2,918 m). It might have reminded him of Mount Hermon, whose height was similar, and the road to Damascus. But there was one great difference. In Greek mythology Olympus was the throne of Zeus and the home of the gods. It symbolized everything to which Paul was opposed. Did its impregnable massiveness remind him of the tremendous effort that would be necessary for the victory of the Cross?

South to Achaia   5

ALL that can be said of the roughly 300-mile (480-km) sail along the mountainous east coast of Greece is that the prevailing wind would have been favourable, and that, in consequence, the trip should not have taken too long.[1]

No matter where Paul disembarked, his goal was certainly Athens (Acts 17: 15). During his studies in Tarsus, he could not have avoided hearing of its great university rival, the cultural centre of Greece, beloved of philhellenic Roman benefactors. It seemed to be the ideal place in which to begin his ministry in Achaia.

Anxiety in Athens

Paul's first concern, however, was with those whom he had left behind in Thessalonica. He had no reason to think that his converts would escape the persecution that he had avoided by flight. He did not fear that the Thessalonians would give in to physical pressure from their fellow citizens (1 Thess. 2: 14). The real danger lay elsewhere, and was more subtle. Paul knew that his converts had assumed somewhat naïvely that in their new state they would be exempt from the violence that was endemic to their previous existence as impoverished manual labourers. What he feared was disillusionment, disappointment so profound as to lead to the abandonment of the faith. If the Thessalonian believers felt that they had been deceived, all was lost.

Small wonder that Paul was frantic with anxiety to know what had happened. He attempted more than once to return to Thessalonica, but nothing came of it. Why? His response is unsatisfactory, to say the least: 'Satan hindered us' (1 Thess. 2: 18). The providential explanation might cover an illness with a prolonged convalescence that left him too weak to travel. Once he had recovered sufficiently to manage by himself, he sent Timothy (and Silas?) from Athens to Thessalonica to find out what was happening (1 Thess. 3: 1).

Then began a long period of waiting. The modern highway from Athens to Thessalonica is 320 miles (512 km); the ancient routes are not well known. At a good consistent speed day after day, Timothy could have made the journey in two to three weeks. The same time must be allowed for the return trip. And, of course, Timothy could not just rush in and out of Thessalonica. He had to stay for at least a couple of weeks to feel the real temper of the community. Thus Paul had some two months in which to possess his soul in patience.

In the interval Paul attempted to preach at Athens. His ministry was not a success. His silence regarding converts there confirms the basic thrust of Luke's account in Acts 17. It is not impossible that Paul's distracted state—his preoccupation with the fate of Timothy and the Thessalonians—contributed to his failure at Athens. His anxiety inhibited the whole-heartedness that effective preaching demands.

Planning for the Future

Paul must have recognized rather quickly that it had been a mistake to come to Athens.[2] It was now an old sick city living on the memories of its glorious past. For several centuries it had been neither productive nor creative. No great native minds emerged, and those who came from abroad to give it a semblance of cultural life were mediocre. Essentially a university town dedicated to the conservation of its intellectual heritage, it viewed new ideas with extreme reserve. Those proposed by outsiders encountered a wall of impregnable complacency. Tradition, enshrined in a rigid hierarchy, was its main safeguard against the threat of novelty.

At Athens Paul could not have avoided hearing about Corinth, on the other side of the Saronic Gulf. The mere thought of their infinitely more prosperous neighbour made Athenians go green with envy. In the fourth century BC Athenian writers vented their spleen by inventing words based on 'Corinth' to convey different aspects of commercialized love: for example, *korinthiazesthai*, 'to fornicate'; *korinthiastês*, 'a pimp'; *korinthia korê*, 'a prostitute'. And things went downhill from there. At the time of Paul there were those who claimed that the moon was more beautiful in Athens than in Corinth.

The disparaging remarks of the Athenians about Corinth would have set up very different resonances in Paul's mind, oriented as it was to the future rather than the past. 'Lack of culture' evoked energetic efficiency in business; 'money grubbing' suggested a focus on the real rather than the ideal; 'no intellectual life' implied an openness to new ideas, because profit can be found in the most unexpected places; 'lucky in its situation' elicited the image of a crossroads with travellers going in all directions. It would be surprising if Paul had not decided that Corinth would be a much more fruitful mission field well before Timothy returned.

The latter's absence would then have become a further source of frustration. Given Paul's temperament, he would have wanted to move immediately, but that would have made it impossible for Timothy to reach him, and so would further delay the news from Thessalonica. How could Timothy ever find him in a large strange city, where (like all others) houses had no numbers and streets no names?

Finally Timothy did appear—and with good news! The Thessalonians had remained steadfast in the midst of affliction. The danger over, Paul exploded in joy, and this was the occasion of his first pastoral letter (1 Thess. 2: 13–4: 2), which he was to write only after settling down in Corinth.[3] The sense of profound relief is palpable in the warm affectionate compliments that he showers on the Thessalonians. The tenor of his encouragement is that they can do no wrong: 'you learned from us how you ought to live and to please God, just as you are doing, do so more and more' (1 Thess. 4: 1).

Timothy's visit to Thessalonica and this letter are the first evidence of any follow-up on Paul's part. Prior to this he had been content to leave his foundations to be nurtured by the Holy Spirit. In this instance, the motivation was personal. He had reached out because he was emotionally involved. It brought home to him, however, that he had to remain in dialogue with his absent converts. A father could not abandon his children (1 Thess. 2: 11).

Corinth the Crossroads

When Paul, Timothy and Silas set out from Athens for Corinth, they had a walk of some 50 miles (80 km) ahead of them, a route rich in religious associations, but whose danger was underlined by the epic deeds of Theseus.[4] At every step of the way there was something to remind the Apostle of the religious and political history of Greece, assuming, of course, that he had paid attention to his pagan professors at Tarsus. For the first 14 miles (22 km) his path followed the Sacred Way to Eleusis, along which passed the great procession each autumn to honour Demeter. Once he reached the shore of the Eleusinian Gulf, he had on his right the salt-water fish-ponds sacred to the Maid and Demeter, and the Rharian meadow, the first place ever sown or cropped, according to Greek legend. To balance such tranquil scenery, memory carried the story of Procrustes, a brigand who made his victims fit his bed by racking the short and amputating the long. One may doubt that Paul wasted time admiring the great sanctuary at Eleusis. His concern must have been to reach Megara, 12 miles (19 km) further on, before nightfall. It would have been a long day's walk.

That night Paul's thoughts would have been concentrated, not on the problems that would face him on arrival at Corinth, but on the first part of his journey next day, which presented a more immediate threat. The 5-mile (8-km) section of the road known as the Sceironian Rocks was no more than a ledge on a cliff face. The physical danger was intensified by the presence of bandits in the vicinity. The place got its name from a legendary robber called Scciron who forced travellers to wash his feet and, as they finished, kicked them over the cliff. In turn he was dispatched by Theseus. In Paul's day it was a place in which he certainly experienced 'danger from robbers ... dangers in the wilderness' (2 Cor. 11: 26).

Crossing the Isthmus

At Schoenus Paul had his first experience of the dynamism of Corinth. If the 4 mile (6.4 km)-wide Isthmus was a land-bridge, permitting trade to flow easily between the Peloponnese and the Greek mainland, it was a barrier to east–west shipping, and mariners needed an alternative to the long route around the Peloponnese. As early as the sixth century BC the Corinthians thought of cutting a canal. Like later plans, this project came to nothing, and an ingenious, provisional solution remained in place for 1,300 years. The Corinthians laid a paved road, the *diolkos*, to join the Corinthian and Saronic gulfs. The width varies from 11 to 20 feet (3.4 to 6 m). Grooves cut in the paving 4.8 feet (1.5 m) apart guided the wheels of the wooden trollies on which small boats and goods were hauled across the Isthmus. Pack animals used the earthen tracks on either side.[5]

The jostling, shouting multitude of labourers along this road, through whom Paul had to push his way, would have been his first concrete perception of what life at Corinth was going to be like. Thus far he had encountered nothing similar. The provincial towns of Asia and Macedonia were, by comparison, sleepy oases of leisure, in which his preaching would have been an agreeable distraction. Corinth had more business than it could comfortably handle. The immense volume of trade was augmented by huge numbers of travellers. Wealth came easily to those prepared to work hard, and cutthroat competition ensured that only the committed survived. 'Not for everyone is the voyage to Corinth' was one of the famous proverbs of the ancient world. No doubt, Paul wondered whether people so busy and preoccupied, so eager in their pursuit of gain, would have any time to listen to his message.

Once through the crowds, Paul found himself in a different world. The road led to the temple of Poseidon at Isthmia. Even though the restoration of the great sanctuary was just beginning, the site must have evoked the Isthmian Games, one of the four great pan-Hellenic festivals, which was celebrated every second year in the late spring. Perhaps there were still traces of the games of AD 49 celebrated some nine months earlier. He was too mature for his blood to stir at the thought of the dry celery crowns awarded the victors (1 Cor. 9: 25). If anything, he thought of the unity that the festival achieved among Greeks from all over the known world. As he marvelled at what the games did for Greek identity, did he pray that the members of his far-flung churches would feel united by a bond equally vivid and secure?

Such spiritual thoughts would have been complemented by the grateful realization that he should have little difficulty finding work in Corinth. During the week of the Isthmian Games, visitors thronged the area, and all Corinth went out to serve and to celebrate with them. The former needed tents in which to stay, and the latter brought booths in which to display their wares. A good tent-maker would find plenty to do. Repairs were as necessary as the manufacture of new tents, and the next Isthmian Games were only fifteen months away. The lift of the heart caused by the solution to one of his many problems carried Paul easily up the final 6 miles (10 km) to the city.

Paul's City

As Paul climbed, the skyline ahead of him was dominated by the height of Acrocorinth (1,885 feet; 580 m), which from time immemorial had been the citadel of Corinth. It is one of the strongest natural fortresses in Europe.[6]

Were Paul to have ascended to the summit, the city would have been laid out before him like a model. The mountain anchored a 6-mile (10-km) ruined city wall, which builders exploited as a quarry. It enclosed a plateau of some 1,000 acres (400 hectares). The lower slopes of Acrocorinth were the coveted suburb of Craneum. Beyond it, where the ground levelled off, one of Julius Caesar's best city planners had laid out a magnificent grid-patterned Roman city centred on the old Greek agora dominated by the temple of Apollo. Just to the left, the high back wall of the 14,000-seat theatre blocked the view of the swimming pool of Lerna and the adjoining temple of

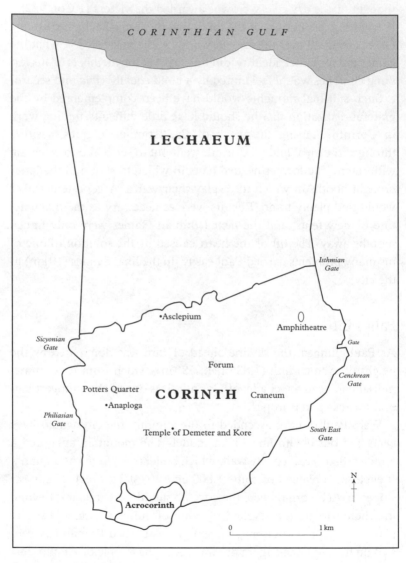

FIG. 3 Corinth: The Walls (based on D. Romano in The Corinthia in the Roman Period, JRA Suppl. 8, ed. T. E. Gregory (Ann Arbor, 1993))

Aesclepius on the edge of a steep drop-off to the coastal plain. From both ends of the north wall the long walls reached out to the blue waters of the Corinthian Gulf to protect the route from the city to Lechaeum, the third largest port in the Graeco-Roman world.

The wind coming off the sea would have carried to Paul's ears the driven cacophony of the polyglot city below. Having been refounded as a Roman colony by Julius Caesar in 44 BC, it soon attracted entrepreneurs from Greece and the major trading cities of the eastern Mediterranean. Such infusions of new capital in a prime commercial situation quickly won back for Corinth the title of 'wealthy' that it had enjoyed since the time of Homer (*Iliad* 2. 570).

Corinth, in consequence, was a lodestone for those seeking fame and fortune. Real wealth, however, tended to be concentrated in relatively few hands. There were many who, despite their best efforts, had not fulfilled their hopes and dreams. Their number explains the enduring popularity of the Sisyphus myth at Corinth. A legendary king of Corinth, Sisyphus, was called by Homer 'the craftiest of men' (*Iliad* 6. 154), and, in order to keep him busy and out of trouble in Hades, he was condemned to roll a stone up a mountain. Each time he neared the summit, it slipped from his hands, and he had to start all over again. He became a symbol of the absurdity of human existence. Those who had failed realized that there was no necessary relationship between effort and achievement. It was an age of anxiety. The arbitrariness of chance generated an interior world inhabited by dread and uncertainty. Hope had vanished. Success was a chimera.

When he arrived in this bustling city, Paul may have feared that the absorbing commercialism of Corinth would deny him a hearing. He would soon have learned, however, that there was a void of pessimism to be filled with the good news of the gospel.

Meeting Prisca and Aquila

There must have been many tent-makers' workshops in Corinth, but by an extraordinary coincidence Paul found employment with Christians. Prisca and Aquila were freed slaves of Jewish origin, who had been converted in Rome, but who had decided to leave Italy in AD 41, after the emperor Claudius had closed down a Roman synagogue as a result of continuous turmoil centring on the figure of Christ.[7] They had feared a persecution of Christians.

The trauma kept them silent about their faith in Corinth. At first they knew Paul only as a competent craftsman. It must have been an extraordinary moment when Prisca and Aquilla first heard him preaching, and realized that it was the same message to which they had responded in Rome. Paul, used to operating in virgin territory, would have been as disconcerted as they were overjoyed. Having had to struggle for years with only rudimentary information about Christianity, they now found themselves hosts, not only to an authorized emissary, but to one who had been in Jerusalem.

The sort of little shops which artisans such as Prisca and Aquila occupied were scattered all over the city. They lined busy streets, and were concentrated in specially built commercial developments. Shortly before Paul arrived, the North Market was completed, and its arrangement is so typical as to serve as a valid illustration of the conditions under which Paul lived and worked in Corinth and later in Ephesus.

The shops gave on to a wide, covered gallery running round all four sides of a square. They had a uniform height and depth of 13 feet (4 m). The width varied from 8 feet (2.8 m) to 13 feet (4 m). There was no running water or toilet facilities. In one of the back corners, a series of steps in stone or brick was continued by a wooden ladder to a loft lit by an unglazed window centred above the shop entrance, which at night was closed by wooden shutters. Prisca and Aquila had their home in the loft, while Paul slept below amid the tool-strewn work-benches and the rolls of leather and canvas.

The workshop was perfect for initial contacts, particularly with women. While Paul worked on a cloak, or sandal, or belt, he had the opportunity for conversation which quickly became instruction, and further encounters were easily justified by the need for new pieces or other repairs. As his ministry expanded, however, something more suitable was required. The space in the workshop was so limited that work had to stop if Paul addressed a group, and the assembly inevitably attracted the attention of passers-by. The lack of privacy precluded intimate discussions. Only the house of a relatively wealthy believer with its atrium and public rooms would provide the necessary space and seclusion.

The First-fruits of Achaia

Curiously, Paul's first converts at Corinth were precisely the sort of people who could meet this need. 'I am thankful that I baptized none of you except Crispus and Gaius . . . I did baptize also the household of Stephanas. Beyond that, I do not know if I baptized anyone else' (1 Cor. 1: 14–16).

The household of Stephanas was 'the first-fruit of Achaia' (1 Cor. 16: 15). The leadership role that they assumed in the community implies a degree of leisure difficult to associate with those who had to sweat for every morsel of food. This is confirmed by the freedom of Stephanas to take part in the delegation to Paul in Ephesus (1 Cor. 16: 17). He was either successfully self-employed or did not need to work. Since nothing is said of their spiritual qualities, the contribution of Stephanas and his family probably consisted in benefactions in one form or another.

Crispus is identified in Acts 18: 8 as an *archisynagogos*. This is an honorific title awarded by a Jewish community in gratitude for a donation to their place of assembly and prayer. The fundamental qualification to be a patron was to have surplus wealth. Crispus certainly was not a poor man.

Gaius is mentioned in Romans 16: 23 as 'host to me and to the whole church'. The adjective 'whole' would be unnecessary if Corinthian Christians always met as a single group. There must have been subgroups: namely, house-churches on a smaller scale. An extra large house was necessary in order to accommodate the entire community. Gaius, in consequence, must have been wealthier than the average believer.

It can hardly be a coincidence that the few whom Paul recalls having baptized at the very beginning of his ministry in Corinth should be just the sort of people who could be of use to him. These conversions happened so quickly that they must be understood to have been the result of a carefully thought-out strategy. The contrast between Paul's experiences at Philippi and at Thessalonica brought home to him the urgent need in each city of a solid nucleus of converts who were in a position to furnish facilities. Moreover, he had been forced to recognize that, while the gospel was offered to all, only those with leisure, education and initiative could function as effective assistants in spreading it. Slaves might be model Christians, but they were not their own masters, and could not dispose of their time as they wished. Neither could Prisca and Aquila, who had a living to earn.

At Corinth the three just mentioned were followed by other converts, who were obviously financially independent. The affairs of the church at Cenchreae were managed by Phoebe, whose house and purse were open to believers (Rom. 16: 1–2). The city official of Corinth, Erastus (Rom. 16: 23), could offer protection and assistance.

Why did they Heed the Gospel?

The church at Corinth clearly got off to a flying start. What made the gospel message so attractive there? One possibility can be excluded immediately. Paul explicitly asserts that he did not use his formidable rhetorical skills to make the gospel palatable. 'When I came to you I did not come proclaiming the testimony of God in lofty words or wisdom. For I decided to know nothing among you except Jesus Christ and him crucified . . . my message was not in persuasive words of wisdom' (1 Cor. 2: 2–3). Another possibility is that the paradox of a crucified saviour resonated in the lives of prominent Corinthians and gave them meaning.

Take, for example, the case of Erastus. The inscription that he erected to himself near the theatre does not include his father's name. This means that Erastus had once been a slave. Yet he had achieved Roman citizenship, and had the surplus income that public office demanded. None the less, however much Erastus may have achieved, he would never have felt fully at ease among the free-born. As with others of his class, the stigma of his servile origins blighted every pleasure.

The fear of being patronized provoked an injudicious aggressiveness. The sense of insecurity of the successful freedman became a favourite topic in literature. Corinth had its own celebrated example, which Paul could not have avoided seeing. A small circular structure on the agora carried the same inscription on both the pedestal and the band above the columns, 'Gnaeus Babbius Philinus, aedile and pontifex, had this monument erected at his own expense, and he approved it in his official capacity of duovir'. The absence of his father's name identifies Babbius as a freedman. He had risen to high office, but he was not prepared to take the chance that his successor as chief magistrate might refuse this little exercise in self-recommendation!

The root of such insecurity was the bitter awareness that one was not recognized for what one had achieved. Contemporaries, it was felt, imposed on the reality an unflattering portrait drawn from other sources. Erastus imagined that those who looked at him saw not the important city official but merely an ex-slave. Freedmen, however, were not the only ones to feel the discomfort of ambiguous status. Phoebe of Cenchreae, though of sufficient independent wealth to be a patron to Paul and many others (Rom. 16: 2), would have been seen first and foremost as a woman, with the social and political disadvantages her sex implied. Crispus was a distinguished and generous figure, but to his pagan contemporaries he was above all a Jew, who lived among them on sufferance.

The central message of the gospel, that the saviour of the world died under torture, spoke to the contradictions of the lives of such people. Though classed as weak, they knew their own power, and thus could understand without difficulty the idea, revealed in the life of Christ, as in that of Paul, that 'power is made perfect in weakness' (2 Cor. 12: 9). To them Christianity made sense of the ambiguity of their lives, and at the same time introduced them into a society committed to looking at them primarily as unique individuals, all equally valuable and valued. It gave them a space in which they could flourish in freedom.

These individuals, and perhaps others whose names Paul does not mention, formed a group, whose members Paul qualified as 'wise, powerful, and well-born' (1 Cor. 1: 26). The 'wise' were the educated, and in particular those with a reputation for prudence and moderation, who exhibit sound judgement in politics or commerce. The 'powerful' were the influential, those whose opinions carry weight in civic life. The 'well-born' are those born into the aristocracy of wealth created by the freedmen who were sent by Julius Caesar to refound Corinth in 44 BC. With admirable brevity Paul evokes a privileged élite, whose impact on Corinth was quite out of proportion to its numbers. Its members were a minority in the city, as were those from this class who became Christians. These latter no doubt played a dominant role in the affairs of the church. Those who take their authority for granted do not need official positions to reinforce it.

The Make-up of the Corinthian Church

The majority of believers were not so fortunate, but neither were they at the bottom of the social scale. Of the members of the church at Corinth we know sixteen individuals by name. Two of them (Prisca and Aquila) are married to each other. Two are women (Prisca and Phoebe). Six are explicitly of Jewish origin (Aquila, Crispus, Prisca, Sosthenes, Jason, Sosipater). Three are certainly Gentiles (Gaius, Erastus and Titius Justus). Others are not so easy to pigeon-hole (Achaicus, Fortunatus, Lucius, Quartus, Stephanas and Tertius), but Tertius, as a professional stenographer, may have been a slave, and the Latin nickname Achaicus, 'the man from Achaia', indicates that he had been a slave in Italy before returning home to make good as a freedman. The 'households' of Stephanas and Crispus most probably contained slaves. While legally disadvantaged, such house slaves often enjoyed a standard of living and education denied to those born free and poor. Their status was very different from that of the degraded field or mine slaves.

The one certain deduction that can be made from these random names is the minimum size of the community, which was between forty and fifty. As regards its composition, if Paul can say without qualification, 'you know that when you were Gentiles you were led astray to dumb idols' (1 Cor. 12: 2), the vast majority of the Corinthian church were converts from paganism. This is confirmed by the type of problems that subsequently arose in the community. Jewish converts were a small minority.

The church at Corinth was definitely a heterogeneous group. Most members had in common only their Christianity. They differed widely in educational attainment, financial resources, religious background, political skills and, above all, in their expectations. A number were attracted to the church because it seemed to offer them a new field of opportunity, in which the talents whose expression society frustrated could be exploited to the full. They were energetic and ambitious people, as were Euodia and Syntyche in Philippi, and there was little agreement among their various hidden agendas. A certain competitive spirit was part of the ethos of the church from the beginning.

For Paul such diversity made the church at Corinth a microcosm. It was integrated into its environment on a variety of levels that should enhance its missionary appeal. What Paul appreciated above all, however, was the willingness of the Corinthians to accept the responsibility of internalizing Christianity, of working out how to give the following of Christ practical expression in their daily lives. No fear of making a mistake dampened their enthusiasm. In fact their self-confidence ruled out error as impossible.

Subsequent events were to show that Paul gravely underestimated their capacity to get things wrong. He himself was not exempt from blame. The imprecision of his preaching exacerbated a positive genius on their part for misunderstanding him. Virtually every statement he made took root in their minds in a slightly distorted form, and from this defective seed flowered bizarre approaches to different aspects of the Christian life. While present, of course, he could nip such developments in the bud. But once he left, the garden ran wild.

Given the vitality of the church at Corinth and its willingness to take initiatives, there must have been a missionary dimension to its life. Unfortunately we know little or nothing about it. Paul includes 'all the saints who are in the whole of Achaia' among the addressees of 2 Corinthians. At only one point can we lift the veil of this vague generality. There was a community at Cenchreae, the eastern port of Corinth, which was headed by a woman, Phoebe (Rom. 16: 1–2).

Correspondence with Thessalonica

Traffic in, out and through Corinth was intense. The city sat at the centre of a web of trade routes reaching out to all points of the compass. This was a definite advantage to Paul, not only in terms of missionary outreach, but because there would rarely be difficulty in finding a group going to wherever he wanted to send a messenger. I suspect that he availed himself of one such opportunity to confide his first letter to the Thessalonians (1 Thess. 2: 13–4: 2) to a Corinthian convert of his who was going north into Macedonia.

This messenger brought back a rather ambiguous report about the community at Thessalonica. On the one hand, they were profoundly committed believers, whose lives radiated the gospel (1 Thess. 1: 6–8), but on the other, they seemed to have misunderstood Paul when he spoke of the breaking in of the new age. The practical result was that some of them had stopped working because they were convinced that they had enough to live on until Christ appeared in glory. Others worried about the salvation of believers who had died since Paul had left them. Should they not have stayed alive because Paul had said that they now possessed new life? Did their death mean that they were lost for ever?

On a more personal level, the messenger diffidently conveyed to Paul that he was not universally popular in the church of Thessalonica. There were no specific accusations, but he had picked up an amorphous feeling of dissatisfaction with Paul's performance. This criticism may have been no more than a casual throw-away remark, but the mere fact of its being made might suggest that there were already rumblings of opposition to Paul at Thessalonica.

The letter (1 Thess. 1: 1–2: 12 and 4: 3–5: 28) that Paul wrote in response to this, his first serious maintenance problem, is very reve-latory. The tone is markedly different from that of his first letter (1 Thess. 2: 13–4: 2). Effervescent warmth and unqualified praise have given way to grave admonition and measured advice. This hint of emotional distance is reinforced by the absence of any expression of desire to see the Thessalonians once more. Clearly Paul has moved on. His affectivity has been absorbed by the nascent Corinthian community. The Thessalonians were no longer in the forefront of his mind.

Contrary to what we might have expected of a pastor, Paul does not deal first with the major issues of eschatology, but instead offers a sweeping refutation of any and all possible accusations regarding his behaviour while at Thessalonica (1 Thess. 2: 1–12). Despite the dispassionate tone, it is surprising to discern such sensitivity to even a hint of criticism in a man in his mid-fifties, who had been an active missionary for more than ten years, and who certainly had dealt more than once with failure. It may have been an unfortunate personality trait, but it may also have been the obverse of his complete identification with his message (1 Cor. 4: 10–11). It was not healthy for Paul to interpret any attack on himself as an affront to the word of God, which justified—required?—a response.

Half-way through the letter, Paul finally gets around to dealing with the problems of the Thessalonians. Instead of offering theological justification to those who had lost loved ones, he both instructs and consoles them by painting a dramatic picture of the Last Day. 'The Lord himself' will descend from heaven with a cry of command, with the archangel's call, and with the sound of the trumpet of God. And the dead in Christ will rise first, then we who are alive, who are left, shall be caught up together with them in the clouds, to meet the Lord in the air' (1 Thess. 4: 16–17). Paul knew instinctively that to assuage their anguish, they needed certitude, not speculation.

There were others in Thessalonica, however, whose belief in an imminent return of Christ in glory abolished the gap between 'now' and 'then'. Paul had to remind them that the gap did exist, and that what they did in the interval determined their fate in the other world. Thus, the unruly, idle element should go back to work and earn their living, just as Paul had always worked when he was with them. From Paul's perspective, what the Thessalonians saw him do should have enabled them to resolve correctly any possible ambiguity in what he actually said. In other words, in the 'gap', life should carry on as before, but now according to the much higher standard set by the self-sacrifice of Christ.

From Ambiguity to Confusion

Like many people, Paul believed that his hearers understood what he wanted them to hear. It does not appear to have entered his mind that this might be at variance with what he actually said. If the problem was brought to his attention, he would have replied with exasperation, 'They should have worked out what I meant!'

Paul's failure to make himself absolutely clear when preaching at Thessalonica certainly contributed to the confusion in the community regarding the implications of the proximity of Christ's return. The letter we are discussing, which was supposed to clarify the situation, did not have the desired effect, because the Thessalonians, who wished to maintain their own contrary opinion, could have read certain statements of the letter as supporting their position. Paul was not careful enough in his formulation.

As an illustration of how the Thessalonians could have taken a meaning out of Paul's words that he in no way intended, let us examine one text. Paul wrote, 'God has not destined us to wrath but to obtain salvation through our Lord Jesus Christ who died for us so that whether we wake or sleep we might live with him' (1 Thess. 5: 9–10). The main clause is 'God has destined us for salvation'. What God decides, however, will necessarily take place. The Thessalonians could legitimately conclude, therefore, that their salvation was guaranteed.

The corollary was equally obvious. How they lived was irrelevant, because nothing that they did could modify the divine decision. They could even find explicit justification for this further deduction in the phrase 'whether we wake or sleep'. Paul intended this to mean 'whether we are alive or dead' (cf. 1 Thess. 4: 13–15). But just previously in this very context he had used the same words in a different sense, 'Let us not sleep as others do, but let us keep awake and be sober' (1 Thess. 5: 6). Here 'sleep' and 'wake' mean carelessness and vigilance with respect to moral observance. This facilitated the Thessalonian understanding of 'whether we wake or sleep' as meaning 'whether we are good or bad'.

Those whose words have been misunderstood will have little difficulty in identifying with the mystified irritation with which Paul reacted to the report brought back by his messenger of what he was supposed to have said. Whatever the explanation—honest misunderstanding, deliberate distortion?—it was not something that he could afford to let pass. He had to respond, and did so with somewhat icy clarity in his third letter to Thessalonica, which we know as 2 Thessalonians.[8] He highlights the signs that must precede the glorious return of Christ, in order to demolish the belief of some of the Thessalonians that the Parousia had already taken place but secretly, and he admonishes the unruly idlers much more sternly.

The view attributed to Paul was so alien to his thought that he seriously considered the possibility that the letter which the Thessalonians received might have been a forgery (2 Thess. 2: 2). This would have been relatively easy, because Paul did not write his letters himself (Rom. 16: 22). If the Thessalonians noted variations in the handwriting of the three letters, they would simply have assumed that Paul had used different professional scribes.[9] In order to exclude forgery in the future, Paul added a note in his own handwriting at the end of 2 Thessalonians, thereby explicitly signing a letter for the first time. 'I, Paul, write this greeting with my own hand. This is the mark in every letter of mine. It is the way I write' (2 Thess. 3: 17).

Financial Matters

The need to keep up correspondence with another church in addition to catering to the needs of his Corinthian converts greatly exacerbated Paul's problem of finding enough time to earn a living (1 Cor. 4: 12). He had not been able to make ends meet when he was at Thessalonica, and now there were many more distractions. In theory there should have been no problem because, unlike in Thessalonica, Corinth had many believers capable of supporting him. Paul, however, refused to make any demands on them. His boast was that he preached the gospel 'free of charge' (1 Cor. 9: 18).

Paul's survival would be a mystery if we did not know that he continued to be subsidized by Philippi. 'When I was with you and was in want, I did not burden anyone, for my needs were supplied by the brethren who came from Macedonia' (2 Cor. 11: 9). The flustered tone of the context reveals a very embarrassed Paul replying to a Corinthian criticism, 'Why did you not ask us to help you? You took money from Philippi! Why not from us?' While in Corinth, Paul had somehow managed to give the impression that he was earning enough to live on. Prisca and Aquila must have conspired with him in this deception. After all, he was their employee. But why did Paul consider it necessary to be so devious?

The cement of the Graeco-Roman world was the exchange of benefactions.[10] Mere possession of wealth was nothing. Only in being distributed was it transmuted into prestige and power. A gift was a public gesture laying claim to superiority, and calling for honour from the recipient. A gift had to be reciprocated. If the return was superior in value, the original recipient gained the advantage. If of equal value, both remained equal. If, however, the return was of less value, the recipient became a client with an unrequited obligation to the giver. To refuse a gift was not a real option, because the consequence would be bad blood.

It is only against this background that Paul's acceptance of money from Philippi, and his refusal of support from Corinth, become intelligible. It was not arbitrary, but a consistent missionary strategy. He would accept financial aid from a community only after he had departed, never while he was still present. Distance made the difference.

The Philippian gift represented a community effort. The church created a common fund to which all could contribute. The sum of money was brought by an official delegation, and presented in the name of the church. The implication, as far as Paul was concerned, was that all members of the church had participated, even though some may have given more than others. The individuality of each contribution was assumed into a whole, which symbolized the unity of the community. The subsidy could be accepted by Paul as an offer of abiding friendship. He incurred no debt to any individual. His gratitude goes to the whole church (Phil. 4: 10–20).

At Corinth, on the contrary, because Paul lived there, all gifts were highly personal. Benefactions were necessarily particular, not only because they were handed over by specific individuals, but because

94

they were in kind. Lodging meant someone's house, a meal some-one's table. How was Paul to react to a multitude of individual gifts? According to the ethos of Graeco-Roman society, he would have had to parcel out his time and energy in such a way that those who had contributed the greatest amount received the most. The needy poor would have had little chance against the resources of the élite. Even with the best motives in the world, the latter would have monopolized Paul's attention to the detriment of the real needs of the whole community.

Perhaps after contrasting his experiences at Philippi and Thessalonica, certainly before he arrived in Corinth, Paul saw that to accept a single gift would put him in an impossible situation. It is hardly surprising that he repudiated all offers, despite the ill feeling this engendered. He was damned if he did, and damned if he didn't, and no doubt he cursed the perversity of human nature.

A Crucial Date

Jewish opposition to Paul in Corinth increased in proportion to the number of 'God-fearers' he won over to Christianity. This loss of pagans sympathetic to Judaism was seen by Jews as a threat to their existence. Those whom they had counted on as their defenders if trouble arose were being decimated. They could not afford to let Paul continue his depredations. Thus one day, 'when Gallio was procon-sul of Achaia, the Jews made a united attack on Paul and brought him before the *bema*' (Acts 18: 12).

The head-high *bema*, or speaker's platform, stood in the centre of the vast open space of the agora. From here public proclamations were read. Here the magistrates sat. A struggling Paul would have been placed on the low, square, stone platform in front of them, with the tall statue of Athena at his back. Unlike what happened at Philippi, this affair did not turn out badly for Paul. Gallio dismissed the charges as being a purely Jewish internal matter in which he had no interest.

The importance of this episode is that it shows that Paul's ministry in Corinth overlapped, at least in part, with the term of office of

L. Iunius Gallio, the brother of the philosopher Seneca. Gallio took up his appointment as proconsul of Achaia at the beginning of July, AD 51. He did not serve his full term of a year, but left Corinth on the excuse of illness in September, Paul, in consequence, can only have met him in the late summer of AD 51.[11]

Shortly after this encounter, Paul left to return to Antioch-on-the-Orontes. He had spent eighteen fruitful but testing months in Corinth (Acts 18: 11), and it was time to leave the community to its own devices. As long as Paul was present, everything was referred to him. The Corinthians had to develop their own understanding of Christianity, and the community needed space for its own leaders to emerge. The overpowering personality of Paul inhibited normal social development.

Antioch and Jerusalem 6

WHEN Paul left Corinth, he did not go straight to Antioch-on-the-Orontes. His experiences in Macedonia and Achaia had taught him a number of important lessons. The first, as we have seen with respect to Thessalonica, was the need for maintenance. He had to remain in touch with his foundations in order to enable them to work through the problems they encountered. The second was the great advantage of having a prepared base when he entered a strange city. He had been lucky at Philippi in finding Lydia, who throughout his stay there provided lodging and support. He was not as fortunate at Thessalonica, where he had to struggle to survive. In Corinth, however, he had struck gold. Prisca and Aquila were well-established Christians who offered him a home and work.

By the time he left Corinth, Paul had decided that, when he returned from Antioch, he would settle at Ephesus. In terms of maintaining contact with his churches, his choice could not be bettered. As the crow flies, Ephesus is equidistant from Galatia and Thessalonica (288 miles; 445 km). If we use this distance as a radius with Ephesus as the centre, we circumscribe a circle within which Corinth (240 miles; 400 km) and Philippi (267 miles; 445 km) fit very comfortably. Moreover, the land and sea routes radiating out from Ephesus were excellent. Finally, the city would fit into the missionary strategy of Antioch, which had been decided some five years earlier.

Once that decision had been taken, the next step followed logically. On his way to the east, Paul dropped off Prisca and Aquila in

Ephesus (Acts 18: 18–19). They were the advance team whose job it was to prepare a comfortable base against the day when Paul would finally join them. It was a wonderful plan as far as Paul was concerned, but he was asking a lot of Prisca and Aquila. They would lose the business which they had laboriously built up in Corinth, and with it the support of their life-style. They would have to begin anew in a strange city, scraping a living as they struggled to attract clients.

They had started from scratch before, however, and they knew that they could do it again. And this time they operated under a much more profound imperative than economic survival. The intense involvement implied by Paul's encomium, 'they risked their necks for my life' (Rom. 16: 3), indicates that they had become an integral part of the Pauline mission. They were members of his permanent team, and all that mattered was the spread of the gospel. Financial loss and personal sacrifice were alike irrelevant.

In order to be sure of finding them again, Paul had to stay in Ephesus until Prisca and Aquila found a place to live. When he rejoined them a year later, he found a thriving church. Much, however, had happened in the meantime.

A Law-free Mission

In the early autumn of AD 51 Paul had been away from Antioch-on-the-Orontes for some five years. What had begun as a mission to Ephesus had been providentially transformed into a series of successful campaigns in Galatia, Macedonia and Achaia. The vast majority of the converts that Paul made in these provinces were pagans, and their conversion process was a very simple one. They had to renounce the idols which they had once worshipped. They had to confess Jesus Christ as the only saviour (Rom. 10: 9). And they had to manifest their belief socially by submitting to the rite of baptism.

Given Paul's recognition that in terms of salvation it was *either* the Messiah *or* the Law, it certainly never entered his mind that his converts should be subjected to the demands of the Law. Belief in

Jesus Christ sufficed. This had been the policy of the church at Antioch when he left, and we must presume that it was also the practice of Barnabas, his erstwhile missionary companion.

The sea journey of some 521 nautical miles (965 km) from Ephesus to the coast of Palestine is dismissed by Luke in two sentences (Acts 18: 21–2). With favourable winds it would have taken less than a week. The destination of the ship, however, was Caesarea, much too far to the south for Paul's liking. As part of his policy of binding Paul as closely as possible to Jerusalem (Acts 22: 3), Luke takes advantage of this fact to insinuate that Paul made a visit of respect to the mother church. In point of fact, Paul probably set out immediately for Antioch-on-the-Orontes. He knew from experience that he still had some 300 miles (480 km) to cover, and that contrary winds would make coastal sailing a slow business.[1] Why would he waste time and energy going up to Jerusalem? It was not his church.

When Paul finally reached Antioch-on-the-Orontes, he no doubt expected a triumphant welcome for bringing the gospel so far and so successfully. It must have come as a tremendous shock to discover that the policy of a Law-free mission that he had implemented was being called in question. The basis of his life-work was under attack. The Antiocheans were less interested in what he had done than in the question of whether he had the right to have done it.

Members of the mother church in Jerusalem had arrived in Antioch, and were insisting that all Gentile converts had to become Jews before they could be accepted as Christians (Acts 15: 1). Pagans must be circumcised and observe the dietary laws in order to become followers of Jesus.

Paul was furious (Gal. 2: 4–5). These trouble-makers were 'false brethren' who were 'secretly smuggled in' in order to 'spy' and then to 'enslave' the Antiocheans. The loaded language of this emotional outburst might make it appear that the Jerusalem Christians were completely in the wrong, that they were propagating a completely false theology. This was not in fact the case.

Even Paul would have admitted that salvation was related to the chosen people, who worshipped the one God, and to whom he had sent his Messiah. The Jerusalemites would have gone on to point out that, during his lifetime, Jesus the Messiah had been circumcised (Luke 2: 21) and had obeyed the Law—for example, when he went on pilgrimage to Jerusalem. Moreover, that same Messiah had proclaimed the eternal validity of the Law—for example, 'Amen, I say to you, until heaven and earth pass away, not an iota, not a dot, will pass from the Law until all is acomplished' (Matt. 5: 18). Finally, the Messiah had commanded obedience to the Law—for example, in saying to the leper, 'go, show yourself to the priest, and offer for your cleansing what Moses commanded' (Mark 1: 44). If Jesus the Messiah had been so scrupulous about the Law, argued the Jerusalem Christians, his disciples could not be otherwise. Therefore, all his followers had to submit to the Law's demands.

For Antiochean Christians who knew something about the life of Jesus, this argument had tremendous force, because the facts on which it was based were incontrovertible. If they looked to Paul for a refutation, however, they were disappointed. To him such arguments were simply irrelevant. He saw things from a completely different perspective. For him the *identity* of Jesus was much more important than anything he had said or done. As Messiah, Jesus inaugurated a new age; he introduced humanity into a new world, in which none of the old standards or criteria or demands or values mattered any longer. 'In the new creation, the old has passed away, the new has come' (2 Cor. 5: 17). The Messiah was the alternative to the Law.

The church at Antioch thus found itself the arena in which two totally convinced adversaries struggled to fight without ever coming in contact with each other. Their blows passed in mid-air. The arguments were on parallel tracks that never met. Both spoke, but there was no dialogue.

Such tension could not be endured for long. The church at Antioch saw only one way of breaking the deadlock. Representatives of the community would have to go to Jerusalem, and present their policy regarding pagan converts to the mother church. Not surprisingly, the choice fell on Paul and Barnabas, the two who had done most to bring Gentiles to Christ. They were accompanied by Titus (Gal. 2: 1), who here appears in Paul's company for the first time.

Titus was a Gentile, and probably an Antiochean, but he was not part of the delegation. It would appear that Paul brought him along deliberately as a test case. Had he merely wanted an assistant, the much more experienced Timothy was available, but he had been circumcised (Acts 16: 3).

A Meeting in Jerusalem

It was with troubled minds that Paul and Barnabas tramped towards Jerusalem. They would be on the road for some two weeks, and had much to talk about. They were fully convinced of the rightness of the case that they were deputed to argue, but there were larger issues. We cannot speak for Barnabas, but Paul, for his part believed, not that circumcision was wrong, but that it was completely irrelevant, and that its acceptance gave a false impression. It appeared to accord continuing validity to the Law, which in his view had been supplanted by Jesus the Messiah. What disturbed the two missionaries was that the simple fact of their mission implied that Antioch was prepared to accept the decision of Jerusalem regarding the circumcision of pagan converts to Christianity.

A Worrying Problem

Paul was fully capable of closing his mind to the possibility of failure, of refusing to believe that the Jerusalem decision could go against a Law-free mission. He had no gift for projecting himself into the minds of others and appreciating their perspective. He *knew* that he was right. Barnabas was probably more pragmatic, and would have forced Paul to face the consequences of an adverse decision. If they lost, what was Paul to do?

Should he sacrifice his understanding of God's revelation in obedience to the moral authority of the mother church? Should he accept the decision of Jerusalem to the extent of demanding that his pagan converts accept circumcision, while remaining inwardly convinced that it was completely meaningless? Should he break completely with both Jerusalem and Antioch and refuse to circumcise his pagan converts? Such questions revolved ceaselessly in his mind as he interminably debated the pros and cons.

If Paul took the last option, which seems the most likely in terms of his temperament, the consequences were clear. Jerusalem could destroy what he had achieved, and systematically oppose any future missionary activity on his part. Envoys could be sent to the communities that he had founded to inform them that Paul was an isolated, unrepresentative maverick, since all authentic followers of Jesus observed the Law.

The threat was very real. Paul had few illusions about his converts' loyalty to his theological principles. His experience with the Thessalonians had shown him how easily his teaching could be misunderstood. Moreover, the few who had grasped what he was about were unlikely to resist pressure to conform to the majority. Finally, Paul knew the difficulties of making moral decisions in full freedom, and as a Pharisee he had experienced the seductive power of the security that rules and regulations offered. In a world where his converts were battered by forces that they could neither understand nor control, the Law could easily be made to appear a lifeline to save them from being swept under by waves of anxiety as to the rightness or wrongness of their choices. The more he thought about it, the more Paul's apprehension increased.

As the gleaming masses of the Temple and the Palace came into view above the ramparts of Jerusalem, Paul would have been reminded of his previous visit some fourteen years earlier (Gal. 2: 1). Then he had come to Cephas full of questions about the historical Jesus. Now he came with just one question. The answers of Cephas had satisfied his curiosity about Jesus. Now the answer on how Jesus should be followed could change his whole life.

Peter no Longer in Charge

If Paul had expected Cephas to be in the same unrivalled position of authority as on his first visit, he was disappointed. And his anxiety increased. On that occasion, Cephas had recognized the divine origin of Paul's mission to the Gentiles (Gal. 2: 7), and no doubt

Paul had counted on his support this time. To his consternation, he and Barnabas were confronted by a committee composed of James the brother of Jesus, Cephas and John (Gal. 2: 9).

Fourteen years earlier, James had been a rising figure in the community (Gal. 1: 19). Now he might not have eclipsed Cephas completely, but he had moved up to be the head of the leadership group in Jerusalem. In a number of ways his career paralleled that of Paul. Initially both men had been hostile to Jesus' ministry, James during the lifetime of Jesus (John 7: 5), Paul when he first heard the gospel preached. Both were converted by a post-resurrection appearance of the Risen Lord (1 Cor. 15: 7–8). By force of personality, both rose to positions of authority in the Jesus movement. Of course, the family relationship of James to Jesus would not have hindered his promotion. James' successor as leader of the Jerusalem church, Symeon, was a cousin of Jesus, being the son of his uncle Clopas, the brother of Joseph.

In contrast to the cosmopolitan Paul, who had travelled widely, James was a parochial Galilean who had moved no further than Jerusalem. He had always lived as part of a Jewish majority, and thus, without questioning, he continued unchanged his Jewish lifestyle, even after accepting Jesus as the Messiah. Baptism and Eucharist, as ritual and meal, were familiar additions, not radical substitutions. Paul had every reason to think that James was behind the Jerusalemites who had troubled the church at Antioch by their insistance that Christians should first become Jews.

Undoubtedly James agreed with the theological arguments that his followers had put forward in Antioch. He might even have added others. A number of prophecies of the Old Testament, for example, spoke of the Messianic age as a time when the whole Gentile world would come on submissive pilgrimage to Jerusalem (e.g. Isa. 60–2). James could have drawn attention to the words that one such prophecy puts in the mouth of pagans: 'Let us go up to the mountain of Yahweh, to the house of the God of Jacob that he may teach us his ways so that we may walk in his paths. For the Law will issue from Zion and the word of Yahweh from Jerusalem' (Isa. 2: 3). Since Jesus had inaugurated the Messianic age, James could have argued,

103

now was the time for those Gentiles who acknowledged Jesus as the Messiah to accept the Law.

In one sense, this line of argument moved James closer to Paul, who had based his position of freedom from the Law on the fact that Jesus was the Messiah. From another perspective, it should have made any compromise impossible, because they should have drawn diametrically opposed conclusions from the same premiss. But this did not happen. Paul held firm, whereas James astonishingly agreed that Titus did not need to be circumcised (Gal. 2: 3), thereby releasing all pagan converts from the yoke of the Law, and implicitly affirming that faith in Jesus was alone necessary.[2]

Why did James Agree with Paul?

Even in the unlikely event that Paul had pulled out all his rhetorical stops, I cannot think that he was so naïve as to believe that James had been won over by the brilliance of his presentation. There must have been other factors which, as far as James was concerned, outweighed the theological arguments in favour of Judaizing Gentile converts. Somewhat surprisingly, I suspect that these were political rather than religious.[3]

In the Roman Empire, to which Judaea now belonged, Jews had privileges which were precisely defined and protected by Roman law.[4] In the fifteen years or so before the Jerusalem meeting in AD 51 there had been a series of serious incidents in which Jewish rights had been violated without any action on the part of the Roman authorities. On certain occasions the authorities themselves were responsible. The emperor Tiberius had expelled the Jews from Rome. His successor, Gaius, attempted to transform the Temple in Jerusalem into a pagan imperial shrine by having a statue of himself as Jupiter erected there. The prefect of Egypt fanned the flames of a violent outburst of anti-Semitism in Alexandria. His colleague, the procurator of Judaea, removed from Jewish control the garments without which the high priest could not function. The inevitable consequence of such repeated incidents—many others may not have been recorded—was a profound sense of insecurity among Jews.

Matters came to a head in Judaea in AD 51. The procurator did nothing to punish the Samaritans who had slaughtered Galilean pilgrims *en route* to Jerusalem. So their friends and other Jews took the law into their own hands and wreaked vengance on the Samaritans. Things had reached such a pass that any perceptive observer could have predicted growing tension between the Jews and Rome, with an ever increasing potential for violence. Clearly it was imperative for Jews to stand together. Only if they were totally united could they survive. Any diminution of commitment could be fatal.

The dilemma in which this placed politically conscious Jewish Christians is obvious. They were first and foremost Jews. All that separated them from their brethren was their acceptance of Jesus of Nazareth as the Messiah. Even without pressure from their co-religionists, their own instincts would have told them that the beginning of the fifties was a time to affirm, not to dilute, Jewish identity. Which end would the circumcision of Gentile converts achieve? Manifestly the latter. To circumcise Gentile converts was to accept them publicly as Jews, even though they had no attachment to Judaism; they were followers of Christ, not of Moses. So what loyalty to the Jewish people could be expected of such individuals when hostile pressures began to take their toll? In a crisis, could any nationalistic Jew really trust them? Would such nominal Jews be prepared to sacrifice their lives for the Temple and the Law?

Questions such as these must have occurred to the more far-sighted members of the Jerusalem church. What seemed to be right in the present could be seen to be a dangerous threat in the not-too-distant future. James, I suggest, was one of these. As the leader of the Jerusalem church, he was swayed, not by theological reasons, but by practical considerations. Those who demanded the circumcision of Gentile converts might be correct in theory, but it was not the moment to insist on principle.

Whatever his personal inclinations, historical circumstances conspired to make James want to find justification for not circumcising Gentile believers. This need made him receptive to Paul's personality and arguments. No more than he had fourteen years earlier (Gal. 1: 19), could he doubt the sincerity with which Paul explained the implications of the way he himself had been converted. Nor could he deny the grace manifested in the number of Gentiles who accepted the Pauline gospel (Gal. 2: 9a). Similar success, presumably, was duplicated by Barnabas elsewhere. Such signs of the presence of the Holy Spirit manifested the divine will that Gentiles should be admitted to the church as Gentiles. But James could not have given such evidence its true value without the pressure of political events.

The Collection for the Poor of Jerusalem

The poverty of Jerusalem was known throughout the Jewish world. Perhaps as many as two-thirds of the inhabitants were supported by public or private charity (Acts 4: 34–7).[5] Some times were worse than others, but no time was good. Visitors to the city were encouraged to bring as much in alms as they could afford. Both Paul and Barnabas had had first-hand experience of conditions in the Holy City, and they certainly supported the initiative of the Antiochean church to take up a collection, which they could bring as a financial present for the Jerusalem church when they went up to discuss the issue of circumcision (Acts 11: 29–30).

At the end of the meeting, James, Cephas and John asked Paul and Barnabas to continue the subsidy from the church of Antioch (Gal. 2: 10a). The leadership in Jerusalem had recognized that, despite its commitment to Judaism, the Christian community in the Holy City was beginning to acquire a distinctive social identity that set it apart from the mainstream. There was a growing possibility that at some point Christians might no longer have access to institutionalized Jewish charity. It was imperative that the Christian diaspora should act like the Jewish diaspora in financially supporting its co-religionists in Jerusalem.

Paul and Barnabas had no hesitation in committing the church they represented to such continuing support. They did not need to consult. It was the duty of all Christians to love their neighbours. Paul, however, took the commitment personally. His enthusiasm was no doubt inspired, at least in part, by the deprivations that he had experienced as a poor Pharisee. How he would then have appreciated a generous donor! But he was also mentally committing his own foundations to the support of Jerusalem. As we saw, he had no intention of staying in Antioch. The day the snows melted in the high country, he planned to be on his way west to Ephesus. There was no reason why the daughter churches of Antioch should not contribute to such a worthy project. It would have been a highly appropriate reciprocal gesture for the recognition that Jerusalem had accorded their freedom.

Trouble at Antioch

Paul and Barnabas were light-hearted as they returned to Antioch-on-the-Orontes. They no longer had the responsibility for a significant sum of money. They could cheerfully turn out their pockets if accosted by bandits. More importantly, a tremendous burden of worry had been lifted from their shoulders. What they had been doing had been accepted as God's will. No changes were necessary. They could continue as before preaching the gospel to Gentiles.

The news of their successful mission was welcomed with gladness by the church in Antioch, whose missionary policy had been officially vindicated. This was the moment for the Antiocheans to appreciate a report from Paul on his great expedition into Europe. He may have played down the hardships that he had undergone, but he would not have stinted on any other details. His audience would have been minutely informed regarding the route he had taken, the cities in which he had preached, the techniques of evangelization that he had employed, the number of his converts, and the sort of communities that had come into being. He had five years' worth of material. The saga no doubt went on for several days.

This was not self-aggrandizement. Paul certainly felt that he was boasting in the Lord (1 Cor. 1: 31; 2 Cor. 10: 17). He would have made it clear that he was simply the channel through which divine power became operative in the world (1 Cor. 3: 5–9). Apart from glorifying God, the point that Paul would have wanted to make was that, if others at Antioch did not offer themselves as missionaries, there would be that many fewer channels to transmit grace. It is easy to visualize him expanding on the inspiring example of the dynamic evangelism of Philippi. The community at Antioch had plenty of time to assimilate what Paul had achieved in its name.

Cephas in a Mixed Community

No reason is given for the arrival of Cephas in Antioch (Gal. 2: 11). I suspect that it was sheer curiosity. At the meeting in Jerusalem he had been intrigued by Paul's vivid description of the community at Antioch, and perhaps at Corinth, where Jewish and Gentile converts lived together in harmony. Cephas had never lived in a *mixed* community.

James, it will be remembered, was not opposed to the conversion of Gentiles. The only point at issue was how they should be incorporated into the Christian community. For Paul, faith and baptism sufficed. For James, circumcision was also necessary. In terms of creating a stable community, James was the wiser man. The communities of Christian Jews, over which he presided, were only nominally mixed. The Gentile members had in fact become Jews. If they had accepted the extremely painful operation of circumcision, they certainly submitted to all the other demands of the Law. Such unity of vision as to what was necessary in terms of day-to-day living guaranteed the permanence of the community.

A genuinely mixed community in which Gentiles remained Gentiles and Jews remained Jews was inherently unstable. As we saw in the case of Antioch, its very existence depended on fragile compromises ever open to renegotiation. Any interference with the life-giving circulation of goodwill was the equivalent of cutting off the blood supply to the heart.

Cephas was an unknown variable in this delicate equation. At first Paul must have wondered whether his impact on the community would be for good or ill. Were Cephas merely to stand aloof and observe, it would be natural for the community to detect a whiff of hostile criticism, and to react accordingly. This fear was quickly dissipated. Cephas integrated perfectly. Although a Jew, he adopted the normal pattern of table fellowship at Antioch, and ate with Gentiles. Given his background and formation, it must have cost Cephas dearly to make this gesture of trust. He was strengthened to take the risk by the power of grace made tangible in the exemplary love of the Antiochean believers.

Trouble-makers from Jerusalem

The sense of triumph and fulfilment that Paul and others experienced at this successful experiment did not last long. Trouble-makers arrived from Jerusalem. Paul does not make it clear whether they were sent by James or whether they took it on their own initiative to represent his mind. In either case, the basis of their intervention was the corollary of James' decision at the meeting in Jerusalem. If the deteriorating political situation made it inopportune to dilute Jewish identity by circumcising Gentile converts to Christianity, then it was the time to reinforce the Jewish identity of converts from Judaism.

This was seen by the Jerusalemites as particularly important in mixed communities —of which Antioch was a supreme example— where integration had gone as far as it possibly could. From their perspective, it was practically assimilation. Their primary objective was to drive a wedge between Jewish and Gentile Christians, because Jews believed that only in isolation could they preserve their traditional values. The first practical step, therefore, was to disrupt the table fellowship of the Antiocheans. The obvious place to begin was by insinuating that Jewish believers were incredibly naïve to imagine that Gentile Christians would offer them acceptable food. It was easy to play on the common Jewish assumption that Gentiles would pollute Jewish food and drink if they got the slightest chance. This fear was much more deeply rooted than the imperative of charity on which the Antiochean compromise was based.

This scare tactic did not succeed immediately. It met the opposition of those who defended the honour and decency of Gentile members against such blanket and unwarranted criticism. In response, the Judaizers ratcheted up the pressure by insisting on ever higher standards in the application of the dietary laws.

In addition, they could have hoisted Paul with his own petard. His tendency to focus on only one point at a time without considering the full implications had done him a great disservice. In the circumcision debate, Paul's one concern was to avoid circumcising his Gentile converts. Thus, he had insisted passionately that only faith in Jesus Christ was necessary for salvation. This permitted the Judaizers to draw the simple and obvious conclusion that social contacts, and particularly table fellowship, between Jewish and Gentile believers were irrelevant.

This, of course, is not at all what Paul intended to convey, but he should not have expected others to read his mind. It was now a little too late for him to insist that what he *really meant* was 'faith working through love' (Gal. 5: 6). This sort of thing would happen again and again.

By now the tension of the debate had made Jewish believers extremely anxious. From their perspective there was much to be said on both sides. But they did not have the tools to make a choice. Thus they watched and waited to see what Cephas would do. Not only was he a Jew, but he was a member of the Jerusalem community, which set the standards for the comportment of Christian Jews.

Eventually Cephas cracked, and the contagion of his example swept all away. Paul records with burning indignation, 'Before certain people came from James, he ate with Gentiles, but when they came he gradually withdrew and separated himself, fearing those from the circumcision. And with him the rest of the Jews acted insincerely, so that even Barnabas was carried away by their play-acting' (Gal. 2: 12–13).

Paul's lack of empathy with those who did not agree with him is manifest. Instinctively he produced the most uncharitable explanation. He could not believe that Cephas might have had good reason for changing his mind. He is dismissed contemptuously as having acted out of 'fear'. Paul could not think that the other Jewish believers had followed their consciences. They were 'hypocrites', who acted out of expediency, not principle. He makes a faint-hearted effort to excuse his old comrade-in-arms, but the pathos of 'even Barnabas' reveals the depth of Paul's disappointment, and he can only suggest that his friend was 'carried away' by emotion.

This is the negative side of Paul's single-minded commitment to Christ. To him the truth was so clear and unambiguous that he could not imagine Cephas or Barnabas agonizing over their decisions. Paul failed to appreciate that Cephas was in a situation where he had to take sides. Neutrality was not an option. Intellectually, he may have agreed with Paul, but his heart made him line up with those who needed him most. The strength of the Gentile church was evident in Antioch, and it had dynamic leaders. The Jewish church, on the contrary, was struggling, and would be shattered by the defection of one of its most revered figures. Barnabas may have reasoned in a similar way, or the nationalistic appeal of James may have touched his Jewish heart. They could have explained themselves for ever, and Paul's only response would have been a contemptuous glance.

Farewell to Antioch

Despite, or perhaps because of, his vehement protests, Paul lost the battle to preserve Antioch-on-the-Orontes as a genuinely mixed community. The Jewish element maintained its refusal to have table fellowship with Gentiles. How did the latter respond? Probably in various ways. Some Judaized completely by accepting circumcision. Others refused circumcision but kept certain basic dietary laws (no pork, no sacrificial meat) in order not to offend their Jewish brethren, and thereby to keep some lines of communication open. Still others would have rejected the Jews as they had been rejected, and paid no attention to Jewish sensitivities.

Was there sufficient unity among the Antiochean Christians to permit a common Eucharist? The optimists striving against hope to bring the different factions together would probably have answered in the affirmative. Paul certainly answered in the negative. The community clearly had not 'put on love which is the bond of perfection' (Col. 3: 14), and so there could be no Eucharist. Only when the community was truly *Christ* in the shared love of all its members could the leader of the eucharistic assembly say, 'This is *my* body' (1 Cor. 11: 24). When judged by Paul's idealistically high standards, Antioch had become a travesty of what a Christian community should be.

111

Paul no longer wished to be part of the church of Antioch, and he could not in conscience continue to represent it. This was the most decisive moment in his life, after his conversion. It was the catalyst that forced him to rethink his position on two fundamental issues: his role as a missionary and the place of the Law in Christian communities. He came to decisions that determined the rest of his missionary career.

Authenticating an Apostle

Apart from a brief period in Arabia, all Paul's missionary work up to this point had been carried out under the auspices of Antioch. It was the church that had commissioned him and sent him out (Acts 13: 3; 15: 40). This relationship could no longer be maintained, and the consequences are clear in the change in the way Paul addressed his letters.

When Paul wrote to the Thessalonians, he was still working on behalf of Antioch. The addresses of two of the three letters have been preserved, and in both of them Paul identifies himself only by his name: 'Paul, Silvanus, and Timothy to the church of the Thessalonians' (1 and 2 Thess. 1: 1). Here we have the simplicity of the confident. Paul knew who he was, and presumed that his interlocutors knew also.

The next letter that Paul wrote was after his break with Antioch. It begins: 'Paul an apostle, not from human beings nor through a human being, but through Jesus Christ and God the Father, who raised him from the dead' (Gal. 1: 1). When we recall that the Galatians knew perfectly well who Paul was—he had spent the better part of two years among them—this elaborate introduction implies that a dramatic change had taken place in the interval. He distances himself from Antioch, under whose aegis he had in fact converted the Galatians, by asserting that Antioch did not originate his commission as an apostle, nor in the strict sense, did it mediate his commission. The one mediator of his divine commission was the Risen Lord, whom he had encountered on the road to Damascus. Such self-justification betrays Paul's awareness of a very serious problem.

By ending his relationship with Antioch, Paul had lost his apostolic accreditation and his legitimizing base. He felt his isolation keenly. This was not grief for his break with Antioch. Paul had put that disaster behind him; he never mentioned it again. On the contrary, he looked always to the future, and saw everything in missionary terms. His isolation meant that he had no defence against the charge that he was a maverick who represented no one but himself. Anyone could plausibly claim that Paul was no different from the charlatans who set themselves up as religious authorities in order to fleece the credulous. In horror, Paul saw himself being dismissed as the inventor and sole member of a rather bizarre religion centred on a crucified criminal in a far-away land.

If Paul was to have any credibility, it was imperative for him to cover himself by rooting his authority. His only option was to refer to a higher power, and claim that he had been sent directly by Jesus Christ. He does this in every subsequent letter with the exception of that to the Philippians. While theologically true, it goes without saying that this was an extremely fragile guarantee. Would he have accorded equal status to any stranger who walked up to him claiming to have encountered Christ? How could that claim, and his own, be verified?

Paul must have been tempted to suggest to his critics that they should check with Christ himself in prayer. If so, he resisted it. He did in fact have an utterly convincing answer. 'Do we need, as some do, letters of recommendation to you or from you? You yourselves are our letter of recommendation, written on your hearts to be known and read by all men. And you show that you are a letter from Christ, delivered by us' (2 Cor. 3: 2–3). In other words, Paul's answer to his critics was to invite them to make a pragmatic test: look at what I am, and then look at what I have achieved!

There was no proportion between the apparent cause (a foreign Jewish manual labourer) and the effect (vital communities in important urban centres whose members were transformed). The evident discrepancy disappeared only when one recognized that Paul was not the real cause, but merely 'God's co-worker' (1 Cor. 3: 9). 'We have this treasure in earthen vessels in order to show that the transcendent

113

power belongs to God and not to us' (2 Cor. 4: 7). As a visible channel of grace, Paul was patently accredited to proclaim the authentic gospel. God would not empower a selfish liar.

Paul, obviously, had no problem with being asked for verification. It was one of the very few areas where he could empathize with a questioner. A healthy scepticism was an integral part of his character, and he could appreciate it in others. Any claim was immediately countered by 'Show me!' Thus, unless grace was manifest, it did not exist. The gifts of the Spirit had to be evident before he would recognize them. This is why he never appointed leaders in his communities. Believers claimed the role by leading effectively. 'We beg you to identify those who labour among you, and take the lead in the Lord and admonish you, and to esteem them highly *because of their work*' (1 Thess. 5: 12–13; cf. 1 Cor. 16: 15–16).

The Law a Rival to Christ

The other major change wrought in Paul by the crisis at Antioch concerned his attitude towards the Law. It has been noted that he had already gone through three stages with respect to the Law. The ambivalence of the adolescent in Tarsus had given way to the total commitment of the Pharisee in Jerusalem, and that had been replaced by a tolerance that permitted Jewish converts to continue their ethnic customs, while denying the Law any salvific authority.

What happened at Antioch forced Paul to realize that such tolerance gave the Law an opportunity to become a dangerous rival to Christ. He saw for the first time that once the Law under any form had been given a foothold in a Christian community, it would sooner or later assume the dominant role. The following of Christ would be buried under an avalanche of legal prescriptions.

Recognition of this danger came to Paul late, and only because the betrayal of Cephas had obliged Paul to reflect on his Pharisaic experience in a way that he had not done before. It can be taken for granted that Paul, like all other Pharisees, believed that the basis of Jewish life was election by a gratuitous divine act. This was the supreme truth. Antioch stimulated Paul to ask himself how this truth had been honoured. Had the greater part of his day as a young Pharisee been devoted to its contemplation? Had he been encouraged to formulate prayers of gratitude for the divine mercy? Had he been initiated into profound theological speculation as to why God had chosen the Jews to be his people?

The answer to each of these questions was negative. As the Pharisaic sources reveal, all the attention of young Pharisees focused on the interpretation of the demands of the Law.[6] Paul the pragmatist looking back at Paul the Pharisee now realized that the way time was allotted differentiated real priorities from theoretical ones. Lip-service was paid to the centrality of election and grace, but in reality it was pushed to the irrelevant margins of life by casuistic debate. One did not win respect among Pharisees by elaborate theological reflections on election, but by a capacious legal memory exploited by formidable forensic skills. Law bred legalism.

Once Paul reflected on his pre-conversion experience and coupled it with what had happened at Antioch, he realized that precisely the same thing not only could happen, but would happen in a Christian community, if the Law was given any say. The real priority, the following of Christ, would be replaced by the practical priorities of obedience.

Human nature being what it is, Paul knew that specific limited demands would be much easier to handle than the challenge to imitate the self-sacrificing love exhibited by Christ. One knew when one had fulfilled a legal obligation, but how would one know if one had measured up to the standard set by Christ? For most people, when salvation was at stake, clarity and certitude were preferable to an ideal whose implications had to be worked out in each individual situation without any guarantee that the solution would be correct.

Paul, in consequence, decided that the Law in any shape or form should have no place in any of his communities. In other words, after the incident at Antioch, Paul abandoned the intrinsically unstable mixed Christian community where Gentiles lived as Gentiles, and Jews as Jews. Henceforward, as far as he was concerned, Jews who wished to follow Christ would have to give up the observances in which their Jewish identity was rooted. The reputation this won him was formulated with perfect accuracy by James in Jerusalem several years later: 'They have been told about you that you teach all the Jews who are among the Gentiles to forsake [the Law of] Moses, telling them not to circumcise their children or observe the customs' (Acts 21: 21). Inevitably Paul incurred the animosity of Christian Jews everywhere, but particularly at Antioch. Paul had burnt his boats, and there was no going back. Neither he nor they could see any basis for reconciliation.

Even while condemning the Law, Paul's attitude towards it remained complex and subtle. He made a distinction between what God intended the Law to be and what had been done to the Law by the Jews. 'The very commandment which promised life proved to be death to me' (Rom. 7: 10). He venerated the Law as the Word of God, and quoted it more than ninety times. The Scriptures exhibited the divine plan of salvation, and offered directives regarding authentic human living. It proposed guide-lines to 'life'. By transforming these directives/guide-lines into binding precepts—that is, commandments that had to be obeyed—the Jews brought the Law into being as an instrument of 'death'. What Paul condemned was this radically distorted understanding of the Law, not the Law as such or in itself.

Henceforth for Paul there was only 'the law of Christ': that is, the law which is Christ (Gal. 6: 2). God's will is now embodied in the comportment of Christ, which both exemplifies the demand made on, and models the response expected of, humanity. As the immediate context indicates—'Bear one another's burdens' (Gal. 6: 2)—love is the sole binding imperative of the new law. It was the salient feature of Christ's humanity, and is the content of the one true precept which remains (Gal. 5: 14; Rom. 13: 8–10), because it is of the very essence of Christian life (1 Thess 4: 9; 1 Cor. 13: 2).

Pastoral Instruction

If Paul's flat refusal to accept the Law of Moses as a collection of precepts was because of the inevitability of legalism, then, logically, he had to say that *law as such* had no place in the life of a Christian.

116

The lives of Christians were not to be determined by any commandments or statutes, no matter where they originated or by whose authority they were promulgated. This had profound consequences for the way Paul interacted with the churches he had founded.

He was the authority figure, but he could not give his words a coercive force which he denied to the commandments of God in the Law. He could not insist on being obeyed, since he had argued that to submit to the Law was to become a transgressor (Gal. 2: 18). Thus he could not rule by precept. He could not constrain his converts to live their lives in a particular way. And he would not permit anyone else, even Jesus Christ, to lay obligation upon them.

Paul twice quotes commands of Jesus. The first quote concerns the prohibition of divorce, in 1 Corinthians 7: 10, which Paul accepted in a particular case (1 Cor. 7: 11), not because he felt bound by it, but because he disagreed with the reasons for the divorce. In another instance, however, he found the reasons for separation compelling and permitted a divorce (1 Cor. 7: 15), thereby revealing that, despite the imperatival form, he refused to give the prohibition of Jesus the force of a constraining precept.[7]

Paul's attitude towards the second command he quotes is even clearer. The form in which he quotes it—'I command those who proclaim the gospel to live from the gospel' (1 Cor. 9: 14)—makes it an obligation for the minister to receive, not for the community to contribute financially. Yet Paul immediately goes on to insist that he has not obeyed and will not obey; he will continue to earn his own living (1 Cor. 9: 15–18). The citation of the two dominical commands underlines the value they had for Paul, and the respect in which they should be held; but Paul's practice indicates that he did not see them as imposing a binding obligation.

Since habits of speech are not automatically altered by ideological conversion, it was perhaps inevitable that Paul should occasionally command that something be done. In some cases he catches himself and introduces a correction, but in others he does not. In this he cannot be accused of inconsistency. A distinction can be made between the two sets of situations. He speaks in the imperative mood regarding conjugal relations (1 Cor. 7: 5) and generosity in giving to the poor of Jerusalem (2 Cor. 8: 7), but in both instances he immediately adds, 'I say this not as a command' (1 Cor. 7: 6; 2 Cor. 8: 8).

The issues on which Paul does not correct his imperatives concern change of social status subsequent to conversion (1 Cor. 7: 17), issues raised by the Corinthians (1 Cor. 11: 34), and the mechanics of the transmission of the collection to Jerusalem (1 Cor. 16: 1). Paul, in other words, is careful to avoid imposing strictly moral judgements, but has no hesitation in making administrative decisions. The latter concern purely practical matters, whereas the former involve inter-personal relations, which are of the essence of Christian life. On basic moral issues Paul is prepared only to offer advice, 'I say this for your advantage, not to lay any restraint upon you' (1 Cor. 7: 35).

The assumptions behind this attitude should be clear from what has already been said about the 'death'-dealing version of the Law, but Paul none the less makes them explicit in two passages. He refuses to oblige anyone to contribute to the collection for Jerusalem, because 'Each one must give as he has decided in his heart, not reluct-antly or under compulsion, for God loves a cheerful giver' (2 Cor. 9: 7). The freedom of the decision is stressed both positively and neg-atively. It must come from the 'heart', which in biblical terms is the core of the personality. The choice must well up from within. It can-not be forced in any way. What one is compelled to give will always be given with regret, and cannot be pleasing to God (Prov. 22: 8).

The second passage is even more explicit. Paul writes to Philemon, 'Even though I have full authority in Christ to order you to do what is fitting, yet for love's sake I rather beseech you' (vv. 8–9a). Paul knew that he had the personal authority to command Philemon to do the right thing concerning Onesimus, his runaway slave: namely, to receive him back without any punishment. In a sub-tle *captatio benevolentiae* Paul expects Philemon to recognize that only love is always 'fitting' for Christians. But there was also another reason: 'I preferred to do nothing without your consent in order that your good act might not stem from compulsion but from your own free will' (v. 14). The opposition between 'compulsion' and 'free will' is absolute; the same act cannot be both voluntary and forced. To consider oneself as bound by a precept is to make oneself incapable of acting freely with regard to the act in question. The constraint of a command makes a free choice impossible. If Philemon is to love Onesimus, the decision must be entirely his.

Only when the consistent pattern of such Pauline passages is perceived, does it become clear just how radical was Paul's antinomian stance. He would not give obedience to any law, and he would not exact submission from his converts to any precept, be it from God, Jesus or himself. In consequence, he was strictly limited in his guidance of the community. He could indicate what he expected of its members. He could attempt to persuade them to modify their behaviour. He could propose his own example (e.g. 1 Cor. 8: 13, 11: 1). But that was all! In terms of saving time and energy, it would have been much more efficient for him to have forcibly imposed the comportment he desired. But his experience at Antioch had taught Paul that to operate through binding precepts would necessarily bring him and his converts back into the orbit of the Law.

The First Year in Ephesus 7

COMPLETELY disgusted at the behaviour of the church at Antioch-on-the-Orontes during the crisis provoked by the trouble-makers from Jerusalem (Gal. 2: 11–14), Paul decided that he could no longer be part of that community. None the less, even though he had surrendered his commission from Antioch, he was determined to go ahead with his plan to return to Ephesus, and make it the centre of the next phase of his missionary activities.

Thus in the spring of AD 52, when travellers brought word that the pass through the Taurus mountains (the Cilician Gates) was open, and that most of the snow had gone from the high country, Paul left Antioch never to return. His travel plan was the same as six years earlier—north through the Cilician Gates of the Taurus mountains, and then west along the 'Common Highway'—but this time his visit to the Galatians would not be an accident.

A Return Visit to Pessinus

Under ideal conditions it would have taken Paul and the ever-faithful Timothy between three and four weeks to cover the 510 miles (816 km) separating Antioch-on-the-Orontes from Pessinus. Occasionally, no doubt, Paul wondered what they would find. It was the first time that he had returned to any of his foundations, and a lot could have happened in four years.

Temperamentally, the Galatians were completely different from the Corinthians. The latter were only too eager to take up the challenge of finding appropriate ways to integrate Christianity into their daily lives. Their self-confidence was such that they did not even envisage making mistakes. The Celts were the exact opposite. They were slow, prudent and very much averse to being caught in error. They preferred to be told what to do, so that they bore no responsibility for any mistakes. They were dismayed when Paul left them with only a few general guide-lines. These they would have followed to the letter, but the need to make independent moral judgements in uncharted territory made them extremely anxious.

The Galatians welcomed Paul and Timothy with open arms. Now all their questions could be answered. What struck Paul, however, was their lack of vitality. Their deeply rooted instinct to play it safe had bred stagnation. He regretted their lack of courage and imagination, and he tried to energize them into action by insisting that they use their freedom creatively. His words fell on deaf ears. Their concern was to avoid making mistakes. They craved security.

Individual members of the community no doubt took him aside in order to extract answers to their specific questions. It took all Paul's tact and forbearance to be both patient and unyielding. To give them anything that looked like a new law would have contradicted his concern that they should mature into independent adults. All that he would permit himself was to prod them with questions that forced them to weigh various options and then decide.

Paul also solicited the Galatians for a financial contribution for the poor of Jerusalem (1 Cor. 16: 1). Even though he had made the promise to James and the others as a delegate of Antioch, he accepted the responsibility as a personal commitment (Gal. 2: 10). He had known what it was to be poor in Jerusalem, but his motivation was more complex than mere sympathy. The gift would be a unifying act of charity, which was at the same time sweet revenge for the trouble that Jerusalem had caused at Antioch. The words of the book of Proverbs may have echoed in his mind, 'If your enemies are hungry, give them bread to eat; and if they are thirsty, give them water to drink; for you will heap coals of fire on their heads, and the Lord will reward you' (Rom. 12: 20).

With a clarity that would have greatly pleased the Galatians, Paul then laid down the procedure that he wanted them to follow. This prosaic, business-like side to his character rarely surfaces. He knew that they did not have large reserves of cash, but he wanted a generous contribution. Thus every member of the community should start saving up. When Sunday came round each week, it should remind each individual to set aside what he or she intended to contribute from whatever small surplus they had accumulated that week. When Paul returned, the private accumulations should be pooled, and Paul would write letters of introduction for the emissaries chosen by the community to carry the contribution of Galatia to Jerusalem.

The benefits of this arrangement were multiple. Paul protected himself against any possible accusation of misappropriation of funds. There was safety in numbers when carrying a considerable sum in coin. Jewish believers in Jerusalem would get the chance to meet Gentile Christians, perhaps for the first time.

Circumstances conspired to ensure that Paul never went back to Galatia. In terms of his own instructions, this would imply that the collection there never came to fruition, and that the Galatians ended up with unexpectedly large disposable incomes. Undoubtedly, after a period of mental turmoil the Celts found a suitable way of spending it.

Ephesus

Had Paul been able to see into the future, he would have stayed in Galatia in order to counter the attack on his community that was soon to come, but the gift of second sight was not given him. He had spent the better part of the summer with the Galatians, and it was time to set off if he was to reach Ephesus before winter set in. He had to cover 340 miles (540 km).[1]

Last time when he left Pessinus, Paul had gone north-west to Dorylaeum. This time he had to backtrack to the south-west to pick up the 'Common Highway' in the vicinity of Antioch-in-Pisidia.

From Apamea (modern Dinar) it was an easy downhill walk to the upper reaches of the valley of the River Lycus (modern Çürük-su). It must have been a relief to Paul to leave the bleak uplands of Anatolia and to come into lush pasture land. His eye long accustomed to unrelieved brown would have been caught by unexpected flashes of colour. The flocks of sheep that roamed the valley were of two unusual types. The wool of one was cyclamen purple, while that of the other was a glossy black.[2] From across the river came the gleam of a frozen waterfall. For millennia, mineral-saturated hot water had poured down the steep slope, gradually building up a deposit that shone a brilliant white in the sun. It was Hierapolis (modern Pamukkale), where a Christian community would be established within a year or so.

The Lycus flowed into the Maeander (modern Menderes), of which Strabo wrote, 'its course is so exceedingly winding that everything winding is called "meandering"' (*Geography* 12. 8. 15). It is said to have given the legendary artist Daedalus his idea for a labyrinth. Paul's road ran along the north bank in the foothills of Mount Messogis (modern Aydin Daglari). Many travellers must have contrasted the straight road with the twists and turns of the river. Did Paul see a parallel between his own unequivocal commitment to Christ and the tortuous efforts of others to avoid the claim of his love?

The 'Common Highway' left the broad valley at Magnesia-on-the-Maeander and crossed a low pass from which the travellers to Ephesus could see their goal. Not the city itself, which was hidden in a valley between two hills, but the 7 metre-high wall on the crest of Mount Pion (modern Bülbül Dagh), which Lysimachus had built about 286 BC. For the last 3 miles (5 km) the arches of the great aqueduct, the *Aqua Troessitica*, marched on Paul's right to the city. It was the end of the summer of AD 52.

The grid pattern of streets that Lysimachus had given Ephesus made it easy for Paul and Timothy to find Prisca and Aquila.[3] If Paul had been too abstracted on leaving them a year earlier, Timothy had certainly noted the co-ordinates with reference to some monument that he was sure he would remember. The alternative would have been a wearisome and frustrating search on top of a tiring two weeks on the road from Galatia. As it was, they were able to go straight to a home in which they were assured of a warm welcome. Paul no doubt took pride in the foresight that guaranteed him such comfort. Instead of having to look for lodgings and work, he had a job plus bed and board awaiting him. He even had a congregation primed to give full attention to his sermons! It is inconceivable that Prisca and Aquila had not hyped Paul's qualities to their converts. Paul was to remain in Ephesus for two years and three months (Acts 19: 8–10).

Hearing about Apollos

In all probability one of the first topics of conversation between Prisca and Aquila and Paul concerned Apollos, who shortly before had left for Corinth.[4] He was a convert Jew from Alexandria in Egypt, who had been trained in rhetoric (Acts 18: 24–8). His developed intellectual formation, therefore, was similar to that of Paul, but he would have surpassed Paul in one respect. He had had the immense good fortune to study with Philo, the great intellectual leader of Alexandrian Jewry, whose life-work was to give Hellenized Jews, such as Apollos, a perspective on the Law that would enable them to accept both it and their ambient pagan culture.

Apollos, in consequence, not only had the ability to relate religious ideas to philosophical concepts, but he was interested in doing so. This was something that Paul considered a complete waste of time. He proclaimed a crucified Jesus as the exemplar of authentic humanity (1 Cor. 2: 15), and saw no need for any speculative development. He was more concerned with evidence of the power of transforming grace in his life and in that of others. In a word, his preaching was consciously and deliberately a stimulus to action, not food for thought.

Some Christian merchants from Corinth were in Ephesus on business and heard Apollos preach at the weekly liturgical assembly. They were highly impressed. By using Philo's methods of interpretation and his philosophical framework, Apollos provided intellectual fulfilment for those who desired it by building a rich synthesis of the elements that Paul provided but refused to develop. Moreover, Apollos' polished eloquence made him a religious leader of which to be proud. The Corinthians had no hesitation in inviting him to return with them to Corinth (Acts 18: 27). They left just before winter closed the sea to commercial traffic.

We can be sure that Paul's reaction to this information was ambivalent. What his head told him conflicted with what his heart felt. In theory, he should have been delighted that Corinth now had a leader whose gifts complemented his own. Paul had planted the seed, why should not God send another to water the crop? In reality, Paul resented Apollos. On the personal level he dreaded losing the affection and respect of the Corinthians to an intruder, whose brilliance Paul could only think of as superficial pandering to convention. Paul was extremely possessive of his converts.

On a much more serious level, Paul feared that speculation about God would replace the following of Christ. As an ex-Pharisee, he knew the pleasures of endless debate and discussion. As a Christian, he was aware that the self-sacrificing love of the crucified Jesus posed a dauntingly unambiguous challenge to believers, which could be avoided by concentration on the will of God, a subjective interpretation susceptible of manipulation to justify virtually anything.

But Paul could do nothing. Autumn had already arrived, and there would be no contact between Ephesus and Corinth until late the following spring, when the end of winter storms and dark days opened the sea to ships, and the land route through the mountains of Macedonia to travellers. It would be eight months before he had any chance of finding out what was going on in Corinth. He had no choice but to possess his soul in patience. Fortunately there was plenty to distract him.

Johannite Disciples of Jesus

Paul's first winter in Ephesus (AD 52–3) was marked by an event that brought him back to the very beginnings of the Jesus movement. Somehow he came into contact with a small group that considered themselves followers of Jesus of Nazareth, but who had never heard of the Passion, Resurrection or descent of the Holy Spirit. They knew only the baptism of John (Acts 19: 1–7).

These were Ephesian Jews who, while on pilgrimage to Jerusalem, had received a baptism of repentance for their sins at the hands of Jesus.[5] They knew him only as the senior assistant of John the Baptist. When John and Jesus moved their prophetic mission to reform Judaism to the more densely populated west bank of the Jordan, the former as the leader took the more difficult task of preaching to the Samaritans, while Jesus went to the Judaeans (John 3: 22–4). Both believed that the time was short, and that maximum exposure was imperative. Thus John baptized at the springs on the eastern slope of Mount Gerizim (as near as he could get to the ruined Samaritan Temple on the summit), and Jesus went to the heart of Jewish life, the Temple in Jerusalem. There, to grab attention, he overturned the tables of the money-changers (John 2: 13–16). It was during this ministry that Jesus encountered the visiting Ephesian Jews and won their repentance.

Peter could have spoken to Paul in Jerusalem about this period in the life of Jesus because he had shared it, but that meeting was fifteen years ago. Paul's questions then, and certainly his preaching since, would have focused on the subsequent period, when Jesus had come to the realization that he was the Messiah.

It was now Paul's task to convince these Ephesian Jews that Jesus was in fact the Messiah for whom they had longed. He would have spoken of the Resurrection as the authentication of all that Jesus had said and done, and of the power of the Risen Lord as displayed in the growing number of believers.

Once the Ephesians had accepted Jesus as the Christ and had been baptized, Paul would have been eager to hear their memories of a crucial day in their lives a quarter of a century earlier. There were new fragments to be fitted lovingly into his mosaic portrait of Jesus.

Apart from this group, nothing specific is known about the composition of the church at Ephesus. Since the city was similar to Corinth in so many ways, we can assume with confidence that the two communities resembled one another, both in size and make-up (1 Cor: 1: 26–9). Each was the city in microcosm: more Gentiles

126

than Jews, a few relatively wealthy members, the majority trades people and slaves, possibly more women than men.

Missionary Expansion in Asia

Even though Paul had chosen Ephesus as his base because of the facility it offered him in keeping in touch with his previous foundations, he did not restrict his activity to maintenance in the twenty-seven months he spent there (Acts 19: 8–10). It would have been impossible for him to do so. He was by vocation a missionary (much more effective in founding churches than in running them), and believed that churches should reach out to unbelievers. The compliment he paid to the community at Thessalonica in fact described his ideal church: 'you became an example to all the believers in Macedonia and in Achaia, for not only has the word of the Lord sounded forth from you in Macedonia and Achaia, but your faith in God has gone forth everywhere' (1 Thess. 1: 7–8). Verbal proclamation ('the word of the Lord') was given power by the quality of their grace-transformed life-style ('your faith in God').

The missionary outreach of the church of Ephesus is confirmed by the greetings sent by 'the churches of Asia' to Corinth (1 Cor. 16. 19). Paul himself mentions the names of three of these churches: Colossae, Laodicea and Hierapolis (Col. 4: 13). This list, of course, is not exhaustive. Laodicea and Hierapolis were mentioned only because, as neighbours of Colossae in the Lycus valley, they were in danger of being infected by the false teaching that had divided the church at Colossae.

Paul did not evangelize the Lycus valley personally (Col. 2: 1). The communities there were founded by Epaphras, a native of Colossae (Col. 4: 12–13), who had been commissioned by Paul. The choice reflected Paul's developing missionary strategy. From personal experience in Asia Minor and in Macedonia he knew the difficulty of starting from scratch in a strange city. He had found a solution to that problem by sending Prisca and Aquila ahead of him to Ephesus. It was they who had carried the burden of loneliness and alienation. No doubt there were many others who were prepared to make the same sacrifice for the gospel. But, reflected Paul, why not select missionaries who had by nature the advantage that Prisca and Aquila had created for him? The fewer the obstacles, the more efficient the mission.

Thus, Paul concluded, the prime agents to preach the word were energetic and enterprising men and women, like Lydia or Epaphras, who had encountered Paul while travelling on business, and had been converted by him. As enthusiastic believers, they returned home—one to Colossae, the other to Thyatira—to a network of acquaintances rooted in long-standing family, social and business contacts. They had a home. They did not have to look for work. They were known and trusted. The respect they had earned guaranteed that there were always at least some sympathetic ears to hear their first stumbling sermons.

Since two of the seven churches of the Apocalypse (Rev. 2: 1–3: 22) were Pauline foundations—namely, Ephesus and Laodicea-on-the Lycus—and since a third, Thyatira, was probably founded by Lydia, a Pauline convert in Philippi (Acts 16: 14), it seems logical to attribute the creation of communities at Smyrna, Pergamum, Sardis and Philadelphia to the missionary initiative of Ephesus. To these cities we should probably add Magnesia and Tralles in the Maeander valley, which are known from the letters of Ignatius in the early second century AD. All were within a 120-mile (192-km) radius of Ephesus and linked by excellent roads.[6] Colossae, the furthest away, could be reached in a comfortable week's walk.

Paul never wrote to any of these churches. With one exception, he wrote only to the churches that he founded on his first great journey from Antioch-on-the-Orontes to Corinth. Clearly he had learnt, not only that he could not do everything, but that he did not even have to try. He adopted a policy of delegation. He trusted the missionary who had founded a particular church to deal with any maintenance problems that might arise there. No doubt Paul was available for consultation, but he maintained direct contact only with the churches he had founded personally. The one exception was the church at Colossae, but the circumstances there were exceptional.

Crisis in Galatia

As Paul strode away from Antioch-on-the-Orontes in the spring of
AD 52, he thought that he had finished with the community that had
disappointed him so bitterly. Certainly he had no intention of returning. All his attention was focused on the foundations in the west that
awaited his attention. He did not know that Antioch was also thinking of those same churches, and in a way that would cause him enormous trouble and anxiety during the next three years.

Antioch claims her Daughter Churches

When Paul founded the churches of Galatia, Philippi, Thessalonica
and Corinth, he had been a missionary commissioned by Antioch
(Acts 15: 40–1). We must assume, therefore, that as far as Antioch
was concerned, such daughter churches were its responsibility. Paul
had been merely an agent. If Paul had rejected Antioch, some
argued, then he had abandoned all rights in these churches. More
importantly, the Law-free version of Christianity that he had given
them now needed correction in order to bring them into line with the
new Judaizing ethos of the mother church.

Unfortunately, the basic spiritual arguments for taking control of
Paul's foundations—truth must prevail, and the Christian movement
must be seen to be unified—coincided perfectly with the all-too-
human desire for domination. The case for intervention would have
been immeasurably strengthened if an erstwhile proponent of the
Law-free mission, such as Barnabas, had agreed to go personally to
reform his foundations. In the eyes of the majority, this would have
put Paul completely in the wrong.

In the elation of his triumph after the meeting in Jerusalem, Paul
had given Antioch the complete story of his success. The
Antiocheans were aware of the cities in which he had founded
churches. They probably even knew the names of those who had
emerged as leaders in the various communities. Knowledge of such
details would have enhanced their claim to be a superior authority,
to which Paul had reported on his return. Thus Antioch decided to

send a reforming delegation to follow Paul's route through Galatia into Macedonia and down to Achaia.

Since Paul had undoubtedly explained his plan to base himself in Ephesus, the Antiocheans realized that their paths would cross at only one point. Thus, the delegation gave Paul plenty of time to get a good head start before heading for Galatia. From Paul they had learned how long it took to get there, and probably planned to arrive towards the end of August. Paul would certainly have left by then, if he was to reach Ephesus before winter set in.

The Antiocheans, for their part, were content to spend the winter months in Pessinus. Everyone they wanted to reach would be accessible because of the travel restrictions imposed by winter, and they were fully aware that the reform process had to be done slowly and delicately. They took it for granted that Paul's foundations would be loyal to him, and they could not be sure that Paul had not prepared the Galatians for their arguments.

Paul would certainly have done so, had he anticipated what was going to happen, but he had no idea that Antioch would take the line it did. They were *his* churches. He was the father who had given them birth, the nurse who had nurtured them (1 Thess. 2: 7 and 11). No matter how deeply troubled Paul had been about developments at Antioch, he was far too shrewd to have further complicated the lives of the timorous Galatians by informing them that there were competing visions of Christianity. That would only have increased their sense of insecurity.

Reporting to Paul

No matter how subtle the delegation was, it would not have taken the Galatians very long to recognize that a very different vision of Christianity was being proposed to them. And this meant trouble. It had been stressful enough trying to work out how to incarnate Paul's vision of the following of Christ. Now they were being asked to choose between two competing visions. The enormity of the decision effectively paralysed them. They took refuge in passive resistance, and sought to win time by insisting that Paul be consulted.

Word about what was happening in Galatia could not have reached Paul in Ephesus before the late spring or early summer of AD 53, depending on when the messenger began his three-week walk. The delegation from Antioch would have strongly opposed the mission, stressing Paul's irrelevance, and pointing out that the road was long and dangerous. They also had a financial argument. The mission was going to cost a poor church a considerable sum of money. The messenger would lose a minimum of six weeks' earnings, and other believers would have to indemnify him. None the less, the Galatians persisted. This time their excessive caution worked in Paul's favour.

Since the delegation from Antioch had been hammering at the Galatians for several months, there was plenty of time for the messenger or his handlers to remember, and perhaps even record, the precise arguments that were being used to overturn Paul's position. In broad outline, the delegation first prepared the ground by attempting to discredit Paul; then they contrasted the shallowness of Paul's gospel with the rich and varied roots of their version in God's plan of salvation.

Paul, the delegation argued, should not be trusted, because he did not faithfully present to them the gospel that he had been taught in Jerusalem by the ultimate authorities in the Jesus movement, those who had known the Saviour during his lifetime.[7] They chose Paul and sent him out to preach their gospel. It was only when Paul, who of course had been circumcised, realized that he would be a much more successful missionary among Gentiles if he omitted those aspects of the Jerusalem gospel which pagans found unacceptable: namely, circumcision and the dietary laws. This he did entirely on his own initiative. The truth, argued the Antiocheans, was much less important to Paul than popularity. These omissions were never approved by his superiors, and his position was strongly challenged at Antioch by Cephas, the senior companion of the Lord. In a word, Paul represented no one but himself. His views were not shared by anyone else.

In contrast to Paul's presentation of the gospel, which focused entirely on the crucified Jesus Christ, the Antioch delegation proposed a version which spoke only of God.[8] Abraham, they said, was the first monotheist. With him God made an unbreakable covenant, whose terms were circumcision and observance of the feasts. Abraham, in consequence, was the first to live in obedience to the Law. God also made a promise to Abraham that in him all the nations would be blessed, and that his descendants would be as numerous as the stars in heaven. The delegation confirmed Paul's identification of Jesus as the Messiah, but insisted that his only importance was to have inaugurated the new age in which the salvation promised to the descendants of Abraham would be extended to the Gentiles. In order to be saved, however, the Gentiles had to live like Abraham; that is, they had to accept the Law with its manifold obligations.

The final point made by the delegation would have been particularly attractive to the Galatians. Paul had been wrong, the delegation continued, when he gave only a few general directives and insisted on personal moral decisions. That bred only uncertainty and fear. The 613 commandments of the Law, on the contrary, covered all aspects of human life. They offered peace of mind and complete security. The Galatians did not have to think or worry any more. They had only to obey.

A Sophisticated Strategy

It is easy to imagine the shock experienced by Paul by the news that people from Antioch were bent on taking over his foundation in Galatia, and that some of his converts there were proving receptive to a Law-observant gospel. The sense of bewilderment (Gal. 5: 7), even of despair (Gal. 4: 11), comes through very clearly in his response, but the dominant emotion is restrained anger.

It was clear to Paul that the situation was much too serious for an outburst which would serve only to relieve his feelings. To vent his spleen on already bewildered Galatians would play into the hands of his adversaries; expostulation is often a sign of guilt. He realized that he had to produce a carefully crafted response to each detail of the arguments urged against him. It was not merely a question of reassuring the Galatians that his gospel was the truth. The intruders were still in Galatia (Gal. 1: 7, 5: 10), and it was much more important to persuade them that their perspective on the gospel was not at all as well founded as they imagined.

Although addressed to the Galatians (Gal. 1: 2, 3: 1), the letter could not be kept from the delegation, and Paul was certainly aware of this. In fact, it became the basis of his strategy. Inevitably he speaks directly to the Galatians, but the delegation is his real audience. If their presence in Galatia was but the first step in an effort by Antioch to recover what it considered its daughter churches, Paul could not content himself with dealing with the symptoms by detaching the Galatians from the Judaizers. He had to go to the root of the problem by developing a long-term solution. The only way to deter any further advance into his territory, and to secure permanently the future of the Galatians, was to undermine the convictions of the Judaizers. Thus he made the crucial decision to focus on the Judaizers, leaving the Galatians in the background. The recovery of the latter was to be a by-product of the defeat of the former.

Paul could not have expected the Galatians, who were converts from paganism (Gal. 4: 8), to grasp the force of arguments which depended on a detailed knowledge of Jewish tradition. Such carefully calculated thrusts were designed to throw the intruders into disarray. The ensuing consternation, Paul hoped, would be the most persuasive argument as far as the Galatians were concerned. He counted on re-establishing his authority among them by reducing the Judaizers to silence. Of course, if the Galatians caught the drift of his arguments, so much the better. Moreover, his evocation of their conversion experience kept them in the picture. They could understand the thrust of such an appeal; but so could the intruders, whose conversion to Christianity was in no way related to the Law.

The sophistication of this approach to a dangerously volatile situation both confirms what was said above regarding the detailed information that Paul had of his opponents' arguments, and at the same time underlines his mental capacity and intellectual formation. Only someone totally convinced of the quality of his rhetorical ability and literary skill would have attempted to carry out such a delicate strategy by letter. It would have been much easier in person. If Paul did not take this latter option, it can only be because something made a visit to Galatia impossible (Gal. 4: 20). Perhaps the moves which led to his imprisonment in Ephesus had already begun; in which case flight might be taken as evidence of guilt. Or there may have been sensitive problems within the Ephesian community, which made it necessary for him to stay there.

Self-defence

The delegation had made a bad tactical mistake by insisting on Paul's dependence on Jerusalem, which, they claimed, was the source of the authentic gospel. Things would have been very different had they dwelt on the long association of Paul with the church of Antioch. Not only had he lived there for considerable periods, but he had been co-opted into missionary work by Barnabas. It would have been impossible for Paul, who insisted so strongly on the importance of community, to deny having belonged to Antioch. And such belonging, from his perspective, implied dependence.

In the letter he wrote to the Galatians, however, it was easy for Paul to document how little time he had in fact spent in Jerusalem *as a Christian*. The italicized words are important, because, of course, he had spent some fifteen years there as a Pharisee. If the Judaizers had not mentioned this, Paul was not going to complicate matters by bringing it up. The situation demanded a certain economy with the truth. And it was a basic rhetorical rule, with respect to the statement of facts in a speech for the defence, that while anything that might be disadvantageous to the defendant should not be omitted, it did not have to be emphasized. Thus, as regards his first contacts with Christians, Paul speaks only of having persecuted 'the church of God' (Gal. 1: 13) and 'the churches of Christ in Judaea' (Gal. 1: 22). The Holy City is not mentioned.

Subsequent to his conversion Paul had made only two visits to Jerusalem, both very brief. Some three years after his conversion, he had spent fifteen days in Jerusalem, and his contacts had been limited to Cephas and James (Gal. 1: 17–19). The second was fourteen years later (Gal. 2: 1), when he had argued as an equal with James, Cephas and John, and emerged victorious. The Law should not be imposed on Gentile converts. Syria and Cilicia (Gal. 1: 21) are mentioned as his mission fields in the interval, but we know that he went much further. In this silence we catch a glimpse of Paul's rhetorical skill. Quintilian had advised orators, 'Whenever a conclusion gives a sufficiently clear idea of the premises, we must be content with having given a hint which will enable our audience to understand what we have left unsaid' (*Institutio Oratoria* 4. 2. 41). It is precisely because Paul had been to the Galatians, and was heading west when he left them, that he could afford not to mention his movements. Such discretion would have made his presentation all the more convincing, because it betrayed a confidence that carried its own persuasive power. To have given details which, from the point of view of the Galatians, were unnecessary, might have created an impression of anxiety. The assumption of shared knowledge flattered his readers.

Although nothing had been said about his relationship to the church of Antioch, Paul had to pre-empt the option by asserting from the outset that his apostolic mandate did not come 'from men or through a man' (Gal. 1: 1). His commission did not derive from any community, nor from any church leader, but came directly from Jesus Christ, whose authority was guaranteed by his resurrection. The unstated implication was that Jesus alone had the right to judge whether Paul was a faithful envoy (1 Cor. 4: 1–4). The miraculous character of Paul's conversion was not something that his opponents could deny; the Galatians were aware that his first contacts with Christians had been as a persecutor (Gal. 1: 13).

If Paul had proved his independence of Jerusalem, could he claim that his gospel was not dependent on the Christian tradition most authoritatively represented by Jerusalem? In response, Paul insisted that 'the gospel preached by me is not worked out by man; for I did not receive it from anyone nor was I taught it, but it came through a revelation of Jesus Christ' (Gal. 1: 11). Here it would be easy to charge Paul with being somewhat less than honest, because he had learnt much from the Christian communities of Damascus, Jerusalem and Antioch in which he had lived. He was thinking, however, of the core of his Law-free gospel, which, as we have seen, flowed directly from the rearrangement of his ideas caused by his encounter with the Risen Lord. What he absorbed from believers in Damascus, Jerusalem and Antioch was so thoroughly sifted through his mental filters that it became merely the confirmation and elaboration of his intensely personal fundamental insight.

It is doubtful that Paul was conscious of the selectivity operative in his appropriation of the embryonic Christian tradition. That which harmonized with his perspective was integrated, but that which did not fit was ignored without being repudiated. He was consistent only in what he positively chose from the Christian tradition. What he tolerated or permitted, however important it might be to others, implied no commitment on his part. His focus on what he considered essential was, from another angle, tunnel vision. What he saw was clear but severely limited. The obscure periphery ever retained its capacity to surprise him.

Growing in Knowledge

If it was relatively easy to be clever in demolishing the attempt of the delegation to denigrate him personally, it was much more difficult to refute the substance of their argument. Not that Paul was shaken even for a moment in his conviction of the centrality of Christ. He *knew* that he was right, and that they were wrong. But he could not simply assert this. No doubt he had already done so at Antioch, without success. If he was going to interact with the delegation, he had to accept their starting-point, and then show them that from it there was a road that led in a different direction.

As soon as Paul focused seriously on Abraham, he realized that Abraham had first been blessed because he had accepted God's word

(Gen. 15: 6). This act of faith was the basis of the fidelity that characterized the subsequent life of Abraham. Faith, therefore, was fundamental. All else was secondary, and in particular the Law, which
was given 430 years after the promise to which Abraham responded
in faith (Gal. 3: 17).

Then Paul noticed that the promise to Abraham, on which the
delegation laid such emphasis, used 'descendant' in the singular.
With superb legalistic aggressivity, he insisted that the reference
was to Christ (Gal. 3: 16). He is *the* descendant of Abraham. Hence
it is those who belong to Christ who are the genuine descendants of
Abraham. The delegation, of course, correctly understood 'descendant' to be a collective noun, but Paul's bold insistence on taking
the singular literally cut the ground from under them. It was a
perfect debater's argument, simple, unambiguous, impossible to
refute.

Recognition of the importance of the faith/fidelity of Abraham
led Paul to think of the faith/fidelity of Christ, which is both the
cause and exemplar of the faith/fidelity of believers to the point
where the two are identified. 'It is no longer I who live, but Christ
who lives in me. And the life I live in the flesh I live by the
faith/fidelity of the Son of God, who loved me, that is, gave himself
for me' (Gal. 2: 20). Faith/fidelity is self-sacrificing love. In the act of
loving, Paul is Christ in so far as he makes present in the world the
very being of Christ. But the same is true of all committed believers.
Hence, they are together Christ. They have 'put on Christ', and are
'one person in Christ Jesus' (Gal. 3: 27–8).

This insight was a radical breakthrough in Paul's understanding of
the relationship between Christ and his followers. It contained the
seeds of two further developments in Paul's Christology: the giving
of the name 'Christ' to the believing community (e.g. 1 Cor. 6: 15)
and the clarification of its nature as 'the body of Christ' (e.g. 1 Cor.
12: 12). It would take another crisis, however, to force them to the
surface of his mind. In Paul's character a certain intellectual lethargy
was the enemy of progressive logic. He never pursued a line of
thought for its own sake. He functioned most effectively in reaction,
but only to the limit of the concrete problem. Yet he had a tenacious

mind, and was instinctively consistent. Each new problem, in consequence, stimulated greater profundity; it did not lead to fragmentation. His Christology grew as a coherent whole, and what at first might appear to be *ad hoc* solutions can always be traced back to basic interrelated insights.

The Second Year in Ephesus

ONCE Paul had handed the letter to the messenger to take back to Galatia, he could only hope and pray. He had done what he could. It was now in the hands of God. It would be a long time before he could possibly get news of how the letter was received by the Galatians. He lived with the worry that he might have done better. The time for introspective self-indulgence, however, did not last very long. Dramatic events occurred in the summer of AD 53, after he had been in Ephesus about a year. It would turn out to be the busiest period of his life.

Imprisonment

Paul's return to Ephesus was not welcomed by everyone in the Christian community there In the eyes of some members, the founders of the church were Prisca and Aquila, and they resented Paul's appropriation of authority. As far as they were concerned, he was a late comer, and the community had been doing perfectly well without him. Paul would have bristled at the hint of any opposition, and is likely to have made the situation worse by insisting on his unrealistically high standards. This put Prisca and Aquila, who of course had deferred to Paul, in a very awkward position; but they never wavered in their loyalty to him.

Thus certain believers were delighted when Paul was imprisoned sometime in late July, AD 53. They were now in a position to show him that he was in no way necessary to the life and mission of the church of Ephesus. It had grown without him in the past, and could expand without him in the future. While this group was stimulated to increased missionary activity, others were frightened into silence, while still others supported Paul (Phil. 1: 14–15). It was a time of extreme tension in the community.

Paul's arrest was a consequence of his success. The governors of senatorial provinces were changed every year, and the new procon-sul of the province of Asia took office on 1 July. A local, no doubt seeking to make a good impression in the hope of future benefit, informed him of a movement that was gathering adherents. Because it was amorphous in structure, no one seemed to know much about it, and perhaps its intentions were subversive. Since preservation of public order was the prime responsibility of the proconsul, such a warning could not be ignored. The prudent course was to incarcer-ate the leader until the matter was cleared up. If he was to assist the Romans with their inquiries, it was safer to have him close at hand.

There were no hard-and-fast rules governing the conditions of such precautionary imprisonment.[1] The form of detention was entirely at the discretion of the magistrate, whose decision was determined not only by his own personality and the nature of the case, but particularly by the degree of influence the prisoner and his friends could bring to bear. The treatment accorded the rich, particularly in their own city, differed significantly from that meted out to the poor and strangers.

Paul, of course, was one of the latter, and he received corresponding treatment (Phil. 1: 13). He was held in the praetorium, the official res-idence of the proconsul of Asia, in which he exercised his judicial functions. In addition, Paul was chained, perhaps to a soldier or to the wall of his cell, or he was forced to wear handcuffs or leg-irons.

Although his movements were hampered, the conditions of Paul's imprisonment were not too severe. He was not held incommunicado in solitary confinement, but was permitted to receive visitors and pass messages. He had access to a professional secretary for the let-ters he wrote to the Philippians, to the Colossians, and to Philemon.[2]

At the beginning of all these letters Timothy appears as a co-author, but he was not a prisoner, because he was free to go to Philippi, if Paul decided to send him (Phil. 2: 19). One would have expected him to be caught in the same investigative net that ensnared Paul. The endings of the letters to Philemon and to the Colossians are unique, in that they list a number of personalities who send greetings to the house-church of Philemon (v. 23) and to the wider community at Colossae (4: 10–14). Obviously they knew each other well. The lists overlap to a great extent. All the names in Philemon appear in Colossians. Were they all imprisoned with Paul? I think they were, because Epaphras is listed as a prisoner in Philemon but not in Colossians, whereas the reverse is true of Aristarchus. It would have been tiresome to note explicitly that all were prisoners. For a writer as skilled as Paul, a hint sufficed.

Paul and Timothy did not evangelize the Lycus valley (Col. 2: 1). They passed through it, but their faces were set towards Ephesus. The credit is given to Epaphras without any suggestion that he was accompanied by a team (Col. 1: 7; 4: 13). This would suggest that the others listed in Colossians 4: 10–14 and Philemon 23 were part of a delegation from Colossae. They had accompanied Epaphras to Ephesus to seek Paul's advice in finding a solution to a problem that apparently could not be handled at the local level.

When the delegation came to visit Paul, the Roman authorities were shocked to find that the Jesus movement was not restricted to Ephesus. Its tentacles reached far into the hinterland. This made the matter much more serious. A province-wide movement was a definite threat, and a delegation of this size would seem to imply that its adherents were numerous. Thus the group from the Lycus valley also ended up in prison. They all had loved ones in Colossae, however, who no doubt were concerned at their extended absence. Hence the need they felt to send word in Paul's letters that they were all right, but without specifying their situation lest it generate greater anxiety.

Danger of Death

It now becomes understandable why Paul should have thought himself in danger of death (Phil. 1: 20–5). Like all his contemporaries,

141

he knew that the arbitrary abuse of authority was restrained only by the fear of reprisals. As an outsider lacking any high-level local support in Ephesus, there was no way he could create difficulties for the proconsul of Asia. He would simply disappear without official notice. It is at first surprising that Paul should confess that death greatly appealed to him. Only when we recall his intense commitment to Christ does this attitude become explicable. Death would mean definitive, unbreakable union with Christ.

Yet Paul did not wish for death. While theoretically the better thing, in reality it would have been selfish. His converts still needed him. 'To remain in the flesh is more necessary on your account. Convinced of this, I know that I shall remain and continue with you all, for your progress and joy in the faith' (Phil. 1: 24–5). This is a most important indication as to how Paul believed the moral judgement should function. The decisive criterion is not whether a course of action is good or bad in itself, but whether it will empower or injure one's neighbour. This key insight, derived from a tension-filled experience, was to play a critical role in Paul's correspondence with the Corinthians (cf. 1 Cor. 8).

The recognition that he was still needed perhaps contributed to Paul's conviction that Divine Providence would ensure his release in the not-too-distant future. His hope was also fed by the awareness that all those in the praetorium with whom he came in contact were convinced that he was neither a revolutionary nor a criminal (Phil. 1: 13). It would not be long, he imagined, before word of his innocence filtered up to those responsible for the disposition of his case.

Even if he were not executed, Paul had to envisage the possibility that the Romans might expel him from Ephesus. It had happened to him at Philippi. He was not a citizen with guaranteed rights. As a Jew, he had an indirect legal status in so far as he was accepted by the *politeuma*, the official corporation representing the Jewish community *vis-à-vis* the civil authorities. A word from the latter, of course, would make him unwelcome among his own people.

However it happened, Paul was neither executed nor deported. He was released from prison, and a year or so later he was still living in Ephesus (1 Cor. 16: 8).

A Mistimed Gift

We must presume that in the early autumn of AD 51, messengers from Philippi arrived in Corinth with another instalment of aid for Paul, only to find that he had just left for a visit to Antioch-on-the-Orontes. Before his departure, however, Paul had told the Corinthians that Ephesus would be his base for the next few years, after his return from Antioch. Thus, when the messengers went back to Philippi for the winter, they knew that Paul would be in Ephesus at the latest by the end of the following summer (AD 52).

Experience had taught the Philippians that Paul needed aid, not at the beginning of his ministry in a new city, but at a later stage, when the number of his converts began to eat into the time he needed to earn his living. It was in the late spring, therefore, or early summer of AD 53 that Epaphroditus of Philippi turned up in Ephesus with aid for Paul. But no sooner had he arrived than he fell ill, which meant that Paul had to find someone in the Ephesian community to convey his letter of gratitude (Phil. 4: 10–20) to Philippi.[3]

Paul should have been overjoyed to receive this testimony of the loyalty of the Philippians, particularly at a time when he was profoundly disturbed by the fear that the Galatians might defect to the Law-observant gospel of Antioch. Yet his letter has a curiously self-conscious, defensive tone. This is surprising, because Paul was used to receiving aid from the Philippians. If he found the gesture offensive, he had had many opportunities to ensure that it was not repeated. It was not the gift, however, but its timing, that caused Paul embarrassment. He had begun to ask the Ephesians for contributions to the collection for the poor of Jerusalem. Acceptance of a personal gift could make it appear that he was appropriating funds given for another purpose. It became important to emphasize that he had not solicited funds from the Philippians, and that he needed nothing more (Phil. 4: 17–18).

Perhaps only in writing this letter did Paul become aware that his generous gesture toward the church of Jerusalem would make his life, which had never been easy, much more difficult. He lived in a world in which every official stole from the public purse. Questions were raised only when they took too much. Paul had to be extremely careful that his acceptance of the subsidies that made his work possible did not ruin his reputation for integrity. One malicious enemy could spread disastrous rumours.

The Weaknesses of a Pastor

The fact that Paul's first letter to Philippi (Phil. 4: 10–20) was concerned exclusively with the subsidy brought by Epaphroditus might appear to suggest that all was well with his community. At least they had no problems that they felt demanded the attention of Paul. This, of course, did not mean that the community was perfect. There may have been problems of which the community was not aware, because it had failed to appreciate fully the difference between the values of the church and those of its ambient society. The habits of a lifetime were not cast off in the moment when pagans converted to Christianity. There was an inevitable tendency to import the values and structures of society into the believing community. These had to be eradicated if the church was to reach its full potential.

There may have been a moment of drama when Epaphroditus fell ill, but it did not last long. While full of sympathy for the sufferer, Paul saw an unexpected opportunity of discovering exactly how the community at Philippi was maturing. By refusing to wait for Epaphroditus to recover before sending his note of gratitude, Paul killed two birds with one stone. The speed of his reply emphasized to the Philippians his affection for them, and at the same time it enabled him to infiltrate a neutral Ephesian observer into the community in the most natural way possible.

The report brought back to Ephesus by the letter-carrier was in general very good. Two points, however, perturbed Paul. The community at Philippi was coming under pressure from pagans, presumably the Roman authorities (Phil. 1: 28), and there was a quarrel going on between the leaders of two house-churches, which threatened the unity of the church (Phil. 4: 2). In Paul's eyes this was a most serious matter, because he saw society as characterized above all by divisions, social, economic and religious. A divided church was no different from the world. Only by demonstrating its unity could the church empower the unification of society.

Thus Paul felt it imperative to write a second letter to the Philippians (Phil. 1: 1–3: 1 and 4: 2–9). It does address the two problems, but it is most unusual in that it tells us much more about the situation in Ephesus than it does about that in Philippi, and in a way that is definitely unflattering to Paul.

Persecution and Unity

Recalling his fears about the effect of persecution on the Thessalonians, Paul seethed with anxiety about its impact on the Philippians, and desperately needed someone to go to Macedonia to bring back word of the state of the community. Timothy was prepared to undertake the task, but Paul preferred to keep his closest collaborator with him until his fate should be decided. The refusal of others was perhaps motivated by the realization that Paul could communicate with Philippi via the letter he could send with the recovered Epaphroditus (Phil. 2: 25), and that the problems there were not so severe as to need the additional presence of a trouble-shooter. Why, argued Ephesian believers, should they interrupt a fruitful missionary effort in their own city, simply in order to gratify Paul's desire for information? On the contrary, was it not selfish of him to prefer his own consolation to the spread of the gospel? Not unnaturally, Paul did not see the matter in this light!

Paul's tantrum (Phil. 2: 21) betrays a wilfulness that could not bear to be thwarted. The childishness of the identification of his needs with those of Christ needs no emphasis. Were there other outbursts of this type, as he tried to establish his authority at Ephesus, the natural reluctance of the community to accept a newcomer would be intensified, and the opposition discussed above becomes even more intelligible. The hostility which Paul attracted was not entirely due to his theological positions. His own character traits were also a significant factor.

The degree of Paul's self-absorption is even more marked when he deals with the unity issue at Philippi. In his mind the directive 'Do not act out of a spirit of rivalry, nor out of vain ambition, but in humility count others better than yourselves' (Phil. 2: 3) had a specific application to the dispute between Euodia and Syntyche (Phil. 4: 2). As we saw, both of these ladies had participated in the spread of the gospel, and with some reason felt that their talents and devotion had earned them an authoritative role in the nascent church at Philippi. But who was to be pre-eminent? This competitive attitude, which was characteristic of society, engendered a disruptive spirit, which endangered the future of the community.

One wonders what the Philippians made of Paul's call for unity and reconciliation, when he exhibited nothing but contempt for those at Ephesus who disagreed with him? Did he perceive that he was sending contradictory messages when he told them, 'Do what you have heard and seen in me' (Phil. 4: 9)? Even when he recognized that his duty was to rise above hurt feelings, he could not resist a mean aside, 'What then? Only that in every way, whether *in pretence* or in truth, Christ is proclaimed. And in that I rejoice' (Phil. 1: 18). The sincerity of his pleasure is at least open to question. If he recognized that the power of the gospel was derived from its effective incarnation in those who preached it (Phil. 2: 14–16), how could he even admit the possibility that it could be proclaimed with false motives, as part of a plan to hurt a fellow believer?

A Warning about the Judaizers

The final proof of the dominance of the introspective side of Paul's character at just this moment is the fact that he completely forgot to inform the Philippians of the danger posed by the delegation from Antioch-on-the-Orontes. If, as seemed most probable, they were following in the footsteps of Paul when he established the daughter churches of Antioch, they would head for Philippi when they left Galatia.

Thus, as an afterthought, Paul wrote a third letter to Philippi (Phil. 3: 2–4: 1), which reproduces the broad outline of his letter to the Galatians. The autobiographical material (Phil. 3: 4–8) is reminiscent of Galatians 1, but it is not used in precisely the same way. In

Galatians, Paul was concerned to demonstrate his independence of Jerusalem, and thus indirectly of Antioch, whereas here his point is to show that he had once been a strictly observant Jew, but had found something better. The contrast between righteousness acquired by obedience to the Law and righteousness given by God 'through the faith/fidelity of Christ' (Phil. 3: 9 = Gal. 2: 16) is evocative of Galatians 3–4. The admonition that salvation is not an immutable given, but an ongoing struggle towards a future prize (Phil. 3: 10–16), could serve as an accurate summary of Galatians 5–6.

Both letters give graphic expression to Paul's extraordinary sense of union with Christ. In one he bears the stigmata of Jesus (Gal. 6: 17), while in the other he shares in the fellowship of Christ's sufferings (Phil. 3: 10). The concluding exhortation to imitate Paul (Phil. 3: 17) echoes Galatians 4: 12; but in view of the divisions within the church at Philippi, the Apostle coins the word 'fellow-imitators' to underline the corporate dimension of the believers' existence.

Trouble at Colossae

As we saw, Paul's missionary strategy in Ephesus regarding the rest of the Roman province of Asia was to entrust its evangelization to visitors converted in Ephesus who would bring the gospel back to their native cities and towns. This had the advantage of giving the missionaries a running start, but it had one serious disadvantage. The missionaries were completely inexperienced, both theologically and in terms of building community. At home they had family responsibilities and businesses that needed tending. They could not afford to stay with Paul more than a couple of weeks, if that. Their training, in consequence, was strictly limited.

From Paul's perspective they got more than enough. After all, there was the Holy Spirit to guide them! His instructions to the departing missionaries would have been simple: (1) preach the crucified Jesus Christ; (2) tell your converts to imitate the self-sacrifice of Christ in loving one another; (3) tell them to preach the gospel wherever and whenever they could; (4) make a special effort to acquire a convert with a house big enough to accommodate the community.

Despite all the odds, somehow it worked. Paul's confidence was not misplaced. Foundations mushroomed. Regrettably, we know something of the inner workings of only one, the city of Colossae in the Lycus valley.

The church there was founded by a native son, Epaphras (Col. 4: 12). His first convert was Philemon, who was followed into the faith by his wife, Apphia, and by Archippus, whose relationship to the first two is unknown (Philem. 1). They actively participated with Epaphras in the evangelization of Colossae.

Philemon was just the sort of person that Paul himself would have targeted in a new city. He had at least one slave, Onesimus, and a dwelling large enough to contain a guest-room (Philem. 22). His home became a house-church (Philem. 2), and he probably had space to receive the whole church when the occasion demanded.

A Guilty Slave

Philemon did not insist that his servants should adopt his new faith. He left them free to choose. One of them repaid this tolerance by injuring Philemon. He acted in contradiction to his typical slave-name, Onesimus, which means 'Useful'. We have no idea of what happened, except that the matter was very serious (Philem. 18). In desperation, because he had no idea how to compensate his master for the damage, Onesimus asked Epaphras for advice.

According to Roman law, a slave who ran away compounded his offence, but a slave who ran to a friend of his master was not con-sidered a fugitive.[4] Such flight was an admission of guilt, but at the same time it indicated a willingness to seek reconciliation and to make recompense, because the point of the visit was to induce the master's friend to serve as a mediator in the re-establishment of good relations. Afraid that he himself would not carry enough weight, Epaphras advised Onesimus to seek the aid of Paul, and told him where Paul was to be found in Ephesus.

We can be sure that Onesimus headed for the coast at top speed, because time was of the essence. The problem had to be solved before the momentary anger of Philemon solidified into permanent bitterness. On reaching Ephesus, Onesimus must have had a shock when he found that Paul was not in the workshop of Prisca and Aquila, but in prison. He persevered, however, and succeeded, not only in reaching Paul, but in maintaining contact with him for some time. The witness given by Paul in chains touched the heart of Onesimus in a way that the preaching of Epaphras had failed to do, and he became a Christian (Philem. 10).

Before Paul could send Onesimus back to Philemon with a letter pleading for leniency, if not complete forgiveness, Epaphras arrived in Ephesus with the delegation from Colossae, and they were immediately slapped into prison, as we have seen. Paul immediately deduced that something had gone seriously wrong. Six men with livings to earn and families to support were most unlikely to absent themselves from their work for a minimum of two weeks just to make a social visit.

False Teaching

It quickly emerged that false teaching had made such inroads into the community at Colossae that Archippus, one of the leadership group in the house-church of Philemon (Philem. 1), had gone over to the enemy (Col. 4: 17). Epaphras had not had the training to deal with intellectual problems of this type. He was a businessman, not a theologian or a philosopher. The fact that he had brought a delegation with him might even suggest that he was not sure that he had understood the issue fully. It is easy to imagine Paul's frustration as he attemped to synthesize the six reports, which certainly differed in detail.

Eventually a pattern began to emerge. Christians at Colossae were exhibiting an unhealthy curiosity in a Jewish mystical-ascetic movement, which happened to be in vogue in the Lycus valley, because it seemed to offer something at once more elevated and concrete than the unadorned teaching of Epaphras. It was believed that fasting from food and drink, coupled with strict observance of the Jewish religious festivals, could procure a mystical ascent to heaven which climaxed in a vision of angels worshipping at the throne of God.[5]

The preaching of Epaphras, of course, had been modelled on that of Paul. In consequence, there had been a strong, if not exclusive, emphasis on the crucified Christ as the sole means of salvation. Those believers at Colossae who were influenced by the mystical-ascetic Jewish approach took from this Christology only those aspects that were compatible with their cosmic speculation. Didactic hymns were part of the liturgy at Colossae (Col. 3: 16), so one of them in an inspired moment crystallized what they thought of Christ into a two-strophe hymn (Col. 1: 15–20), which Epaphras and the delegation brought to Paul in Ephesus:

> He who is the image of the invisible God
> First-born of all creation
> For in him were created all things
> All things through him and to him were created.
>
> He who is the beginning
> First-born from the dead
> For in him all the Fulness was pleased to dwell
> And through him to reconcile all things to him.

The perplexity of Epaphras now becomes much more understandable. This was far from what Paul had said about Christ, but how could he object to such exaltation of the Saviour? The hymn conveyed an impression of ineffable profundity that left him, a simple businessman, feeling completely inadequate.

No doubt others in the community at Colossae felt the same way. Their humiliation, however, was tinged with pride. They were in the company of great minds struggling to penetrate to the heart of the mystery. They were happy to sing or recite the hymn in the belief that they were articulating central truths whose meaning was beyond them.

The initiates, on the contrary, felt that the milk offered them by Paul's representative had at last been replaced by succulent red meat into which they could sink their intellectual teeth. The ambiguity and ambivalence of the hymn offered material for indefinite debate, in which individuals could shine like angels by the brilliance of their insights.

150

A Pastor at his Best

Even though Paul's dealings with Philippi were separated by only a month or so from his response to the problems at Colossae, he appears in a completely different light in the two exchanges. The prisoner, whose self-absorption risked making the situation at Philippi worse, has been replaced in the same cell by the authentic pastor, whose generous heart pleads eloquently for the rehabilitation of Onesimus, and whose incisive intelligence cuts through 'the beguiling persuasive speech' of the false teaching at Colossae to expose it as 'empty deceit', mere 'shadow', in contrast to the 'substance' of Christ (Col. 2: 4, 6, 17).

A Covering Letter

Contrary to what one might have expected, the letter that Paul sent with Onesimus when he returned to Colossae was not addressed exclusively to his master Philemon, but 'to Philemon, our beloved fellow-worker, and Apphia our sister, and Archippus our fellow-soldier, and the church in your house' (Philem 1–2). Then, despite this communal beginning, the letter speaks only to a single masculine individual, who is undoubtedly Philemon.

This looks very like a subtle form of moral blackmail, in which the manipulative side of Paul's character comes to the fore. The communal address ensured that the letter could not be treated as private. It had to be read out to the house-church. Paul's request to Philemon, in consequence, became known to the other members of the community, whose sympathy with the imprisoned apostle would be expressed as criticism of Philemon if he refused to comply with Paul's appeal, which proves to be much more than one would expect from a mediator.

Paul explicitly recognizes that Onesimus has injured Philemon, and makes himself personally responsible for the damages. 'I, Paul, write this with my own hand, I will repay it' (Philem. 19). Such restitution went a long way towards the rehabilitation of Onesimus, but Philemon still had to be placated for his hurt feelings. Paul does so with graceful compliments, because he needs much more from

Philemon. He wants him to set Onesimus free in order that he might work with Paul (Philem. 11–13). This was not a light petition. An adult, active, competent slave was a considerable asset, and to give him up meant a serious financial sacrifice.

This two-pronged approach (pressure and flattery) to Philemon stemmed from Paul's understanding of his relationship to the churches he had founded. His position gave him paternal authority, but he could not issue orders that were simply to be obeyed. That would be to impose another law, and at Antioch he had clearly seen the legalism that it would eventually lead to. Goodness by compulsion (Philem. 14) was completely repugnant to him. If he was to respect the moral autonomy of his communities and their members, all that he could do was to attempt to 'persuade' them to do what he considered right. Of course, as we see here, he understood 'persuade' in a very broad sense.

Correcting Colossae

From Paul's perspective, the basic problem at Colossae was that the honour offered to Christ effectively marginalized him. He was given cosmic significance at the price of his terrestrial reality. He was elevated to the point where he could no longer be imitated. Believers, in consequence, were no longer challenged by exposure to the agonizing suffering of a crucified Saviour. Instead, they were invited to relax into serene contemplation of the worshipping angels in heaven.

With the skill of a trained rhetorician, Paul cuts straight to the heart of the false teaching by dissecting and correcting the hymn that Epaphras had brought from Colossae. The fact that the hymn focused on Christ gave him the opportunity to hoist the false teachers with their own petard. He accepted their language, and from it drew conclusions that destroyed their position.

The hymn gave Christ a role in the creation and reconciliation of 'all things'. Paul points out that the universal must include angels of all stripes (Col. 1: 16bcd). As the instrument of their creation, therefore, Christ must be infinitely superior to all spiritual beings. Why, then, should the Colossians bother about them? If 'all things' need reconciliation, then it is required, not merely by sinful human beings, but also by angels (Col. 1: 20c). Manifestly, only good angels can be effective mediators with God. But how are terrestrials to know which angels have in fact been reconciled? Angels, in other words, are both irrelevant and useless as far as humanity is concerned. Paul, however, leaves this inference unstated. What the Colossians could deduce for themselves would be a much more effective corrective than a pre-packaged conclusion. A trained orator flattered his audience by assuming their intelligence.

Having sidelined the angels to which the Colossians gave such attention, the field was free for Paul to reiterate the teaching with which he had inculcated Epaphras. Reconciliation is the making of peace, but that was effected 'by the blood of his cross' (Col. 1: 20b). The graphic imagery will be intensified later in the letter by the mention of 'nailing' (Col. 2: 14). Paul will never let anyone forget that reconciliation has been achieved within history at the cost of the agonizing suffering endured by Jesus Christ. Once again the Colossians were expected to work out for themselves that they owed Christ something.

Paul uses the structure of the hymn to introduce in the central position between the two strophes a theme which would become fundamental to his future preaching. 'Christ is the head of the body, the church' (Col. 1: 18a). This is but the logical extension of the insight of Galatians, 'you are all one in Christ Jesus' (Gal. 3: 28). That Paul is here thinking along the same lines is clear from the extremely close parallel between this latter verse and Colossians 3: 11, which speaks of the new man, 'where there cannot be Greek and Jew, circumcised and uncircumcised, barbarian, Scythian, but Christ is all, and in all'.

The 'new man' is in fact a plurality, but one which is unified in a unique way, 'holding fast to the head, from whom the whole body, nourished and knit together through its joints and ligaments, grows with a growth that is from God' (Col. 2: 19). This use of 'head' in the sense of 'source' is better attested than the alternative meaning 'superior', which is certainly the sense in Colossians 2: 10. Paul's insistence that Christ is present in him, and in all members of the church, draws the cosmic dimension of the Christological reflection of the Colossians down into ecclesiology.

Colossians 1: 18a is the first time that Paul articulates the organic unity of the church in terms of a human 'body'. It is most improbable that he merely adapted the Greek philosophical view of society as the body politic. It is psychologically impossible that Paul should have taken over to describe the church a term used to characterize society, which appeared to him as riven by divisions (Gal. 3: 28; 5: 19–20). The basic quality of the church, on the contrary, was unity rooted in love (1 Thess. 4: 9; Col. 3: 14).

It is much more likely that Paul was jolted into thinking of the church as a 'body' by reflecting on the most memorable feature of the temples of Aesclepius scattered throughout the eastern Mediterranean: namely, the ceramic representations of parts of the body which had been cured. The recommendation of Vitruvius (*De Architectura* 1. 2. 7) that such temples be sited only in areas with clean air and pure water made them favourite places of recreation, and there is no reason to think that Paul did not frequent them on occasion. The sight of legs which were only reproductions brought Paul to the realization that a leg was truly a leg only when part of a body. Believers, he inferred, were truly 'alive' only when they 'belonged' to Christ as his members (Col. 2: 6, 13; 3: 4). The 'death' of egocentric isolation has been replaced by the 'life' of shared existence.

Colossians is a very different sort of letter from Galatians. The delegation from Antioch-on-the-Orontes had made a well-thought-out frontal attack on Paul personally, and on all that he believed in. He had to demolish a thoroughly worked-out vision of Christianity, whose coherent arguments were rooted in revelation. Antioch played no role in Colossae. Its representatives, who by now were on their way to Philippi, did not even know that the church there existed.

Paul's opponents at Colossae had nothing like the intellectual depth of the Antiocheans. They described mysteries, apocalyptic visions, whose reality no one could verify. In contrast to the well-rooted representatives of Antioch, they floated in a fantasy world. Paul's concern was to restore a sense of reality, to set the feet of the misguided on solid ground. They grasped at shadows; he had to show them that Christ was substance (Col. 2: 17). The most effective tactic was not to challenge the mystics head on, but to consistently introduce discreet modifications, whose cumulative impact would subvert their teaching completely. He relied on the sobering effect of the calm assumption of authority.

Future Plans

While under investigation at Ephesus, Paul understandably had for-mulated plans for the time after his release. But they were not entirely coherent. He wrote to the Philippians, 'I trust in the Lord that shortly I myself shall come also' (2: 24; cf. 1: 26). Shortly afterwards he made a request of Philemon in Colossae, 'Prepare a guest-room for me, for I am hoping through your prayers to be granted to you' (Philem. 22). These projects were dictated by his heart, not his head. The road to Philippi led north, while the 'Common Highway' to Colossae headed due east. If Paul decided on action, he had to make a choice. We can only guess at his reasoning.

Paul was probably released in the latter part of the summer of AD 53. From the fact that a visit to Philippi was still on his agenda a year later (1 Cor. 16: 5), we can infer that he did not go to Philippi on his rel-ease. This is very understandable. We have seen that there was signifi-cant opposition to his leadership within the church at Ephesus (Phil. 1: 14–15). The round trip from Ephesus to Philippi would have taken a minimum of a month under optimum conditions. This would have brought him dangerously close to the moment when normal sea travel ceased. If ships no longered sailed from Neapolis to Troas, he would be trapped in Macedonia for the winter, with unacceptable consequences. A prolonged absence might guarantee the success of a different vision of Christianity at Ephesus. Moreover, to leave the city at that crucial moment might be interpreted as the flight of a coward.

These considerations would not have militated with the same force against a visit to Colossae. Paul's reason for going to Philippi was essentially for the pleasure of seeing believers who had always been loyal and co-operative. It was intended to refresh his spirit after a tense time under investigation. Apart from the tension generated by the personal competition between Euodia and Syntyche (Phil. 4: 2), there were no problems that imperatively demanded his presence. It would not have been difficult for Paul to rationalize his failure to keep his promise to the Philippians as the repudiation of a selfish decision made in a moment of weakness.

The planned visit to Colossae could not be avoided so easily. An important doctrinal point was at stake, and Paul had accepted responsibility for the work of his agent, Epaphras, by writing letters to the Colossians and to the Laodiceans, which they were to exchange (Col. 4: 16). He needed to know whether the way he had dealt with the false teachers had been successful. If not, it was imperative to make a further effort.

Paul, however, did not have to go to Colossae himself. There were at least two other sources of information available. Tychicus was a permanent member of Paul's entourage (2 Tim. 4: 12). Although it is not stated, it must be presumed that Paul expected him to return to Ephesus with a report on how his letter had affected the situation at Colossae (Col. 4: 7–8). Epaphras would certainly have returned to Colossae the moment he was released, and could be back in Ephesus within two weeks, if the situation warranted it.

Paul must have wondered whether he should rely on second-hand information or go and see for himself. A decisive factor in his internal debate was his conviction of the autonomy of the local community. Whatever needed to be done as the result of his letter would have to be accomplished from within, as a member of the community. In many other churches this would mean no more than slipping back into the niche which he had occupied for a year or more. At Colossae people knew him only by reputation. He had met none of them personally (Col. 2: 1). To know them, and to be known by them, would take time. And there was also Laodicea and Hierapolis to consider (Col. 4: 13). The more he thought about it, the more Paul became convinced that, if he went to the Lycus valley, he would be obliged to spend the winter there.

Could he afford so much time away from Ephesus? On balance, Paul thought not. His personal position there was in danger, and it was the place which he had selected as his base for contacts with other churches. He had just had to deal with a problem in Corinth via the previous letter (1 Cor. 5: 9). Moreover, he had not formally promised the Colossians that he would visit them. Nothing about a visit is mentioned in Colossians, and he did not plan to stay with Epaphras, the leader of the community, with whom he had shared a prison cell. The request for a guest-room was addressed to Philemon (Philem. 22), and could be considered a purely private matter. It would be more prudent, Paul decided, to wait for the reports of Tychicus and Epaphras.

What news they brought him, we shall never know. From the following spring Paul was completely absorbed by the problems of the church in Corinth, and left Colossae to the care of Epaphras.

Conversations with Corinth   9

PAUL renewed his contacts with Corinth in the late summer of AD 53 or very early spring of AD 54 when Apollos returned to Ephesus. The two had never met. Their personalities were very different, and Paul had resented the presence of Apollos among his converts. Yet, once contact was made, they got on well together. Paul realized that their gifts were complementary. 'I planted, Apollos watered, but God gave the growth' (1 Cor. 3: 6).

Formally or informally Apollos gave Paul his impression of the progress of the church at Corinth. He highlighted a discrepancy between what some members believed and their comportment. There were some who continued the immoral practices of their pagan past. The community recognized the situation, but apparently did not know how to remedy it. How should sinners within the community be treated? Their profession of faith had made them brothers/sisters to be loved unequivocally. How could this be compatible with any form of disapproval?

Such dithering infuriated Paul. What should be done was perfectly clear, had the Corinthians accepted their responsibility to each other. He dashed off a now-lost letter (1 Cor. 5: 9) in which he pointed out that all they had to do was to refuse to associate in any way with the individuals in question. We know this much only because the issue was still alive several months later. The letter may also have dealt with other matters.

Situation Reports on Corinth

When the sailing season opened in late April, AD 54, a wealthy busi-nesswoman of Ephesus, Chloe, sent representatives to Corinth, per-haps slaves or freedmen. Corinth was the nub of the trade routes in the eastern Mediterranean, and she obviously hoped to have the first pick of the commodities arriving from the west. The first goods of the new trading season had a brief scarcity value that pushed up their price. It may have been on their own initiative that her people made contact with their fellow Christians in the city, but it is most improbable that Paul would have failed to avail himself of the opportunity to obtain news of a church that he had not seen for three years. An important factor in his choice of Ephesus as his base had been the possibility of using precisely such travellers to carry his messages back and forth.

At this point in his career Paul had dealt with the teething and adolescent problems of a series of churches (Thessalonica, Galatia, Ephesus, Philippi and Colossae). He had a very clear idea of the things that could go wrong, as a church struggled to define itself on the way to maturity. That he should have indicated to Chloe's people the areas of community life that might prove problematic is sug-gested not only by common sense, but by the fact that he does not know them individually. Evidently her representatives were not important enough for him to retain their names, and there is a ten-dency to assume that members of the lower classes needed to have everything spelt out to them. Sexual morality was certainly one of the aspects they were asked to assess, because Paul must have been concerned about the impact of the previous letter.

The Report of Chloe's Employees

The report brought back by Chloe's people stunned Paul (1 Cor. 1: 11–12). The situation at Corinth was much worse than anything he had hitherto encountered as a pastor. Murphy's Law had been imple-mented to the full. Everything that could go wrong had gone wrong.

The greatest injury was to the unity of the community, which was riven into three factions. Apollos of Alexandria (Acts 18: 24–8) had quickly found a niche in the competitive world of the Corinthian church. Paul's preaching was minimalist. He proclaimed a crucified Christ as the exemplar of authentic humanity (1 Cor. 2: 1–5), and saw no need for any speculative theological development. He was more concerned with evidence of the power of transforming grace in his life and that of others (2 Cor. 3: 2). He cut a poor figure by comparison with the orators who attracted followers by their eloquence. He also disappointed those believers who aspired to a real theology. Apollos met these needs. In addition to his oratorical gifts, he had the ability to connect things up, to establish relationships between different aspects of the faith. This was one of the fundamental aspects of rhetorical education. By using Philo's methods of interpretation and his philosophical framework, Apollos provided intellectual fulfilment by building a rich synthesis of the elements which Paul had provided.

Human nature being what it is, the intellectual aspirations of those who clustered around Apollos certainly alienated others, perhaps the less well educated, who, in reaction, insisted on the importance of the bare minimum inculcated by the founder of the church. What mattered most, they insisted, was love of neighbour.

An Apollos group and a Paul group were inevitable once Apollos appeared on the scene. But apparently there was also a third group, which Paul identifies with Cephas (1 Cor. 1: 12). There is no evidence that Cephas ever set foot in Corinth. My guess is that ever since the incident at Antioch (Gal. 2: 11–14), 'Cephas' had functioned for Paul as a symbol for a type of Christian Jew, who had tasted freedom and then rejected it. Thus we should think of a group of Jewish converts who found difficulty in integrating into a predominantly Gentile community (1 Cor. 12: 2). The philosophical style of Apollos' preaching might have contributed to their sense of isolation. In any case, they had little influence within the community.

While such factionalism was of fundamental importance to Paul, in the eyes of Chloe's people it paled into insignificance beside a series of fascinating cameos. The church took pride in an incestuous marriage, the cohabitation of a man with his stepmother (1 Cor. 5: 1–8), because this differentiated them from Jews and Gentiles, both of whom condemned such unions. Paul, after all, had told them that they must be distinctive in order to hold forth the word of life.

Yet, noted Chloe's people, Corinthian believers had no compunction about having recourse to pagan courts (1 Cor. 6: 1–11), and justified their using prostitutes on the grounds that Paul had told them that they were free from all law (1 Cor. 6: 12–20). A similarly childish understanding of Paul's insistence that there was no place for traditional differences in the church found expression in the community's acceptance of a male homosexual with a magnificent female hair-do as a leader in the liturgical assembly (1 Cor. 11: 2–16). After all, Paul had said 'There is no more male and female' (Gal. 3: 28). As if this had not sufficiently scandalized Chloe's people, they found the eucharistic congregation split into two groups, those who had too much to eat and drink, and those who had nothing (1 Cor. 11: 17–34). The sharing that should characterize the Lord's Supper was noticeably absent.

On their return to Ephesus, Chloe's people would be extraordinary if they did not strive to outdo one another in recounting instances of bizarre behaviour among the Corinthians. Paul could not believe his ears. Their excited babble offered him the slender lifeline of hope that they might be exaggerating. There was also the possibility that they might have misunderstood what was going on. After all, they were business people, and inexperienced in church matters.

It would have been unwise for Paul to react on the basis of what was essentially no more than gossip. Before intervening, he had to find out exactly what was going on, and at his side was the man capable of carrying out such an investigation. Timothy had already undertaken a similar mission in Thessalonica (1 Thess. 3: 1–6). He was not only trustworthy, but experienced. Fortunately, he had not yet left for Philippi (Phil. 2: 19–24).

As soon as possible, Timothy took passage on one of the many ships plying between Ephesus and Corinth. The duration of the voyage is uncertain. It depended on many factors: notably, fine weather, fair winds and good omens. On official business and using naval equipment, which meant no cargo delays, it took Cicero from 6 to 22 July, 51 BC, to sail from Athens to Ephesus (*Letters to Atticus*

161

5. 11–13). To allow Timothy two weeks in each direction is probably a minimum. He could hardly spend less than a fortnight in Corinth. Hence, we can safely assume that he was away from Paul for six weeks, probably from the beginning of May to the middle of June.

The Corinthian Letter and Delegation

The Corinthians no doubt learnt from Chloe's people that Paul had in fact carried out his plan to settle in Ephesus. Shortly after Timothy had left for Corinth, a delegation, comprising Stephanas, Fortunatus and Achaicus (1 Cor. 16: 15–17), arrived from Corinth bearing a letter, in which the church of Corinth asked for Paul's opinion on a number of contested issues (1 Cor. 7: 1).

There was disagreement in the community on the appropriateness of sex in marriage (1 Cor. 7: 1–11), on the legitimacy of eating meat which had been sacrificed to idols (1 Cor. 8–10), on the hierarchy of spiritual gifts (1 Cor. 12–14), and on the resurrection from the dead (1 Cor. 15). Each side of every issue had its partisans. Debates were charged with an intensity that endangered fraternal charity. Motives were imputed, and ill will mounted. Paul, who had shuddered at the report of factions, was devastated by the news of further divisions at much more basic levels.

The presence of the delegation meant that all the information which Paul had expected to acquire through Timothy was now immediately available, and from a representative, trustworthy source. He had access to people who could speak authoritatively about the state of the community and its problems, and thus support or deny the gossip of Chloe's people. The precision of his information was such that in his letter he was able to quote the 'slogans' that different groups used to state or justify their positions. Paul, therefore, was in a position to formulate his response, not only to what the Corinthians saw as questions, but to aspects of their lives which did not bother them but which Paul considered problematic. The urgency of the situation brooked no delay. Sometime before 2 June, the date of Pentecost (1 Cor. 16: 8) in AD 54, Paul wrote the letter we know as 1 Corinthians.

First Corinthians

Such a bewildering series of complex issues might have paralysed a less able personality. Paul dealt with them all in precisely 6,829 words! His organization of the material betrays his formidable rhetorical skills. He had been taught that a long discourse should treat the most important issues at the beginning and at the end. Everyone is awake when the speaker starts, and comes to life again when the subconscious picks up the words, 'And now in conclusion'.[1]

Thus, as one might have expected, Paul treats first the divisions in the community (chs 1–5) and concludes with a defence of the Resurrection (ch. 15). A divided community is no different from society, and without the Resurrection, Christ is meaningless. Were Paul to let go these fundamental points, the church at Corinth would be nothing but another secular organization. In between these basic topics he groups related issues, whether reported by Chloe's people or raised by the Corinthian delegation. He deals in turn with the importance of the body (chs 5–6), problems caused by social status (ch. 7), problems arising from the pagan environment in which the church lived (chs 8–10), and problems in the liturgical assemblies (chs 11–14). He covers each point in a business-like manner, clearly, forcefully and succinctly.

The Spirit People, the Root of All Evil

If we look closely at 1 Corinthians 1–4, where Paul is most explicitly concerned with divisions in the community, a group emerges whose members believed that their possession of 'wisdom' made them 'perfect' (2: 6). As possessors of 'the Spirit which is from God' (2: 12), they were 'spirit people' (2: 15). They thought of themselves as 'filled (with divine blessings)', 'wealthy', 'kings' (4: 8), 'wise', 'strong', 'honoured' (4: 10). They looked down on others in the community who had not attained their exalted spiritual status as 'children' capable of imbibing only 'milk' (3: 1), and as 'fools' who were 'weak' and 'dishonoured' (4: 10). For convenience I call them the Spirit People. They were drawn predominantly from the wealthier and better-educated section of the church at Corinth. It is they who would have had the leisure and ability to indulge in religious speculation.

The language of the Spirit People evokes Philo of Alexandria's distinction between the heavenly man and the earthly man.[2] All the key elements mentioned in the previous paragraph appear in two passages of a single work by the great Jewish philosopher, *De Sobrietate* 9–11 and 55–7. Hence, we are entitled to assume that other elements integral to Philo's understanding of the heavenly and earthly man also formed part of the religious outlook of the Spirit People, and that Paul has these latter in mind when he argues against such points.

The body was a fundamental point of disagreement between the heavenly and the earthly man. The wisdom possessed by the former revealed to him that 'the body is evil by nature and treacherous to the soul' (*Legum Allegoriae* 3. 71), whereas the earthly man was 'a body lover' (*Legum Allegoriae* 3. 74). If the body is 'a plotter against the soul, a corpse and always a dead thing' (*Legum Allegoriae* 3. 69), it is natural to infer that the Spirit People were those who denied the Resurrection (1 Cor. 15: 12). Death, from their perspective, was liberation from the weight and defilement of the body (*De Somniis* 148). To recover the body after death would have been meaningless. It is highly unlikely, therefore, that the Spirit People could have accepted Paul's preaching of Jesus as the Risen Lord in the sense that he intended. Perhaps they thought of him as a purely spiritual 'Lord of Glory' (1 Cor. 2: 8). In reality, they had no sense of the historical Jesus; their attitude to him in effect said 'Anathema Jesus!' (1 Cor. 12: 3). In keeping with their sapiential orientation, they were theists, and, in every instance where Paul confronts them, he has to remind them of the importance of Jesus Christ (1 Cor. 2: 16; 3: 23; 8: 6; 10: 16; 15: 3–5).

When Philo's disparagement of the body is associated with his dictum that 'only the wise man is free' (*De Posteritate Caini* 138), which means that 'he has the power to do anything and to live as he wishes' (*Quod Omnis Probus Liber sit* 59), we see the basis for the Corinthian slogans 'all things are lawful to me' (1 Cor. 6: 12; 10: 23) and 'every sin which a man commits is outside the body'

(1 Cor. 6: 18). Their belief in the moral irrelevance of the body enabled the Spirit People to indulge their sexual appetites (1 Cor. 5: 1–8; 6: 12–20), and to eat what they wished (1 Cor. 8–10).

The importance that some Corinthians attached to glossolalia (1 Cor. 12–14) is drawn into this pattern when it is recognized that, for Philo, possession of the prophetic spirit expressed itself in ecstasy and inspired frenzy, since 'the mind is evicted at the arrival of the divine spirit' (*Quis rerum divinarum Heres* 264–5). When speaking of tongues, Paul specifically mentions 'frenzy' (1 Cor. 14: 23) and the inactivity of the mind (1 Cor. 14: 14). Mysterious, unintelligible speech flattered the conviction of the Spirit People that they were superior.

The Spirit People, in other words, were at the root of the problems dealt with in thirteen of the sixteen chapters of 1 Corinthians.

Apollos, the converted Alexandrian Jew, was the obvious channel by which Philo's philosophical framework had entered the community.[3] What he said, however, and what his followers understood were not necessarily identical. If they mistook Paul's meaning so badly, it is improbable that they understood Apollos adequately. Certainly Paul's quarrel was with the practical implications of their interpretation of Apollos, rather than with the personality or teaching of the latter (1 Cor. 16: 12). Indeed, Apollos may have left Corinth, and come to live with Paul at Ephesus, specifically because he had become dismayed at the uses to which his teaching was being put.

A Most Unchristian Strategy

When Paul recognized that the Spirit People were at the root of virtually all the problems in the Corinthian community, his bias against speculative theology was immeasurably strengthened. It had revealed itself in its fruits. Not only was it unnecessary, it was pernicious. Hence, instead of a sincere effort to get to the root of the problem, and to understand the legitimate aspirations of the Spirit People, Paul's reaction was brutally dismissive. Confident that such intellectuals would always be a minority without popular support, Paul chose to play on the dark side of the majority by turning the

Spirit People into figures of fun. Cruel laughter was the weapon he selected for his campaign.

Perhaps, if left to himself, Paul would not have made what would prove to be a disastrous mistake. The suggestion may have come from his co-author, Sosthenes (1 Cor. 1: 1). Even in that case, we must ask what motivated Paul to accept such an unchristian tactic. Personal factors were probably decisive. The influence acquired by Apollos was an implicit criticism of Paul's leadership. He might content himself with simple proclamation to those incapable of receiving anything higher, but the Spirit People expected much more. A latent note of challenge is easily detected (1 Cor. 2: 15; 4: 3). If Paul did not offer them 'wisdom', might it not be that he was incapable of the soaring religious speculation that they considered integral to true religious authority? Might not the absence of such a gift indicate that he was not fit to lead the community? Such presumption, from Paul's perspective, merited a sharp put-down, and that is what he provided in 1 Corinthians 1–4, which sets the tone for his relationship with the Spirit People.

In 1 Corinthians 2: 6–16 Paul plays a cruel intellectual game with his opponents. His whole purpose is to mystify them, and thereby reduce them to confused silence amid the laughter of all the others who hear the letter read aloud. This he achieves by appropriating some of the most cherished terms in the lexicon of the Spirit People, and giving them a meaning radically opposed to that intended by them. He agrees that they are 'spiritual' and possess 'wisdom', but goes on to insist that their spirit is 'the spirit of the world' (2: 12), and that their wisdom is 'the wisdom of this age' (2: 6). He consents to their self-designation of 'mature' only to redefine it as childishness (3: 1). Those who set themselves up as judges are revealed to be incompetent (2: 14). The unerring precision with which he goes to the heart of their cherished beliefs is inexplicable without the assistance of Apollos, who was with him at the time of writing (1 Cor. 16: 12). The piercing tone of mockery was designed to prick the bubble of the Spirit People's smug complacency.

The savagely sarcastic rhetorical questions with which this initial section terminates (3: 3–4) reappear in 4: 7: 'Who sees anything different in you? What have you that you did not receive?' The Spirit People, Paul insinuates, have no qualities which would make them valuable as allies or supporters. They are recipients, not creators. The contemptuous tone is heightened as Paul goes on to mock them by taking their spiritual language literally, thus transforming their legitimate religious aspirations into absurd social achievements. It takes little imagination to hear the rustle of malicious laughter in the congregation, and to see the contemptuous sideward looks as the reader of the letter gave emphasis to the words, 'Without us you have become *kings*! And would that you did reign, so that we might share the rule with you!' (4: 8).

Having dispatched the letter with the returning delegation, Paul relaxed in the consciousness of a job well done. He had deployed his rhetorical skills so cunningly that he felt real optimisn that his views would prevail. What he needed now was a good holiday. His difficulties in Ephesus apparently having been resolved, a leisurely swing through the churches of Macedonia would refresh his spirits. When he finally got to Corinth at the end of the summer (AD 54), he could tidy up any loose ends that remained (1 Cor. 16: 5–7). The lack of any hint of urgency in these future plans suggests that Paul had completely forgotten that Macedonia was next on the list of the Judaizing delegation from Antioch-on-the-Orontes, who had troubled the churches of Galatia a year ago.

An Unplanned Visit to Corinth

Timothy was still in Corinth when the delegation returned with Paul's letter. He was profoundly shocked when he heard it read in public. The impact was so disastrous that he found it difficult to believe that Paul could have been so stupidly insensitive. He desperately wished that he had been in Ephesus to check him. The kaleidoscope of new theological insights that the letter contained was lost in an emotional explosion. If the Paul party gloated in victory, the majority were repelled by the lack of charity in his treatment of the Spirit People. Paul's venom certainly diminished him in the eyes of the genuine Christians in the community. They felt that he had gone

167

too far. Thereafter his judgement became suspect, and unconditional support problematic.

For the Spirit People it went much deeper. Profoundly wounded by the humiliation of public ridicule, they were completely alienated, and became Paul's implacable enemies. Since they could not attack him directly, they channelled their pain and anger into frustrating his ambitions for the community. It was the Spirit People who offered hospitality when the Judaizers from Antioch-on-the-Orontes, who had troubled the churches of Galatia, arrived in Corinth in the middle of the summer of AD 54, thereby showing that some Corinthians at least were prepared to listen to an alternative vision of Christianity.

Timothy could not return quickly enough to Ephesus to inform Paul of his catastrophic mistake. It was imperative to instigate some form of damage control immediately. Paul might have hesitated if it were only a question of the susceptibilities of the Spirit People. In his book they were snobbish trouble-makers. If they suffered for the confusion they had caused in simple minds, so much the better.

The news that the delegation from Antioch had already reached Corinth was another matter altogether. Not only had they left Galatia, but they had passed through Philippi and Thessalonica. They had completed their mission to the daughter churches of Antioch, and had done it so quickly that Paul could only conclude that the Macedonian churches had abandoned their allegiance to him. He still had no news of how the confrontation in Galatia had worked out.

Paul found himself on the horns of a dilemma. The churches in Macedonia were just as much his responsibility as Corinth was, and he had planned to visit them (1 Cor. 16: 5). But he could not be in two places at once, and time was of the essence. He had to make a choice. His decision fell on Corinth.[4] The Judaizers had only just arrived there. If Paul lost no time in getting there, he could confront them in person, and destroy their Law-observant vision of the gospel before it made a serious impact on the community. Macedonia would have to wait. The damage there, he believed, had been done. He could, however, send Timothy, as he had promised (Phil. 2: 23), to do what he could to prepare the ground for Paul's eventual arrival.

Timothy's heart must have been heavy as he headed north with Erastus (Acts 19: 22) to take ship from Troas. The impact on Paul of his news from Corinth dismayed him. He had never seen his leader so crushed. He felt keenly the burden of responsibility he carried, and dreaded the hostility that he might face from the Macedonians.

Timothy's anxiety was nothing compared to that of Paul. Profoundly depressed, Paul fretted impatiently as he waited in the harbour for the requisite combination of cargo, favourable wind and auspicious omens. The voyage would have appeared interminable as his restless imagination created one scenario worse than the other, while he mulled over different strategies. If at times he saw himself victorious over his enemies, formulating brilliant arguments that would rout the Judaizers and confirm his position among the Corinthians, the spectre of defeat was always there to haunt him. If he lost Corinth, his adversaries would have completed their encirclement, and Ephesus at the centre, together with her daughter churches in Asia, could not long survive. The whole future of the Gentile church was at stake.

Confrontation at Corinth

Paul's frame of mind when he arrived in Corinth is easily imagined. Waves of righteous anger, paralysing fear and maudlin self-pity washed over him. Such swirling, confused thoughts cannot have enhanced his presentation when he encountered the leader of the delegation from Antioch. The line taken by the latter must have been very similar to the one he took in Galatia. Paul, he asserted, was a dishonest representative of the church which had sent him out to proclaim the common faith. A traitor to his commission, Paul preached his own ideas, not the common gospel. The dismissive tone in which the slanders were pronounced added insult to injury. Paul leaves us in no doubt that he had been deeply humiliated, and his authority challenged in the most radical way possible.[5]

Yet what perturbed Paul most was the attitude of the Corinthians. Their failure to support him cut him to the quick. From the perspective of an outsider, this is not really as disconcerting as Paul found it.

169

The attitude of the church of Antioch was irrelevant as far as the Corinthians were concerned. They were confident of their own identity, and they had absorbed Paul's teaching on the autonomy of the local community. The idea of a claim based on a remote genetic connection with another church far to the east would have seemed rather unrealistic to them. The success of Jerusalem in imposing its ethos on Antioch was no concern of theirs. It might matter to Paul, but in that case he could fight it out with the intruder on a purely personal level.

Naturally Paul did not see the episode in this light. His vanity had been seriously wounded. Those whom he had engendered through the gospel (1 Cor. 4: 15) should have preferred him above all others. Moreover, the 'neutrality' of the Corinthians induced the suspicion that they were prepared to listen to the Judaizers. No doubt Paul asked them to reject the intruders out of hand. To which the Corinthians replied that no one should be condemned without a fair hearing. This, of course, was precisely what Paul wanted to avoid. The report from Galatia had revealed to him the seductive character of the message of the Judaizers. One might reasonably suspect that the Spirit People were behind the refusal to let Paul lord it over their faith (2 Cor. 1: 23); the wounds caused by his treatment of them in 1 Corinthians were still open and bleeding.

The obstinacy of the Corinthians put Paul in an extremely awkward position. On the one hand, he wanted to stay in Corinth to counter the arguments of the Judaizers; on the other hand, he believed himself to be needed in Macedonia. He could not stay indefinitely in Corinth, and perhaps he recognized that his presence was only exacerbating the situation. The beneficial effects on everyone of a breathing-space may have been a factor in his decision to leave.

Paul announced that he was going to Macedonia, but that he would return to Corinth as soon as he had finished his business there, and then there would be a final show-down with the Judaizers.

Faithful Macedonia

It is most improbable that Paul sailed north from Corinth. Not only was the voyage long and dangerous, but the Etesian winds began to blow strongly from the northern quadrant in mid-June and continued for three months, making northward navigation difficult if not impossible. The overland route from Corinth to Thessalonica is 363 miles (580 km). At an average of 20 miles (32 km) per day, the journey would have taken between eighteen and twenty days. Whether Paul would have been able to maintain this average is another matter. He had to slog across the great double plain of Thessaly, which in summer is one of the hottest places in Europe. The mountains which ring it harboured bears, wolves and wild boar. These, he feared, were awaiting him in the passes to the north, and apprehension must have intensified the exhaustion of the trek across the sun-seared plain.[6]

There can be little doubt that Paul's exhausted physical state was an accurate reflection of his dispirited frame of mind as he trudged into Thessalonica sometime around mid-July, AD 54. The trouble he anticipated, however, did not materialize. There is no hint that he had to confront the Judaizers either there or in Philippi. On the contrary, the commitment of the Macedonians to his cherished project of the collection for the poor of Jerusalem reveals them to have been entirely on his side (2 Cor. 8: 1–4).

Paul now knew how and why the delegation from Antioch had reached Corinth so quickly. They had received very short shrift from the Macedonians once they had revealed their hostility to Paul and his gospel. The contrast between the fidelity of the believers in Thessalonica and Philippi and the mocking neutrality of the Corinthians intensified the bitterness that Paul felt towards the latter.

Perhaps under the moderating influence of Timothy, who is likely to have stayed on in Macedonia, Paul had the good sense to realize that it would be unproductive to return to Corinth with bile seething within him (2 Cor. 2: 1). It could only lead to another explosion, and even greater damage. Hence, he decided to return directly to Ephesus, even though this would give the Corinthians another stick with which to beat him. He had already changed his travel plans twice in their regard. It would be easy to make a charge of inconsistency stick.

171

A Letter Written in Tears

With luck Paul could have been back in Ephesus by mid-August, AD 54. Even though he had decided not to return to Corinth, Paul felt that he owed it to himself and to the Corinthians to explain how he felt about what had happened during his visit. It was not an easy letter to write. 'I wrote you out of much distress and anguish of heart and with many tears' (2 Cor. 2: 4). Unfortunately this letter has not survived, but Paul gives us enough hints to work out his approach.

The letter was in no way similar to the one he had written to the Galatians. He did not deal with the arguments of the Judaizers, but focused exclusively on his own relations with the Corinthians (2 Cor. 2: 9; 7: 12). His strategy was to win their sympathy by revealing their treachery through the description of his hurt. The letter was designed to tug at the heart-strings, while at the same time administering a severe shock. The missive had to be strong enough to shake the Corinthians, but not so brutal as to alienate them. Effective reproof had to be blended with the assurance of his affection. The delicacy of the decisions made the writing an agonizing business. Even after it had been despatched, Paul fretted about the impact of the letter. It might do more harm than good. It might have stood a better chance of achieving his goal, had he said this rather than that. The uncertainty weighed upon him terribly.

The letter was entrusted to Titus (2 Cor. 2: 13; 7: 6). It would not have been tactful to send Timothy, who at the least had been the occasion of the blow-up between Paul and the Corinthians. No matter what other assistants may have been available, Titus had a special qualification. He had been with Paul at the Jerusalem conference (Gal. 2: 1–3). Titus, in other words, made an admirable foil to the Painful Letter, in which Paul had poured out his anguished deception. He was in a position to report authoritatively on the agreement between Paul and the mother church, and thereby to refute any claims, or highlight any distortions, of the Judaizers.

Macedonia and Illyricum 10

HOW the Corinthians would react to his letter written with so much anguish was only one of the problems that weighed on Paul's mind in the late summer of AD 54. He feared that he would be forced out of Ephesus. Evidently the 'hostility of many' (1 Cor. 16: 9; cf. 15: 32), which he noted at the beginning of the summer, had increased. Presumably it was these enemies who were at the root of 'the affliction we experienced in Asia', a trial so grave that 'we despaired of life itself; indeed we felt that we had received the sentence of death' (2 Cor. 1: 8–9). We do not know what happened, but it must have been extremely frightening.

An Emergency Plan

Before Titus left with the Painful Letter, Paul prepared an emergency plan in case the worst happened. Even though it was much quicker, and Paul was desperate for news from Corinth, he instructed Titus not to return from Corinth by sea. He was to take the long land route through Macedonia and to cross over from Neapolis to Troas, thence to take the coast road south to Ephesus. Were Paul obliged to leave Ephesus, he would go north on that road and begin a new ministry in Troas. That way they would be certain of encountering each other.

The selection of Troas as Paul's next missionary centre was an obvious one. The outreach of the church of Ephesus had previously been limited to places within a week's walk of the city, the capital of

Asia. The evangelization of the area around the 'Common Highway' to the east could be left to the initiative of the churches already established along it. Cities to the north of Ephesus, such as Smyrna, Thyatira and Pergamum, had already been targeted as part of Ephesus' program of evangelization. Miletus to the south had its attractions; it was an important city.[1]

It could not, however, compare with Troas, which Paul knew personally. Having passed through it twice—on his first foray into Europe, and on his return to Ephesus from his abortive visit to Corinth—he recognized that it was precisely the sort of large urban setting in which he operated most effectively. Troas had another advantage.[2] A Christian community there could serve as a link between the churches of Asia and those of Europe. The guarantee of Christian hospitality there would facilitate communications. Finally, it was a base from which the gospel could be preached the length of the Hellespontus (modern Dardanelles) and along the southern coast of Propontis (modern Sea of Marmora) reaching east towards Bithynia.[3] It was fortunate that such valid reasons harmonized with Paul's desire to be as far as possible along the road to Titus and the crucial news that he would bring from Corinth.

Paul did in fact have to leave Ephesus before Titus returned. The precise circumstances escape us.[4] He says only, 'When I came to Troas to preach the gospel of Christ, a door was opened for me by the Lord. But my mind could not rest, because I did not find my brother Titus there. So I took leave of them, and went on to Macedonia' (2 Cor. 2: 12–13). Paul was torn between a fruitful ministry (Acts 20: 7–12) and a desperate anxiety to hear Titus' news. As each day passed, the danger grew that they would find themselves trapped on opposites sides of the Sea of Macedonia. Paul waited until the last possible moment before taking a ship for Neapolis, the port of Philippi.

Once Paul had disembarked, one source of anxiety evaporated. He would not be cut off from Titus for the winter. But, as the days slowly passed, the stress of the delay began to wear him down. He mentions a period characterized by 'every kind of affliction, disputes without and fears within' (2 Cor. 7: 5). The strain of the uncertainty of how the Corinthians would react was exacerbated by his fears for the safety of Titus, now seriously overdue, and by squabbles of various sorts. Paul by now was in a state of extreme tension, where everything was an irritation. His emotional state inflated questions into accusations, and discussions into disputes.

It would have been impossible for Paul to have passed through Philippi without stopping to visit the believers. Were Titus not there, his stay would have been short. It is entirely possible that he had walked the 90 miles (144 km) to Thessalonica before Titus appeared. The joyful reunion could have taken place anywhere.[5]

Now that winter was setting in, Paul and his companions settled down in the nearest Christian community until good weather returned in the spring. He had plenty of time to assimilate the report of Titus, and to formulate an appropriate response with the aid of Timothy. Paul was not going to repeat the terrible mistake of 1 Corinthians.

The Report of Titus

Titus could well have begun his report with 'Well, I have good news and I have bad news. Which do you want to hear first?' The good news, of course, was what Paul eagerly wanted to hear. The Painful Letter had had precisely the effect he had hoped for. The sincerity of the Corinthians' contrition for letting Paul down was underlined by the action they took against the leader of the delegation from Antioch (2 Cor. 2: 5–11). The nature of the punishment is not specified, presumably because there was but one possibility: namely, complete ostracization. The believers simply refused to have anything to do with him. He was thrown on the mercies of a society which did not care whether he lived or died. The Corinthians were totally on Paul's side.

Paul's joy, however, was tempered by a series of observations on the life of the community at Corinth, which revealed Titus to be a penetrating and shrewd observer.

Spirit People and Judaizers

The frontal attack on Paul by the leader of the Antiochean delegation had backfired. Titus noted, however, that the Judaizers had not
given up completely. They had made a strategic retreat to regroup,
and to reinforce their links with the Spirit People. At first sight an
alliance between free-thinking Hellenistic pseudo-philosophical
believers, the Spirit People, and Law-observant Jewish Christians
seems rather improbable. History, however, abounds in instances of
minority groups with radically different aims uniting in order to
overthrow a common enemy. When the Judaizers arrived in Corinth,
their first act would have been to probe for weaknesses in the community which Paul had built up. In order to work from within, they
had to be received by someone, and prudence would have indicated
that they search out a group that was already at odds with Paul.

Titus certainly confirmed the report of Timothy regarding the feelings of the Spirit People. There had been no change. Their pride still
sought revenge for Paul's brutal, public humiliation in 1 Corinthians.
Had Apollos remained in Corinth, they might have formed an alternative church, but he had left them to join Paul, and apparently was
not particularly interested in returning (1 Cor. 16: 12). Such betrayal,
for which they may have blamed Paul, could only have intensified
their bitterness. In this frame of mind, Titus insisted, they were fair
game for any of Paul's opponents. The alliance, in consequence, was
one in which both parties gained something. The Judaizers found a
welcome among the élite of the Corinthian community, and the
Spirit People were given the means of damaging, if not destroying,
Paul's achievement.

Titus further pointed out that, while such negative common
ground might be a very fragile basis for concerted action, in this case
both groups shared a positive interest in Moses. For the Spirit People
Moses was the perfect wise man, who epitomized all the Hellenistic
virtues as king, lawgiver, priest and prophet. Moses, in other words,
exemplified everything that the Spirit People aspired to be. For the
Antiochean delegation, on the contrary, the importance of Moses
was that he was the author of the Law, of which he was the living

embodiment. There was a difference, but if the matter were handled adroitly, Titus insisted, Moses could be the key to the hearts of the Spirit People.

Titus also disabused Paul of any idea that the Antiocheans, as uncouth Syro-Palestinians, would be an unwelcome alien element in sophisticated Corinth. They were not devoid of political skills and had recognized that they had to make some concessions to the Spirit People. They had become aware very quickly that the basis of the hostility to Paul among the Spirit People was rooted in his failure to meet their expectations concerning religious leadership. Thus the Judaizers stressed their superior qualifications. They proclaimed their credentials by advertising their visions and revelations, and their miracles. They had adopted the conventions of Hellenistic rhetoric. Themes developed at some length and with a spice of mystery flattered the sensibilities of the Spirit People. None of these 'adaptations' conflicted with the delegation's commitment to the Law.

Inconsistency

Titus went on to report that the atmosphere in the community at Corinth was being deliberately poisoned, by continuous sniping at Paul. The Spirit People dripped malice on his every word and gesture. They falsified his motives, and promoted wilful misunderstanding of his words (2 Cor. 1: 12–14).

The Spirit People, reinforced by the Judaizers, harped on Paul's inability to keep his word. As regards his travel plans, he had told them that he would go first to Macedonia and then to Corinth (1 Cor. 16: 5–6), but in fact he went to Corinth first and then to Macedonia. When in Corinth he promised that he would return there from Macedonia, but in fact he went back to Ephesus (2 Cor. 1: 15–16), whence he merely wrote them a letter. Such vacillation had become the basis for the charge that Paul exhibited the inconstancy of the flatterer, whose criterion of behaviour was the momentary pleasure of the listener. There were people at Corinth saying that Paul was entirely untrustworthy; his word could not be relied upon. In consequence, he could neither be a true friend nor, in this context, an authentic leader.

Paul's attitude towards money was another source of snide remarks. Since the arrival of believers from a sister church could not be kept a secret in the community at Corinth, Paul had had to explain why he accepted financial support from the Philippians while refusing it from the Corinthians. Distance made the difference. He refused it from the Corinthians with whom he was living because it would lock him into a web of patron–client relations. He would become the captive of the wealthy section of the community, to the detriment of the poorer members. Individual contributions, and their consequent obligations, were lost in the subsidy brought from Macedonia. It was a gift of the whole church, and thus acceptable. Paul was prepared to accept that sort of patronage, and repaid it by his letters of advice and support.

This explanation made perfect sense to Paul's supporters at Corinth. But it was easy for his enemies to dismiss the explanation as self-serving and to hammer at the facts. In their eyes, the facts proved only one thing. Paul loved the Philippians. He did not love the Corinthians, because every loving offer of support was refused.

The Collection for Jerusalem

Titus had exhibited such sensitivity in discerning the anti-Pauline feeling in the community that he was kind enough to save a bit of good news for the end. The Corinthians, he told Paul, showed real enthusiasm for the collection for the poor of Jerusalem.

To raise this matter at Corinth was not part of Titus' brief. The Painful Letter had only one very difficult objective, and Paul was far too experienced to complicate an already messy affair by introducing extraneous considerations.

In discussions with the Judaizers, however, Titus had realized that the collection furnished a perfect *ad hominem* argument. The effort that Paul put into it demonstrated in the most practical way possible his love and concern for the mother church, which the Judaizers claimed to represent. They could not refuse the gift of the Pauline churches without endangering the survival of their compatriots in Jerusalem, and without putting themselves in precisely the position which the Corinthians found objectionable in the case of Paul.

Once Titus was convinced that the Corinthians had accepted the reprimand of the Painful Letter, it would have been natural for him to remind them gently of their commitment to the collection, a gesture which the Judaizers could only second (2 Cor. 8: 6)! In that instant at least, Paul, the Corinthians and the Judaizers would have been at one, and an optimistic note in Titus' report becomes more understandable.

A Carefully Crafted Letter

Paul was fortunate that winter had begun by the time Titus reached him in Macedonia. The weather excluded an immediate return to Corinth. And that put paid to a hasty reaction to the situation there, similar to the disastrous 1 Corinthians. Paul had time to dictate and correct many drafts, before a messenger could get through to Corinth the following spring. At the earliest, the letter (2 Cor. 1–9) was sent in March or April of AD 55.[6] Climatic conditions, therefore, forced on Paul a period of reflection on the best strategy with which to handle a very complex situation. This time he had the additional advantage of having at his side Timothy, who proved to be a much better co-author than Sosthenes had been for 1 Corinthians.

Paul's principal objective in writing 2 Corinthians 1–9 was to drive a wedge between the Spirit People and the Judaizing delegation from Antioch. Almost equal in importance was the need to convince the Spirit People that suffering and weakness, not dignified bearing and eloquence, were the distinctive signs of a genuinely Christian leader.

Breaking an Alliance

In order to deprive the Judaizers of their base at Corinth, Paul offers a critique of the Mosaic dispensation in terms to which the Spirit People would be particularly sensitive, while at the same time presenting the Christian dispensation in a light which they should find attractive.[7]

In 2 Corinthians 3: 7–18 Paul focuses on the figure of Moses, which was the lever used by the Judaizers to pry their way into the

179

favour of the Spirit People. The polemic edge in his exposition of 'When Moses had finished speaking with them he put a veil on his face' (Exod. 34: 34–5) becomes explicit in the contrast he establishes between his own behaviour and that of Moses: 'we act with confident boldness, not like Moses who put a veil over his face' (2 Cor. 3: 12–13). By presenting himself simply as he was, without any pretensions, Paul implicitly claimed a whole range of other qualities, which Moses must have lacked because he dissimulated by veiling himself.

Having thus sown the seeds of doubt in the minds of the Spirit People concerning the stature of Moses, Paul goes on to associate Moses' achievement with intellectual blindness (2 Cor. 3: 14–15). The Judaizers had played into his hands by introducing the idea of a *new* covenant, for this enabled him to stigmatize the Law of Moses as the *old* covenant, thereby making it supremely unattractive to those who thought of themselves as in the forefront of religious thought. By using 'Moses' alone, instead of 'the book of Moses', Paul cleverly attaches the pejorative connotation of 'old' to the figure of Moses. Paul then goes on to reinforce this point by a subtle adaptation of Exodus 34: 34, which is nothing more than a simple and effective *ad hominem* argument. The presence of Jews in the Corinthian community showed that they had found something lacking in their previous mode of life based on the Law. They had been blind, and now they see. Why, then, Paul implies, would the Spirit People want to commit themselves to the darkness of intellectual sclerosis, when they could have the light of authentic glory in the gospel?

In 2 Corinthians 3: 17 Paul shifts from indirect criticism to seduction by appropriating two key terms in the lexicon of the Spirit People: 'spirit' and 'freedom'. If Paul earlier had associated the Law with intellectual blindness, the vice that the Spirit People most despised, here he identifies the gospel with the values they most esteemed. 'Spirit' evoked the Philonic heavenly man, and for Philo 'freedom' carried the connotations of virtue, perfection and wisdom.

The sophisticated intricacy of Paul's argumentation here is light-years away from the brutal slashes of 1 Corinthians. It shows that Paul was capable of learning from his mistakes. He took to heart the criticisms of Timothy and, in an extraordinary gesture of humility, he thought his way into the religious world of the Spirit People, almost certainly with the aid of Apollos.

Paul abandoned the frontal assault that had served him so badly in 1 Corinthians. Instead, he chipped away delicately at the convictions of the Spirit People. His subtle denigration of Moses diminished the common ground on which the Judaizers had relied. His reformulation of the gospel was carefully calculated both to harmonize with, and gently but firmly to refashion, the Philonic perspective which the Spirit People had received from Apollos. These latter, as Paul presumably realized, would have been constitutionally opposed to the restrictions imposed by the Law. It needed but little to tip the balance against the Judaizers. Paul's discreet, indirect approach obviated the danger of a perverse reaction such as had been the outcome of 1 Corinthians.

An Authentic Christian Leader

The attitude of the Spirit People to the historical Jesus is summarized by Paul in the shocking phrase 'Anathema Jesus!' (1 Cor. 12: 3). They found the idea of a crucified saviour repugnant, and preferred to think in terms of a superhuman saviour from above, 'the Lord of Glory' (1 Cor. 2: 8). Paul could not accept this separation of Jesus and Christ, because, as one of his oldest commentators most perceptively put it, Jesus is the truth of Christ (Eph. 4: 21). Only a being of flesh and blood, anchored in space and time, can demonstrate the *real* possibility of the restored humanity proclaimed in the gospel. Unless the ideal is lived, it remains a purely theoretical possibility, beautiful to contemplate, but without any guarantee that achievement is feasible. Paul, therefore, had to insist that Jesus *exhibited* love, as opposed to merely talking about it.

The way Christ died was, for Paul, the demonstration of Christ's love for humanity. Thus, even though the preaching tradition of the early church spoke only of the death of Jesus, Paul consistently insisted that Jesus died in a particularly horrible way, although he recognized that a *crucified* Christ was 'a stumbling block to Jews and folly to Gentiles' (1 Cor. 1: 23). The Spirit People preferred to avert their thoughts from this dimension; it cannot be integrated into any philosophical approach to religion. No doubt the Judaizers co-operated. They could assert, with perfect justification, that Paul's stress on the manner of Christ's death was exceptional. Moreover, their adaptation to what the Spirit People expected of religious leaders meant a life-style more compatible with that of the Lord of Glory than with that of a tortured criminal.

These attitudes obliged Paul to defend both his ministry and the historicity of Jesus. An integrated approach was indispensable, and the quest forced Paul's thought into a new dimension. It was in reflecting on the conditions of Jesus' ministry that Paul saw its relevance to his own situation. In the process he gave new depth to the understanding of Christ's ministry reflected in the gospel tradition.

The manner of Christ's ministry was determined by God: 'For our sake he made him to be sin who knew no sin' (2 Cor. 5: 21). In other words, God willed Christ to be subject to the consequences of sin. Jesus was so integrated into humanity-needing-salvation that he endured the penalties inherent in its fallen state. Jesus saved humanity from within by accepting its condition and transforming it. He became as other human beings in order to reveal to them what they had the potential to become. Thus he suffered as others suffer, and died as others die, even though he in no way merited such affliction.

If 2 Corinthians 5: 21 highlights the divine plan, other texts emphasize the freedom of Christ's co-operation: 'he became poor for your sake' (2 Cor. 8: 9), and the reason for his choice: 'one died for all' (2 Cor. 5: 14). His life and death were a deliberate sacrifice of self in order that others might benefit. The fundamental lesson of the self-oblation of Christ is that 'those who live might live no longer for themselves' (2 Cor. 5: 15). Prior to Christ, it was taken for granted that the primary goals of human existence should be survival, comfort and success. In the light of Christ's radical altruism, such a life-style can only be perceived as the 'death' of selfishness. It is the antithesis of genuine 'life', which is totally concerned with benefiting the other.

The presentation of Christ as 'the image of God' (2 Cor. 4: 4) reveals the essence of authenticity to be empowerment, the ability to reach out to enable others. In the chapter of Genesis in which this formula appears (Gen. 1: 26–7), God is presented exclusively as the Creator. In consequence, creativity remains the primary referent in determining the meaning of the phrase. Humans resemble God in so far as they are creative. Like Adam before the Fall, Christ is 'the image and glory of God' (1 Cor. 11: 7) in the sense that he gives glory to God precisely by being what the Creator intended.

The creative power which made Christ the new Adam (cf. 1 Cor. 15: 45) was exercised in and through poverty and ignominy. His whole existence was a 'dying' (2 Cor. 4: 10), but he brought into being 'a new creation' (2 Cor. 5: 17). Once Paul had been led to this insight, it was easy for him to see it as the archetype of his own situation. He was conscious of his 'weakness' (1 Cor. 9. 22), yet he disposed of a 'power' (2 Cor. 4: 7) which created new communities of transformed individuals (2 Cor. 3: 2–3). The basis of Paul's identification with Jesus, which is the distinctive feature of his understanding of ministry in 2 Corinthians 1–9, was their shared experience of suffering.

Hitherto Paul had accepted suffering as integral to the human condition. The harsh experiences he had endured would not have set him apart in the ancient world. Life was brutal, and survival very much a matter of luck. None of Paul's acquaintances would have dissented from Homer's insight, 'The sorrowless gods have so spun the thread that wretched mortals live in pain' (*Iliad* 24. 525). Now Paul saw an opportunity to give meaning to suffering. Even though he thought in terms of his own ministry, his insight is valid for all believers. Suffering can be revelatory when the unchangeable is accepted with grace. If the achievement is disproportionate to the means, the power of God becomes visible.

Paul perceived himself as one of the prisoners of war destined for execution at the climax of a Roman victory parade (2 Cor. 2· 14). His first insight is to see his suffering as a prolongation of the sacrifice of Christ. He is 'the aroma of Christ' (2 Cor. 2: 15). As smoke wafting across the city from the altar conveyed the fact of sacrifice to those who were not present in the Temple, so Paul in his wanderings proclaimed Jesus to the world, not merely in words, but more fundamentally in his comportment. He speaks of himself as 'always carrying in the body the dying of Jesus, so that the life of Jesus may be manifest in our bodies. For while we live, we are always being given up to death for Jesus' sake, so that the life of Jesus may be made visible in our mortal flesh' (2 Cor. 4: 10–11).

This extraordinary statement is the summit of 2 Corinthians 1–9, and the most profound insight ever articulated as to the meaning of suffering and the nature of authentic ministry. Death shadowed Paul's every step; he could die at any moment. As one headed towards a fate which seemed inevitable, he saw his life as a 'dying', which he identified with that of Jesus, who had also foreseen his death (e.g. Mark 8: 31). Paul's acceptance of his sufferings created a transparency, in which the authentic humanity of Jesus became visible. By grace in his comportment, Paul was to his generation what Jesus had been to his.

Paul, of course, did not put himself on the same level as Jesus. What he achieved would not have been possible without Jesus. None the less, he recognized that, were Jesus to have been the only one to demonstrate the type of humanity desired by the Creator, this revelation could have been dismissed as irrelevant, a unique case without meaning for the rest of humanity. Hence, Paul's acceptance of the responsibility of *being Jesus* for his converts. The explicitness of this presentation of the minister as an *alter Christus* is unique in the New Testament. It was forced upon Paul by the Spirit People/Judaizers' denial of the meaning of Jesus' terrestrial existence and their disparagement of Paul's ministry. Christ as he was on earth is the model of authentic leadership.

The Collection for Jerusalem

Since Titus had elicited a positive response at Corinth to the collection for the poor of Jerusalem, Paul decided to strike while the iron was hot. He intended 2 Corinthians 8 to be the final passage of the letter, but when he took the pen in his own hand to write the authenticating last brief paragraph, his heart took over in a fervent appeal for participation (2 Cor. 9).

These two chapters reveal Paul at his best in terms of religious leadership. His consummate skill in the art of persuasion underlines how much he has matured in a single year. Even though he has to stretch the truth to do so, he praises what can be praised—the willingness of the Corinthians (although it was now a year old; 9: 2)—and sedulously avoids even a hint of criticism. He explicitly states that he is not ordering them to contribute (8: 8a), but merely expressing his opinion (8: 10). The example of the Macedonians is introduced in such a way as to permit the Corinthians' self-respect to function as an internal incentive. In order to assuage any possible anxiety on their part as to the sum expected, he is at pains to emphasize that their attitude is more important than the value of the gift (8: 12). Near the end, however, a hint of the old Paul surfaces in the way he highlights the possibility that he and the Corinthians might be humiliated by a much poorer church (9: 4). Once again we catch a whiff of moral blackmail, which is reinforced by the throw-away line that their contribution 'should not be an extortion but a willing gift' (9: 5).

Once before, however, the Corinthians had given their assent, and then done nothing. This time Paul was not prepared to rely on promises alone, and decided to send emissaries to Corinth, whose presence would be a continuous reminder of his invitation. But even such discreet pressure might be resented by the Corinthians as interference in the internal affairs of a local church.

Paul's nervousness is palpable in his presentation of Titus. He emphasizes that he is not really sending Titus, as 8: 6 might imply. The latter had volunteered to return to Corinth in response to Paul's appeal (8: 17)! This little vignette tells us something about Paul's treatment of his associates. He does not order a subordinate, but requests 'a partner and co-worker' (8: 23). Naturally Titus was the bearer of the letter which recommended him so highly.

With Titus will go a brother selected by the churches of Macedonia to act as their delegate in the actual assembling of the money for Jerusalem (8: 19). It is curious that, while his qualifications are given prominence, his name is never mentioned. In light of the contacts between the Corinthian and Macedonian churches (1 Thess. 1: 7–9; 2 Cor. 11: 9), the simplest hypothesis is that he was a Corinthian Christian, who had gone to aid the spread of the church in Macedonia, and who there had established himself as an exceptional preacher of the gospel. When the Corinthians recognized him, and heard Paul's eulogy, they would have been both flattered and relieved. Their contribution to a sister church was publicly praised, and Paul's emissary was not a critical Macedonian (9: 4), but one of their own. His specific role was to guarantee the integrity of the collection (8: 20–1).

The third member of the party (8: 22) is also unnamed. The way he is described suggests that he was a long-time associate of Paul who had some relationship to the Corinthians. He may have been with Paul on the intermediate visit, or he may have accompanied Titus when the latter carried the Painful Letter. It was Paul's practice to travel with others, and it is most unlikely that he permitted Titus to go to Corinth alone. A travelling companion was indispensable, not merely to present a stronger front to robbers, but to guard whatever property they had, while the other went to the baths or elsewhere.

Missionary in Illyricum

According to 2 Corinthians 9: 4, Paul planned to go to Corinth in the near future—that is, during the summer of AD 55—in order to finalize the collection, on which he had now been working for four years. It would have been clear to him, however, that he could not just breeze in, make contact with the Corinthian delegation, and leave for Jerusalem. Despite his optimistic words in 2 Corinthians 7: 5–16, he was fully aware that the re-establishment of relations with the church left a number of serious problems unresolved. An extended stay was imperative. Exactly how long would depend on circumstances, but he could not risk spoiling the process of reconciliation by fixing a premature departure date. The more he reflected, the clearer it became that whenever he went to Corinth, he would have to spend a winter there.

The Macedonians, on the other hand, might not want to delay. It would be natural for them to want to rid themselves as soon as possible of the heavy responsibility represented by the money collected for the poor of Jerusalem. Only in summer could they travel to Jerusalem, and the round trip took several months. Any delay now would mean postponing the trip for a year. Hence, the note of hesitation: '*if* some of the Macedonians come with me' (2 Corinthians 9: 4). The matter had not been decided when 2 Corinthians 1–9 was sent.

The more Paul thought about his plans for the future, the more reasons he found not to hasten to Corinth. Second Corinthians 1–9 demanded time for the subtlety of its message to be assimilated adequately. It could only be to Paul's advantage to have his arguments discussed at length. He could be sure that Titus would nudge reflection in the right direction, and such delicate manipulation should not be hurried.

Paul was prepared to find such reasons convincing, because for five years he personally had done little real missionary work. His agents had founded churches in Asia, and he had begun a new community at Troas. This latter episode was brief, and for the most part his energy had been focused on the maintenance of existing communities. Crisis after crisis in one church or another had demanded his attention. Now all his communities were calm. He could not be sure, however, how long this tranquillity would last. The time to act was now. The long summer stretching out before him was a golden opportunity to again seek virgin territory, and to be what he was divinely chosen to be, a founder of churches, one who preached Christ where he had not yet been named (Rom. 15: 20). The prospect must have been irresistible. In any case Paul did not restrain himself.

Wherever Paul and his associates had passed the winter in Macedonia, Paul would certainly have accompanied Titus and his two companions as far as Thessalonica. From there the latter had the choice of sailing or walking south to Achaia.

Paul headed west. The first few miles of the great Via Egnatia were familiar to him. On a previous visit he had turned south-west to Beroea shortly beyond the River Axios. This time the river crossing symbolized a new venture into unknown territory, something that Paul had not done for some ten years. Did he recall his departure from Antioch-in-Pisidia, and the unforeseen circumstances that had brought him through Galatia into Europe?[8]

In order not to infringe on what the Thessalonians might reasonably have considered their mission field, Paul determined to go as far west as the area occupied by the Illyrians (Rom. 15: 19).[9] If he set off from Thessalonica in mid-April, he would have covered the 200 miles (320 km) to the ill-defined border near Pylon by the end of the month. One cannot be sure how far Paul advanced into Illyrian territory. It depends on how much time he was prepared to spend before heading for Corinth.

If Paul planned only a summer campaign, I would surmise that his eagerness to get to work as quickly as possible meant that he went no further than the first considerable town, which was Lychnidos (modern Ohrid in Serbia), on the shore of beautiful mountain-ringed Lake Ohridsko. On the other hand, were he prepared to invest a year or so, it is more likely that he continued the extra 100 miles (160 km) to the port of Dyrrachium (modern Durrës in Albania). It was the northernmost of the two eastern terminals of the Via Egnatia, and just the sort of crossroads city that enhanced Paul's missionary outreach.

Bad News from Corinth

How much Paul had invested in his plans for the summer of AD 55 in Illyricum can be gauged from the depth of his frustration when news from Corinth forced him to change them.

His previous letter to Corinth (2 Cor. 1–9) had two objectives: first, to drive a wedge between the Judaizers and the Spirit People, and second, to win the latter to Paul's side. How well this latter goal was achieved is an open question, but it appears that he did succeed in isolating the Judaizers. Having lost what they hoped would be a firm base at Corinth, the Judaizers could only redouble their attacks on Paul's person and authority. If there was now little chance of converting the Spirit People into Law-observant Christians, there was always the possibility that they might still be receptive to criticism of Paul.

Titus, or someone sent by him, found Paul in Illyricum and informed him that the old criticism of his unimpressive presence and uninspired preaching (2 Cor. 10: 10) had been revived in a more vicious form. The Judaizers had managed to convince a number that their spiritual gifts raised them far above Paul (2 Cor. 11: 5). The latter's failure to take strong action during the intermediate visit, suggested the Judaizers, perhaps indicated that he did not have the authority. Certainly his flight, and failure to return, could only be interpreted as cowardice.

The importance which Paul attached to the collection for the poor of Jerusalem gave the Judaizers the opportunity to highlight his suspiciously ambivalent attitude towards money. He apparently refused money for himself, but solicited it for the poor. Would it all really go to Jerusalem? All the Judaizers had to do, when questioned by the Corinthians about the poverty of the Jerusalem church, was to shrug their shoulders. They did not have to deny the need for the collection. All they need do was to insinuate that the questioners were a little naive in taking Paul's statements at face value.

A Furious Response

Paul could only take such criticisms as a malicious distortion of his motives and actions. His bitter anger was intensified by the awareness that, if he was discredited, his version of the gospel was at risk. Another gospel might take its place. In a mood of desperate anxiety for the future of the Corinthian community, he dashed off his final letter to his most troublesome community (2 Cor. 10–13). The reasonable tone and subtle arguments of 2 Cor. 1–9 are replaced by a wild outburst, in which Paul gives free rein to his capacity for sarcasm and irony.

The language in which he excoriates the gullibility of the Corinthians is a perfect illustration of the character of this intemperate letter: 'You gladly bear with fools, being wise yourselves! You put up with it when someone makes slaves of you, or eats you out of house and home, or swindles you, or walks all over you, or smacks your face. To my shame, I must say, we were too weak for that!' (2 Cor. 11: 19–21). The 'wisdom' of the Corinthians is to be so lacking in self-respect that they eagerly accept their own exploitation!

The quality of the writing is matched by the authority of the strategy. His opponents have forced him to compare himself with them, and what he does is to display his contempt for their pretensions by turning rhetorical convention upside-down. After noting his breeding (2 Cor. 11: 22–3), he goes on to parody the self-display of the Judaizers by highlighting what should be hidden, and minimizing what should be accentuated (2 Cor. 11: 23–30). Churches and converts are only hinted at; the spotlight is on situations in which he has been degraded. With great dramatic flair he concludes his list of 'accomplishments' with a graphic account of his humiliating escape from Damascus, lowered down the wall like a helpless baby in a basket (2 Cor. 11: 32–3)!

Parody is not the only weapon in Paul's rhetorical armoury. He deflates his opponents' claim to visions and revelations by speaking of his own experience in the third person (2 Cor. 12: 2–4). The technique distances him from the episode, and thereby underlines its irrelevance to his ministry. It did not change him in any way, and did not provide him with any information he could use. The criticism of his opponents is all the more effective for being unstated. If their experience was the same as Paul's, it contributed nothing to their ministry. If it was something about which they could talk, it was less ineffable than his!

Second Corinthians 10–13 is extraordinarily revelatory of a Paul rarely apparent elsewhere. Here the rigid control he normally imposed on his passionate nature dissolves in the heat of his anger. He gives full rein to his emotions, and in so doing betrays the quality of his education, which he usually denied (cf. 1 Cor. 2: 1–5). The fluid creativity of his thought is matched by the masterful facility and freedom with which he employs a number of the techniques of rhetoric. The assurance of his adept use of rhetorical devices can only be the fruit of long study and practice. There can be little doubt that he was brought up in a socially privileged class, which he was formed to adorn.

A Thorn in the Flesh

Paul concludes his defence with a rhetorical *tour de force*, a humble admission which leads into a paradox: 'And to keep me from being too elated by the abundance of revelations, a thorn was given me in the flesh, a messenger of Satan, to buffet me, to keep me from being too conceited . . . when I am weak then I am strong' (2 Cor. 12: 7–10). The nature of the thorn in the flesh has intrigued commentators from the early patristic period to the present day.[10] But a common-sense look at what Paul actually did in the course of his lifetime excludes any bodily or psychiatric disease. No one with a physical ailment could have tramped the thousands of miles that he covered in all sorts of terrain and climatic conditions. He clearly enjoyed robust health and a strong constitution. The few character flaws that we have seen do not betray any hint of mental illness. In fact, he demonstrates impressive mental stamina and control.

The only hypothesis for which a serious case can be made is that by the thorn in his flesh Paul meant opposition to his ministry from within the Jesus movement. His mention of 'a messenger of Satan' implies an external, personal source of affliction, and previously he had identified as 'servants of Satan' (2 Cor. 11: 14–15) his Antiochean adversaries at Corinth. In the Old Testament 'thorns' are a metaphor for Israel's enemies, both within (Num. 33: 35) and without (Ezek. 28: 24).

In every community to which Paul belonged, or which he had founded, there were some believers who caused him grief—the Judaizers at Antioch-on-the-Orontes, idlers at Thessalonica, Euodia and Syntyche at Philippi, those paralysed by prudence in Galatia, the resentful at Ephesus, the mystico-ascetics at Colossae, the Spirit People at Corinth. None of his churches measured up to his expectations. There was no single community on which he could look with complacent pride. Despite the good things to be found in every church, any tendency on Paul's part to conceit, or even satisfaction, was immediately countered by evidence of some sort of dissent. This was a continuous source of suffering, but a type of suffering that had no redeeming value. The divisions that were its cause were opposed to the plan of God, for whom the church should exhibit the organic unity of a living body. Hence, Paul could pray legitimately that these sufferings would come to an end.

The wry humour of his self-assessment continues into the presentation of the divine response to his prayer: 'My grace is sufficient for you, for this power in weakness is perfected' (2 Cor. 12: 9a). The paradox is as extreme as the meaning is profound. The thorn reminds him that he has none of the qualities which the world considered essential prerequisites for the success of his mission. Yet he serves as a channel of divine grace expressed in the power of Christ (2 Cor. 12: 9b), whose 'life' he exhibits (2 Cor. 4: 10–11)—and the world is changed.

Farewell to the East 11

THE messengers who had brought the bad news from Corinth
returned there with 2 Cor. 10–13. In it Paul promised a visit in the
near future (2 Cor. 12: 14; 13: 1–2). Anxiety for the Corinthians
raged in his heart, but he was not free to leave Illyricum immediately.
His experience had taught him that he could not simply abandon
new converts to the care of the Holy Spirit. God acted through
human agents (1 Cor. 3: 5–9), and it was Paul's responsibility to set
the infant community on a secure foundation. It is easy to imagine
the redoubled fervour with which he worked, attempting to pack in
as much as possible before the onset of winter obliged him to start
the long journey to Corinth.

Were Paul in Lychnidos, his best plan would have been to go west
along the Via Egnatia to Dyrrachium, and from there take a coastal
trader going south. Were he already in Dyrrachium, he had a head
start. The ideal would be a boat that would take him at least as far as
Patrae (modern Patras) at the western end of the Gulf of Corinth.
From there it was but 84 miles (135 km) to Corinth. The alternative
was a 290-mile (464-km) rough track along the coast. Either way it
would have taken Paul the best part of three weeks to get to Corinth.[1]

Paul's need to capitalize on the shock effect of 2 Cor. 10–13 makes it
unthinkable that he should have postponed his visit to Corinth until the
following spring. It would have been out of character for him to leave
one of his co-workers to direct the nascent church. Certainly Timothy
travelled with him to Corinth (Rom. 16: 21).

Planning for the Future

As the desperate days succeeded one another on the seemingly interminable journey to Corinth, Paul had plenty of time to reflect on his future. He would spend the winter in Corinth because he had no other choice, but after that he would waste no more time on the childishness (1 Cor. 3: 1; 14: 20) of what should have been the most brilliant of his foundations. It was time to focus his energies on something more profitable.

The exhilarating experience of his brief forays into virgin missionary territory at Troas and in Illyricum had rekindled the fervour of the apostle in the breast of Paul. It reminded him that he had been called by God to spread the gospel, to move ever forward. From this perspective the three years that he had just devoted to crisis management did not seem the best use of his gift. The service he had given to maintenance had been necessary, but enough was enough. He had done his best for the ring of communities that he had established around the Aegean Sea. If by now they had not acquired the maturity to make the decisions appropriate to realizing Christ in their lives, there was nothing more that he could do for them except pray.

A Final Fling

But where was he to go next? The fatigue of the long journey reminded Paul of his age. He could no longer swing along as vigorously as in bygone years. He was now just about 60 and, given the life expectancy of his contemporaries, there could not be much time left to him.[2] What was needed was one final splendid gesture for the honour and glory of God.

Paul had always seen his vocation in prophetic, if not messianic, terms. The key words in what he wrote to the Galatians, 'when he who had set me apart from my mother's womb, and had called me through his grace, was pleased to reveal his Son to me, in order that I might preach him among the nations' (1: 15–16), were designed to evoke not only the vocation of the prophet Jeremiah (1: 5) but, more importantly, the mission of the messianic figure of the Servant of

Yahweh, 'From my mother's womb he called my name.... He said to me... I will give you as a light to the nations that my salvation may reach to the end of the earth' (Isa. 49: 1–6).

What more appropriate climax could there be to Paul's missionary career than to go to 'the end of the earth'? It was not really very far away. Anyone who lived in the Mediterranean basin would have agreed with the great geographer Strabo that the end of the world faced the Atlantic ocean, 'the Sacred Cape (modern Cape St Vincent in Portugal) is the most westerly point, not only of Europe, but of the whole inhabited world' (*Geography* 3. 1. 4; Diodorus Siculus, *History* 25. 10. 1).[3] In a burst of enthusiasm Paul decided that his next mission field would be the Iberian Peninsula.

On reflection he must have recognized that there would be difficulties, but one may doubt that he realized how serious they were. In the eastern Mediterranean, Paul moved in a world whose language he spoke, and which had a network of Jewish institutions of which he could avail himself. In Spain both these advantages were lacking.[4] The Jewish diaspora did not extend westward beyond Italy. This meant that there were no God-fearers whose minds had been prepared for the gospel by the reading of the Scriptures. Nor were there many who spoke Greek. The language survived in the few old Greek colonies along the east coast, but the hinterland was dominated by a bewildering number of Iberian dialects. Latin was the language of the Roman administration, but not of any significant portion of the population.

An Apostle of Rome?

Even if he had not foreseen these problems, Paul must have known that the western end of the Mediterranean would be dissimilar to anything that he had previously experienced. He would not have taken long to reach the conclusion that he needed the expertise of those closer to that strange land. Rome, he decided, would be his springboard to the west.

Paul, of course, knew that Christianity had already been well established in the Eternal City. Not only had his close collaborators, Prisca and Aquila, belonged to a community there, but it would have been most surprising had there been no Roman Christians among the merchants and travellers who thronged Corinth, and who could have provided information on their home community. Thus Paul was certainly aware that he could be sure of finding work and lodging among fellow Christians in Rome. Many of them had been formed in the cultural ethos of the eastern Mediterranean, where hospitality to travellers was second nature.

Yet Paul decided to uproot Prisca and Aquila once again, and to send them ahead as his advance team (Rom. 16: 3). This had made sense in Ephesus, where they had accepted the burden of having a comfortable base ready for him when he finally arrived. This was unnecessary in Rome. Christians there did not need to be placated or warned. Paul, in consequence, must have been thinking of something more important than just a friendly visit.

What Paul desired was to be accepted and to belong. He wanted to be *sent* to Spain as a missionary of Rome (Rom. 15: 24).[5] This was not just a matter of logistic and linguistic support, although these would have been most useful. He needed Rome to *commission* him to act in its name as Antioch-on-the-Orontes had once done. What happened in Galatia and at Corinth had made him conscious of how vulnerable he was to accusations that he was a maverick who represented no one but himself. A new suit of armour, however, was but a fraction of his need.

Paul's developing sense of the unity of the Jesus movement beneath the variety of its concrete expressions in many different lands had brought him to a greater appreciation of the importance of institutional links. A mother church had the authority to challenge her daughters. She could point out that the structures they had chosen in this or that set of circumstances did not really embody the values of the Jesus movement, and could demand reconsideration. Through his letters Paul had played this role with respect to his foundations. But he would not live for ever. What then? He had wrenched his churches free of Antioch. There was no one to take over the responsibility of challenge. He would leave his communities orphans.

Forced to be honest with himself, Paul saw that, by staying outside the system of accredited representatives which established genetic links, he was depriving his churches of a channel of grace. What had been done was done. He might regret it, but he could not change it. The future was another matter. Some church had to have the authority to challenge to be more Christ-like whatever foundations he might make in Spain. He could give this responsibility to Rome only by persuading its community to commission him as a missionary. For the common good he was prepared to sacrifice his proud title, 'apostle of Jesus Christ by the will of God', and humbly become 'an apostle of Rome'.

By the time Paul finally reached Corinth, he had solved his personal problems. He knew what he had to do, and he had worked out how he was going to do it. That gave him new strength to confront the Corinthians and to re-establish his authority.

As it turned out, his apprehension had little basis. His furious letter from Illyricum had had a salutary effect. There is no hint that he had to waste time during the winter of AD 55–6 defending himself or arbitrating internal squabbles. Given the temper of the Corinthians, it would be miraculous if disputes had not arisen from time to time, but at least there were none of the catastrophic explosions that had been a feature of Paul's relations with his Achaean converts.

Decisions on Tactics

It is rather improbable that Prisca and Aquila had accompanied Paul first to Troas, then to Macedonia and Illyricum, and finally to Corinth. It is not the way Paul operated. Timothy and at most one other were his travelling companions. It is likely, therefore, that before Paul was forced out of Ephesus in the late summer of AD 54, he told the couple that if they got into trouble they should head for Corinth, where he would eventually catch up with them.

Prisca and Aquila willingly fell in with Paul's plan to send them to Rome. Whatever he wanted, they would do. The spread of the gospel was all that mattered. They may even have been happy to have the opportunity to return to the Eternal City. Some thirteen years had elapsed since Claudius had acted against the synagogue with which they were associated, and no doubt they were curious as to how things had developed in the interval.

Paul presumably intended Prisca and Aquila to act as his propagandists, so that by the time he got to Rome, the community there would feel that he was one of their own, and worthy to represent the church. The couple, or perhaps Timothy, however, suggested a refinement. Would not a personal letter in which he revealed something of himself and his theology be a useful complement to their efforts? It would be a most tactful and flattering gesture.

Paul must have resisted the idea initially, because he had never written such a letter. All his previous writings had been in response to particular problems in communities whose members he knew. What could he say that would interest members of a strange church in the capital of the empire? Moreover, there was no time to compose such a letter before Prisca and Aquila left.

These objections were quickly beaten down. He did not have to write the letter immediately. It would in fact be more helpful if it arrived some time after his emissaries. Thus he had until the following spring to work out what to say. The assurance that one can procrastinate is often an inducement to acquiescence. In addition, Prisca and Aquila reminded him that he had at least a generic understanding of the Roman church. From their experience its members were predominantly Gentiles who had had close contacts with Jewish synagogues before becoming Christians. Paul had dealt with such God-fearers in most of the cities in which he had preached, and knew their preoccupations and problems. Finally, they promised to send him a report on the Roman community as soon as communications reopened after the winter. It would be most surprising if merchants from Rome did not head for Corinth, the nub of east–west trade, when spring opened the seas to commerce. Such data would permit him to be more personal at the end of his letter. There might even be questions that he could answer.

Eventually a precise strategy was hammered out. If all went according to plan, Paul would have a letter ready to send to Rome in the spring of AD 56. Once he had made the personalizing additions based on data from Prisca and Aquila, the letter could go to Rome with a returning merchant or a compliant Corinthian who had business in the Eternal City. That duty accomplished, Paul would sail from Corinth to Jerusalem with the collection for the poor, which had been a major preoccupation ever since the famous meeting in Jerusalem some five years earlier. The journey should not take very long. A fast boat propelled by consistent winds from the north-west should get him to the Syro-Palestinian littoral within a couple of weeks. In Jerusalem all he had to do was to hand over the money and leave. He had no responsibilities there, and socializing did not rate high among Paul's priorities. If everything worked like clockwork, Paul could be in Rome at the very end of the summer of AD 56. The first part of this scenario went according to plan, but thereafter things went disastrously wrong, and it was to be several years before Paul reached Rome.

A Letter to Rome

When he settled down to write the letter that he had promised Prisca and Aquila, Paul's problem was to find a topic which would be of interest to the Romans and at the same time serve as an introduction to his person and his gospel.

Selecting a Topic

Since the incident at Antioch-on-the-Orontes, the problem of the co-existence of converts from Judaism and from paganism in the church had been forced on Paul's attention again and again. It was not a problem that agitated him personally. The episode at Antioch had reinforced an insight of absolute clarity. If one belonged to Christ, the demands of the Law were completely irrelevant. The only law for Christians was the following of Christ (Gal. 6: 2). But in church after church in which there was at least a number of believers of Jewish origin, the topic surfaced anew.

Through the cut and thrust of many debates in which he had to explain and justify his attitude towards the Law, Paul became more and more adept at expounding his views effectively. He came to know the standard Jewish objections so well that he could have argued their case better than they did themselves. He built up a collection of relevant passages from the Scriptures, which were part of the common ground that he shared with his Jewish interlocutors. The other part, of course, was their shared experience of the grace of Christ. His responses became ever more refined and sophisticated, as he learned which were the most effective in practice.

What Prisca and Aquila had told him about the composition of the community in Rome—the majority Gentiles but some Jews (compare Rom. 1: 13 and 11: 13 with 2: 17 and 3: 9)—encouraged Paul to believe that it must have encountered, and perhaps might still be dealing with, the same type of problem regarding the Jewish identity of converts that regularly reared its head in his churches. If he was correct, the distillation of his experience should be of use to Roman believers.

Moreover, the irenic, detailed exposition of this topic might have a beneficial effect at Corinth. Those who had been bothered by the Judaizing delegation from Antioch, or who were simply interested, could be given the opportunity to assist at the working-out of his reasoning, and then hear the final product dictated to the scribe, Tertius (Rom. 16: 22). As an unexpected bonus, Paul realized that it would be a perfect way to reveal to the Spirit People his mastery of rhetorical technique and the power and sophistication of his intellect!

God's Plan of Salvation

The theme of the letter is set forth with admirable brevity: 'the gospel is the power of God for salvation to everyone who has faith, to the Jew first and also to the Greek' (Rom. 1: 16). The next ten chapters systematically unpack the meaning of this deceptively simple statement. It is the sort of thing that everyone imagines they have understood until the hidden depths and unforeseen implications are gradually brought to light.[6]

In order to puncture the carapace of arrogant presumption which Jews and Gentiles might have donned in a discussion about salvation, Paul begins with a detailed portrayal of the reality of Jewish and Gentile life. Were both to be judged by their works, they would be condemned by a righteous God. Sinfulness was universal, and sinners cannot put themselves right with God.

How, then, can anyone be saved? Only if God takes the initiative. 'Now apart from the law the righteousness of God has been revealed, as attested by the law and the prophets, that is, the righteousness of God through faith in Christ Jesus to all who believe. For there is no distinction; all have sinned and lack the glory of God. They are justified as a gift by his grace through the redemption which is in Christ Jesus' (3: 21–4). Recognition and acceptance of this extraordinary gift is faith, and precisely the same faith is required of Jews and Gentiles. The model believer is Abraham. He did not choose God. God chose him, and not because he was circumcised or obeyed the Law. These came much later than the promise which rewarded Abraham's naked faith (4: 1–25).

Paul then works out the implications of the life of faith for individuals (5: 1–11). They are at peace with God, even though they may undergo suffering. Such pain must be understood against the background of the suffering of Christ, whose death for us reveals the love of God for each one. At this point Paul enlarges his perspective to encompass the whole history of humanity from creation to consummation, as typified by two individuals, Adam and Christ. The former represents sin and death, whereas the latter represents grace and life (5: 12–21).

Having sketched these two major theses, Paul as an excellent teacher goes on to elaborate them in much greater detail. Chapters 6–8 expand 5: 1–11. The crucial realities with which the individual has to deal are sin, death, law and the flesh. 'While we were living in the flesh, our sinful passions, aroused by the law, were at work in our members to bear fruit for death' (7: 5). For Paul these are the structures of unredeemed existence. In one sense believers have put them behind them in baptism, but in another they remain part of the ongoing struggle to be Christ-like, 'sending his own Son in the likeness of sinful flesh and for sin, he condemned sin in the flesh' (8: 3). For his followers Christ's victory is a victory only in principle; it must be translated into reality with the aid of the Spirit.

The wide historical perspective of 5: 12–21 reappears in chs 9–11, but in a form that highlights an issue with which Paul struggled with ever greater intensity as his gospel attracted infinitely more Gentiles than Jews. If God had chosen the Jews, and given them so much, how can it be that it is Gentiles who now predominantly worship him in the way that he wishes? The principle on which Paul works out his answer is stated with absolute clarity: 'it is not as though the word of God has failed' (9: 6). That word, which Israel mistakenly thought was addressed only to itself, in the divine intention had a wider audience. Now that it has been explicitly and clearly addressed to Gentiles, they have responded, as indeed some Jews have.

The intricate argumentation of Romans 9–11 is impressive evidence of Paul's knowledge of the Scriptures. The sophistication of his interpretation again reflects the strength of his intellectual formation. The quality of the writing is also remarkable. The hymn (11: 33–6) in which he sings out his adoration with extraordinary eloquence is arguably his greatest literary achievement.

The outpouring of gratitude is a fitting conclusion to the summation of the argument in 11: 25–32, in which Paul reveals his solution to the problem of the salvation of Israel. He had never wavered in his conviction that God could not deny himself and abandon those whom he had chosen and blessed (11: 1–2). Paul recognized the truth of this in his own ministry. The book of Isaiah had always played a key role in his understanding of his apostolate to the Gentiles. He saw himself as part of the faithful Jewish remnant, which proclaimed salvation to the nations, thereby fulfilling the eschatological obligation laid upon Israel. Not surprisingly, it was in reading Isaiah that he realized the means whereby the Jews would be saved.

In order to support his thesis that 'all Israel will be saved' (11: 26), Paul quotes: 'From Sion will come the Redeemer, he will banish ungodliness from Jacob, and this will be my covenant with them' (Isa. 59: 20–1); 'when I take away their sins' (Isa. 27: 9). The allusion is to the Parousia of Christ. The Jews, in other words, will be saved in exactly the same way as Paul was. His Pharisaic commitment to the Law had not only blinded him to the true role of Christ, but it had engendered bitter hostility. That attitude was changed by a completely unexpected encounter on the road to Damascus, where Christ took the initiative. So will it be for all Israel, at the Parousia when Christ appears in glory. Then the Jews will no more be capable of rejecting him than Paul the Pharisee had been.

Practical Problems

Were the Spirit People to have heard the above part of the letter to Rome as Paul worked it out during the winter of AD 55–6 in Corinth, they would have been impressed by the marvellous rhetorical skill with which he controlled a complex flow of citation and interpretation, which was carefully structured into the justification of a series of interrelated theses. They would have been intrigued by the way he enlivened and varied his presentation by introducing an interlocutor, by posing sudden objections, by formulating false conclusions, and by creating an imaginary dialogue. This was masterly use of the rhetorical technique of the diatribe.

The sharper ones among the Spirit People, however, would have recognized that Paul really did not know much about the local scene at Rome. He was communicating generic ideas, not dealing with specific problems. Especially if they were still smarting from 1 Corinthians, they must have noted the striking difference between the passion with which Paul had handled the concrete 'slogans' of the Corinthians and his calm didactic approach to the stylized objections in Romans.

There is little doubt, then, that Paul had composed Romans 1–11 before he heard from Prisca and Aquila. Their promised message came with the first travellers from Rome who arrived in Corinth in the early spring of AD 56. In the light of the information that they supplied him, Paul added the material in chapters 12–14, which reflects rather precise knowledge of at least some of the problems agitating the church in Rome. He comments on a taxation issue (13: 1–7), and reflects on the tension caused by believers who wish to observe Jewish dietary laws and festivals (14: 1–23). Throughout he underlines his understanding of the community as the body of

Christ, which should be animated by the self-sacrificing love that Christ showed on the cross. 'Christ did not please himself' (15: 3).

Travel Plans

In terms of the political purpose of the letter, chapters 1–14 could be considered a prolonged *captio benevolentiae*, a ploy designed to win the favour of the readers. Only at the very end of the letter does Paul finally return to the question of his forthcoming visit, which he had introduced at the beginning (1: 10–15). He explains why he has not visited them earlier. He was on God's business elsewhere, 'from Jerusalem and as far round as Illyricum I have fully preached the gospel of Christ' (15: 19).

The all-important point that motivated the letter is finally stated: 'Now with no further scope for me in these regions, I desire, as I have for many years, to come to you when I go to Spain. For I do hope to see you on my journey, and to be sent on by you once I have enjoyed your company for a little while' (15: 23–4). Clearly Paul feels that he has done everything he can in the eastern Mediterranean. He does not ask straight out to be commissioned as an apostle by Rome. That would be premature, but the request is delicately hinted at in his use of the verb 'to send on'. The ground is being carefully prepared for his visit.

The skill with which Paul begins to insinuate himself into the Roman community is clear in the series of greetings with which the letter ends.[7] He salutes twenty-six individuals, twenty-four of whom are named. In addition, he mentions three house-churches and two groupings of (ex?) slaves, which also may have been house-churches.[8]

Some of these he certainly knew personally. Prisca and Aquila were with him at Corinth, and later at Ephesus. The qualification of Epaenetus, Ampliatus, Stachys and Persis as 'my dear friend' cannot be an empty formula. If the mother of Rufus had also 'mothered' Paul, he must have known both her and her son. An element of doubt clouds the case of Andronicus and Junia, because 'my fellow prisoners' may mean only that they had suffered imprisonment *as* Paul had done. He was not in gaol when he wrote this letter. There is nothing in the least surprising that Paul, during his ministry in Greece and Asia Minor, should have made the acquaintance of a minimum of eight and a maximum of ten Christians who later ended up in Rome.

If Paul knew where these individuals now were, the information most likely came from Prisca and Aquila. These also provided data on the achievements of members, which gave Paul an opportunity for compliments. The leaders of house-churches are all mentioned by name. Such public acknowledgement would have been welcomed. Women ministers are given particular prominence, 'Mary, who has laboured much for you . . . Tryphaena and Tryphosa, those labourers in the Lord . . . and my dear friend Persis, who has laboured much in the Lord' (16: 6, 12). These would have been flattered that their accomplishments were known overseas. Moreover, such recognition reinforced the egalitarian position of women in the Pauline churches.

Nowhere else in the letters do we see Paul acting like a glad-handing politician. The unusual effort to win over individuals betrays the importance he attached to Roman commitment to his mission to Spain.

Journey to Jerusalem

In the letter Paul informed the Romans that he had one important duty to accomplish before he was free to go to them. His churches in Macedonia and Achaia had fulfilled his dearest hopes, and had come through with significant contributions for his cherished collection for the poor of Jerusalem. To bring this gift to the Holy City would be the climax of his work in the eastern Mediterranean.

This should have been an occasion of great joy for Paul. In fact, it made him extremely nervous. The very thought of going to Jerusalem knocked him off balance to the point where he let slip his anxiety to the Romans. His anxiety blinded him to the fact that the mere hint that he had difficulties with the mother church could damage him in the eyes of those whom he hoped to make his allies.

Paul asked the Romans to pray 'that I may be preserved from the disobedient in Judaea, and that my service for Jerusalem may be acceptable to the saints, in order that I may come to you with joy by God's will' (15: 31–2).

Cause for Concern

'The disobedient in Judaea' is an unusual formulation, but Paul clearly means Jews who have not accepted Christ. The verb he uses evokes a vivid sense of danger. When speaking of his two previous visits to Jerusalem, Paul never suggested that he felt physically threatened (Gal. 1: 18–19; 2: 1–10). It is possible to detect an element of secrecy in Paul's first visit as a Christian—he saw no one but Peter and James—but that may have been due to embarrassment. He did not want to confront those whom he had persecuted not many years earlier. Nothing similar is in evidence during his second visit. The series of meetings with James, Cephas and John must have been known to the whole community. Other Jews apparently exhibited no interest. Were they aware of the decision not to circumcise Gentile believers, one might assume that they welcomed the refusal of Christians to make pagans nominally Jews.

Why should Paul now take it for granted that Palestinian Jews would be hostile to him? I suspect that he was the victim of his gloomiest thoughts. In this minimalist scenario we should envisage Paul the Pharisee assessing and finding guilty Paul the antinomian. Reflection on the way he had once acted towards followers of Christ whose deviations from Judaism were minor, and on the way he would have wanted to act against those who repudiated the Law as irrelevant, stimulated Paul's imagination to the point where the threat from observant Jews became very real. He postulated what he feared.

While there might be some uncertainty regarding the attitude to Paul of Palestinian Jews in general, there is none regarding that of the Jerusalem church. Emissaries from Antioch, as we have seen, had been on Paul's heels for four years, challenging his attitude towards the Law. In Galatia they had the opportunity to read Paul's letter to the churches there, and it is far from impossible that they sent a copy to Antioch. In any case, it is unlikely that they stayed away for several years without reporting back to their home base. At least an oral report of Paul's radical opposition to the Law reached Antioch.

Regular contacts between Antioch and Jerusalem can be safely assumed. Mutual support would have become even more necessary as anti-Semitic pressures intensified in the eastern Mediterrranean. Paul could be quite sure, therefore, that James and his cohorts knew perfectly well that Paul's position had hardened into a stance which was the antithesis of theirs. It was perfectly reasonable, in consequence, for Paul to wonder if James would accept a gift with which he, Paul, was so intimately associated.

In principle, Jews had no compunction about accepting gifts from Gentiles for Temple worship. As relations with Rome deteriorated, however, such pagan participation in the Jewish cult became progressively less acceptable to the more extreme elements in Jerusalem.[9] It is only in this political context that Paul's apprehension regarding the reception of the collection becomes understandable. He had experienced James' nationalistic attitude both positively (Gal. 2: 3) and negatively (Gal. 2: 12), and was well aware that a gesture which could be understood as forging a bond with Gentiles might meet with a rebuff. Paul could not be sure, however, because he did not know how much the Jerusalem community needed the money.

Paul could have decided not to return to Jerusalem. His participation in the delegation was not imperative. The delegates of the contributing churches were with him, and he could have entrusted them with the mission. They were perfectly capable of going without him. The only injury would have been to his pride. His decision to persevere, despite mortal danger and the possible futility of the gesture, underlines how deeply he felt about the relationship between the Jewish and Gentile churches. No one was more conscious than he of the depth of the widening gap between those for whom Christ was central and those for whom he was subordinate to the Law. Yet it was desperately important to fling across the abyss a fragile bridge of charity. Paul would risk all in the attempt.

Transporting the Collection

Exactly how much money Paul collected will never be known. It is certain, however, that the sum was considerable. The symbolic value of the gesture would have been negated were the sum derisory. The Jerusalemites would have seen it as a gratuitous insult. Unless an impressive amount of cash had been assembled, Paul would have considered the exercise a failure, and would have returned the contributions to the communities, accompanied, no doubt, by a bitter comment on their lack of generosity.

This raises the question of how the gift was going to be transported to Jerusalem. The model that would have spontaneously occurred to people of the Apostle's background was the procedure for transmitting the annual half-shekel Temple tax from the Diaspora to Jerusalem. The money collected from the various communities in an area was reduced to the smallest volume by being exchanged for metal of the highest value: namely, gold.

Given the conditions of travel in the first century, Paul's major preoccupation had to be the security of the funds entrusted to him. He was hardly in a position to hire armed guards. Hence we can exclude the use of pack animals to transport coffers of specie or sacks full of clinking coins. Imagine the effect on the bystanders when the containers were unloaded at the first inn, and how quickly word would spread among the local underworld types!

Paul's best protection was absolute secrecy. Each member of the party carried their personal funds for the journey in the usual money-belt or little bag suspended from a cord around the neck, but in addition each had a number of gold coins sewn into his or her garments in such a way that they would not chink. Since gold is heavy for its volume, the danger of distorting the shape of the garment would have limited the number of coins that any one individual could carry. In consequence, the number of Paul's companions was conditioned by the amount of money that had to be transported.

One final question remained: how was the group to travel? In the past Paul had always gone east by ship. In this case it would undoubtedly have been the safer way. The crew and passengers on a ship were a fixed and known quantity, whose movements could be monitored. A thief had a chance of escaping only if the theft went undiscovered until the ship arrived in port.

Security on land was much more difficult. Acquaintances on the road, or fellow guests at an inn, were constantly changing. Paul could never know what they had noticed, or what plans were being made to attack his group. The anxiety level, in consequence, was consistently high, whereas at sea there were long periods of relaxation between ports, provided of course that the sea was calm.

Yet Paul opted for the land route (Acts 20: 3–21: 16)! He and his companions went north into Macedonia, and then down the west coast of Asia Minor. Not only was this less secure, but it was much longer, three sides of a square around the Aegean Sea instead of a fast sail along the southern side.[10] What motivated this extraordinary choice? Despite Paul's optimistic plans for the future as revealed in Romans 15–16, we are forced to assume that the pessimistic side of his nature subsequently gained the upper hand, and he became convinced that he would never return from Jerusalem. He longed to see his churches one last time.

Paul's purpose in going to Macedonia was to say farewell to the communities at Thessalonica and Philippi. They had been his first foundations in Europe, and had been more successful than all the others in living up to his expectations. Not only had they immediately repulsed the Judaizers from Antioch, but the quality of their community lives made them existential proclamations of the gospel. They lived their belief to the point where Paul considered them both model (1 Thess. 1: 6) and message (Phil. 2: 14–16).

Coastal Navigation

According to the 'we-source', the travellers left the land route at Neapolis, and went down the west coast of Asia in a series of coasting vessels. The first stage from Neapolis to Troas was 120 nautical miles, which they covered in five days at the excruciatingly slow speed of one knot (Acts 20: 6).[11] The depression that Paul must have been feeling was intensified by several uncomfortable nights at sea.

His visit to Troas proved a wrenching emotional experience. The church there was one of the two communities to which Paul had not been able to devote much time, the other being Illyricum. Presumably when he crossed to Macedonia to meet Titus, he had promised to return. Now, when he finally did, it was to tell them that it was unlikely that they would ever see him again. Not unnaturally, they clung to him. Even though a ship sailing as far as Assos was ready to weigh anchor, he could not brutally wrench himself away. To give himself a day longer, he told his companions to set sail, after arranging to join them in Assos by cutting across the base of the great headland on foot (Acts 20: 13). It was a walk of 30 miles (48 km), which could easily be done in a day. There was no guarantee as to what winds the ship would encounter as it rounded Cape Lekton.

The 'we-source' continues, 'And when he met us at Assos, we took him on board and came to Mitylene. And sailing from there we came the following day opposite Chios. The next day we touched at Samos, and the day after that we came to Miletus. For Paul had decided to sail past Ephesus, so that he might not have to spend time in Asia, for he was hastening to be at Jerusalem, if possible, on the day of Pentecost' (Acts 20: 14–16). For all its brevity, this is an accurate and vivid picture of coastal navigation among islands in Paul's day, a leisurely sail by day and night in a secure harbour.[12]

From Assos to Mitylene on the east coast of the island of Lesbos was 26 nautical miles (48 km). If we presume twelve hours of daylight sailing, their speed was a slow 2.17 knots, almost certainly a sign of unfavourable winds. Of course, they could have started late and landed early. The next day they covered twice that distance. Once they rounded the south-east corner of Lesbos, they must have picked up a good stern or quartering wind that drove them along at a respectable 4.3 knots.[13] For the passengers at least, entering the channel separating the island of Chios from the mainland would have been a moment of queasy drama. The channel is only 11 miles (17.6 km) wide, and sitting across it is the 7.5-mile (12-km) chain of the Oinousian islands. The pilot had to decide very quickly whether to leave them to port or to starboard. There must have been many sighs of relief as they landed on Chios.

The logical route the next day would have been to head in towards Ephesus, but apparently contrary winds forced them to round the west side of the island of Samos before finding shelter in its lee. That day they covered 69 nautical miles (128 km), which meant that they were thrashing along at an above average 5.7 knots. The howling of the wind and the violent movement of the boat would have frightened many, but to those used to the sea it was exhilarating. The following day, however, the wind dropped, and they barely covered the 17 nautical miles (32 km) to Miletus. For the battered travellers it must have been a great relief.

According to the 'we-source', it was Paul's decision to avoid Ephesus. In reality, of course, he had no control over where the boat went. He and his companions were merely deck passengers. Their arrival at Miletus, however, gave him a choice. He could go to Ephesus to say farewell to the community, or he could invite representatives to come to him.

He opted for the latter (Acts 20: 17). By sending for the Elders of the church, Paul gained four or five days—the round trip was 100 miles (160 km)—in which to recuperate. And he certainly needed the rest. His departure from Troas had been an emotionally draining experience, immediately followed by two rather stressful days at sea. He was exhausted, and he dreaded a repetition of the heart-rending scenes into which the Christians of Troas had plunged him, if he announced to the Ephesians that they were unlikely to see him again. The Elders, he could be sure, would be much more dignified. None the less, when they arrived, he could not bring himself to bid them a formal farewell. The closest he could manage was to share with them his fear as to what might happen at the end of his journey: 'I am going to Jerusalem, bound in the Spirit, not knowing what shall befall me there' (Acts 20: 22), and to alert them to the fact that henceforward they would be responsible for the church of Ephesus (Acts 20: 28).[14]

Paul's apprehension regarding his future led him to make an extraordinary decision that must have broken his heart. Timothy should stay at Ephesus. No doubt Timothy protested violently. He was Paul's closest friend and most essential collaborator, and knew just how much Paul depended on him. Why did Paul want to leave him behind now, just at the time when his support was most important?

No doubt Paul found pastoral reasons to placate Timothy: for example, he would reinforce Paul's supporters in a divided church. But his real motive belonged to a different order. Timothy was closely identified with him, and he was also a Jew. Were Paul to suffer in Jerusalem because he was considered an apostate Jew, the same fate was likely to befall Timothy. Thus, in order to guard his dearest companion from danger, Paul found an excuse to keep him away from Jerusalem. Paul lived the self-sacrificing love that he preached.

We have no way of knowing how long Paul actually spent in Miletus, either conferring with the Elders or waiting for a boat going south. Eventually three daily stages on small coasters at an average of 4.3 knots brought them via Cos and Rhodes to Patera in southern Turkey (Acts 21: 1).[15] There they found what they had been looking for: a ship sailing to Phoenicia. The one they boarded was in fact heading for Tyre. It was not ideal. They would have preferred a port further south, but it was close enough. If, as the 'we-source' tells us, they left Cyprus to port (Acts 21: 3), then it appears that they had a virtually straight run to the south-east at the ship's best point of sailing. Even at the slowest average speed (4.5 knots) for such long open sea passages, the 347-nautical-mile journey would have taken only a little over three days. An average of 6 knots would have cut that time by a day.

According to the 'we-source', the travellers spent a week recuperating in Tyre, before going down the coast by ship, first to Ptolemais (modern Akko in Israel), and then to Caesarea Maritima, where they took another rest period before starting on the two-day march to Jerusalem (Acts 21: 3–15).[16] It seems legitimate to infer a certain reluctance on the part of Paul. He would not be turned from his decision, but he was prepared to dawdle. None the less, it is entirely possible that he reached Jerusalem before Pentecost (Acts 20: 16), which in AD 56 occurred on 11 June.[17]

Reception in Jerusalem

Paul needed to think hard about the reception he would be given in Jerusalem. He had reason to be afraid, but he was unlikely to let that paralyse him. He was not the type who would go quietly like a lamb to the slaughter. On the contrary, we can be sure that his fertile mind sifted through various scenarios that would permit him to achieve his objective whatever the opposition might do.

Paul's objective was not at all complicated. It was simply to hand over to the Jerusalem church the money that his Gentile churches had collected for the poor, and to head back to the west as soon as possible. The key to the solution was James. The community would follow his lead. Although fully committed to a Law-observant vision of Christianity, James had exhibited extraordinary pragmatism at the meeting in Jerusalem, where he had approved Paul's Law-free mission. Paul, therefore, had reason to hope that, even if James had principled objections to receiving the collection, this would not necessarily mean a refusal in practice.

Working out a Strategy

Paul had no illusions as to how much James knew of his radical opposition to the Law.[18] The Judaizers, who had threatened his communities in Galatia and in Greece, would have certainly informed Antioch-on-the-Orontes, which was in close contact with Jerusalem. He could foresee James saying to him, 'You see, brother, how many thousands there are among the Jews who have believed. They are all zealous for the Law. And they have been told about you that you teach all the Jews who are among the Gentiles to forsake [the Law of] Moses, telling them not to circumcise their children or observe the customs' (Acts 21: 21). Clearly James' freedom to manœuvre was limited by the opposition he would face if he was perceived to concede too much. In these circumstances the fundamental question that Paul had to resolve was: what would James require of him in order to make acceptance of the collection politically feasible?

The first step, obviously, had to be to give the lie to the rumours circulating about Paul. A flat verbal denial was excluded by Paul's conscience, and most likely would be ineffective. Words are cheap. Paul cast his mind around for a public action that would affirm his Jewishness, something that only Jews would do and could identify with. Paul had no scruples about such gestures. In his eyes they were completely meaningless. He had written in one of his letters, 'To the Jews I became as a Jew in order to win the Jews.... To those outside the Law I became as one outside the Law ... that I might win those outside the Law' (1 Cor. 9: 20–1). Thus, for him to act like a practising Jew was not a problem. If others chose to understand it as repudiation of his reputed antinomianism, that was their concern.

Once Paul had set up these parameters, the answer became obvious. The simplest act, and the minimum which James could have accepted, would be for Paul to undergo the purification required of all Jews coming from pagan territory who wished to enter the Temple. It was assumed that they had incurred corpse-uncleanness abroad, and this Levitical impurity had to be removed by having a priest sprinkle them with the water of atonement on the third and seventh days (Num. 19: 11–16). Only by going through this ritual would Paul be in a position to relate to the strictly observant members of the Jerusalem community, who, in addition, would have been gratified by the implicit condemnation of Gentiles.

It certainly eased James' mind to know that Paul was willing to undergo the seven-day ritual of purification. As a result, he approached the question of the transfer of the collection in a spirit of co-operation, and he may have been the one to suggest an elegant solution, which certainly pleased Paul, if he had not already thought of it independently. The money would not be given directly to the Jerusalem community. That might have generated acrimonious debate. Instead, it would be spent for the benefit of the community before its members knew what was going on, thereby unfreezing other community funds.

The mechanism for this clever ploy was the institution of the Nazirite vow (Num. 6: 1–21). To acquit oneself of such a vow was an expensive business. The obligatory offering consisted of 'an unblemished male yearling lamb as a burnt offering, an unblemished yearling ewe lamb as a sacrifice for sin, an unblemished ram as a peace offering, and a basket of unleavened loaves made of fine flour mixed with oil, and of unleavened wafers spread with oil, with the cereal offerings and libations appropriate to them' (Num. 6: 14–15).

214

For a poor person the financial burden was considerable, and it might take an excessively long time to assemble the money. Hence, it was considered meritorious of the Jewish community to help out.

James had four Nazirites who needed assistance (Acts 21: 23). The plan was that Paul would pay their expenses. When it became known, the gesture was one which the Jerusalem church could hardly refuse from a Jewish visitor who had been ritually purified. Moreover, it relieved the church of a financial burden. Acceptance, however, meant that the church had already profited by the collection!

In Roman Custody

Tragically, the plan was initiated but never brought to completion. Before the seven days of his purification were completed, and thus before he could do anything for the Nazirites, the second danger that Paul had anticipated became a reality.

While visiting the Temple, non-Christian Jews attempted to lynch him on the spurious grounds that he had brought a Gentile into that part of the Temple reserved to Jews. This was the pre-Herodian 500-cubit square, which stood in the midst of the Court of the Gentiles. To protect its sanctity, it was surrounded by a waist-high wall. Each of its gates carried inscriptions in both Greek and Latin promising death to any Gentile who crossed the barrier.

An alert Roman sentry on the battlements of the Antonia fortress at the north-west corner of the Temple saw the violent movement of the crowd. Fearing a riot, he called the tribune, Claudius Lysias, who immediately intervened, snatching Paul out of the hands of the mob, and sweeping him up the steps into the fortress. He was preparing to interrogate Paul under torture when the latter claimed the rights of his Roman citizenship (Acts 22: 25). This episode must be dated to sometime in the middle of the summer of AD 56.

This notched up responsibility to an uncomfortable level, and the tribune passed the buck to his superior, the procurator of Judaea, who was based in Caesarea Maritima. At this time the office was held by Felix (AD 52–8), a freedman of the imperial household who, we are told by Tacitus, 'wielded royal power with the instincts of a slave' (*History* 5. 9). As in Ephesus, Paul was imprisoned in the praetorium. In Caesarea this was the erstwhile palace of Herod the Great, built out into the sea on a promontory. Some two years later, when Felix was recalled by the emperor Nero, Paul's case had still not been disposed of, and he became the responsibility of the new procurator, Porcius Festus (Acts 24: 27). The probable date of this change of administration is the summer of AD 58.[19]

For these two years Paul was apparently in limbo. It may be that the conditions of his imprisonment were more severe than in Ephesus. In any case we hear of no activity involving his churches. No doubt he exercised the same internal ministry as he had in the praetorium of Ephesus (Phil. 1: 13), but it must have been extremely frustrating not to be able to reach out beyond the walls of his prison. No interrogation had ever lasted so long before. But what could he do? There was no *Habeas Corpus Act* to prevent people being imprisoned on mere suspicion or left in prison for an indefinite time without trial. He had no influential friends to intervene on his behalf. He was totally at the mercy of the procurator.

Paul must have lived with the fear that he would be handed back to the Jewish authorities. This was an incentive not to push too hard for a decision. At the same time he must have hoped desperately for some news from the outside, and in particular concerning the fate of the collection. He had been arrested before he could help the Nazirites, and were he held incommunicado, he could not know what had become of the money that he had collected with so much effort. What had happened to his companions? Had his and James' plan been carried through when the situation in Jerusalem had quietened down? To such questions Paul got no answers, and the weary days dragged on interminably under Porcius Festus.

It could have been another year or so before a decision was forced on the procurator. The Jewish authorities were insistent in their demand that Paul be handed back to them for judgement, and maintained pressure on Festus. Much as it went against the grain, it would have been difficult for him to deny them a hearing. Having delayed as long as he could, he forced them to come to Caesarea. There they laid out their case for a change of jurisdiction. Paul vehemently protested his innocence, but his crucial words were: 'I am standing before Caesar's tribunal, where I ought to be tried' (Acts 25: 10). What he wanted was for the procurator, the representative of Caesar, to make a decision in accordance with the evidence, and set him free. Festus, however, decided to interpret Paul's words as a demand to be judged in Rome by the emperor. It would relieve him of all responsibility, and the decision would certainly irritate the Jewish authorities.[20] In all probability it was the late summer of AD 59.

The Final Years 12

THE inexperience, or perhaps the laziness, of the centurion selected to escort Paul to Rome condemned them to a frightening journey. He could not contemplate the endless miles across Asia Minor and then across Macedonia, particularly in winter. This left only one solution. To go by sea. His friends must have warned him that it was much too late in the year to contemplate such a voyage. He knew better, however, and there were orders to be obeyed. It was his bad luck to find an owner and captain who were prepared to put to sea despite the danger. A calm run as far as Crete built false confidence, and the decision was made to continue. They had not long to wait before the predictable storm struck. Badly scared, they jettisoned the cargo, and ran before it under bare poles. Eventually, they went aground in the region of Malta. The islanders treated them well and, when the sailing season began in the spring, put them on a boat going up the west coast of Italy.[1] They finally arrived in Rome in the late spring or early summer of AD 60.

A Mission to Spain

All that is known of Paul's two-year Roman imprisonment (Acts 28: 30) is that he was eventually set free. How it happened is anyone's guess. A favourable imperial decision? An amnesty designed to make space available in the prisons? The desire of a lower magistrate to shorten the court list by dismissing unimportant prisoners? In any case, after a certain time Paul found himself at liberty, probably in AD 62. That was when his troubles began.[2]

The Roman church did not give Paul the welcome that he had worked to ensure. This was not due to any particular ill will. Simply too much time had elapsed. They had received his letter in the summer of AD 56. Even if the Romans had then meticulously studied his carefully crafted letter of introduction, now they could hardly remember what he had said. Prisca and Aquila had sung his praises when they first arrived, but it would have been pointless to continue when Paul's arrival was so long delayed as to have become highly problematical. It is even possible that a pessimistic estimate of the outcome of his long-drawn-out Caesarean imprisonment had reached Rome.

Paul refused to recognize that the world had moved on. Nothing had changed in his commitment to carry the gospel to the end of the earth. He still wanted Rome to adopt him as its missionary to Spain. The Roman believers did not agree, and could produce a series of perfectly good reasons to justify their position. First, Spain belonged to their sphere of influence. Thus, it was their responsibility to preach the word of God there, and they would choose whom they willed to represent them. It was not for an upstart from the provinces to thrust himself upon them. Second, they were the only ones equipped to communicate with the Latin-speaking colonies in Spain. Paul, on the contrary, would have been severely linguistically challenged. Third, they were the best judges of the most opportune moment to launch a missionary expedition. Finally, Paul's inevitable failure would make it difficult for them to mount their own campaign.

None of these reasons, of course, had the slightest impact on Paul. His tendency to identify himself with his gospel, and his desires with the will of God, has already been noted. Caught out by the impossibility of furnishing a point-by-point refutation, he resorted to bluster, as he had in the dispute over finances with Corinth. In vitriolic terms he contrasted his total commitment with the complacent detachment of the Romans, whose church apparently had no daughters! As both sides dug in their heels, the poisonous atmosphere worsened.

At some point Paul made it clear that he was going to go to Spain anyway. This drew a flat prohibition from the Romans. It would be most presumptuous of Paul to go ahead without their approval. He would be flouting the dignity of the church of the capital of the empire. As far as Paul was concerned, such mundane arguments were as a red rag to a bull. Opposition goaded him. His determination hardened implacably.

Paul did in fact go to Spain. Under the circumstances it would have been totally out of character for him to have done anything else. The sea journey was an easy one. He could have reached the coast of Catalonia in four days, or Gades (modern Cadiz) in seven days on a ship sailing out of Ostia, the port of Rome. Once he landed, he was in trouble and, as the Romans had foretold, he achieved nothing. It was as ignominious a flop as his abortive attempt to convert the Nabataeans immediately after his conversion. While inspired by great enthusiasm, both ventures were ill-conceived and ill-prepared. It cannot have taken Paul more than a summer to admit that, since Greek was hardly spoken on the Iberian Peninsula, he was not going to get anywhere in the foreseeable future in Spain.

Return to Illyricum

The debate and the disaster can easily be accommodated in the summer of AD 62. What was Paul to do now? His experience in Spain had shown him that he could not hope for success on the southern littoral of Gaul or in northern Italy, where conditions were similar. His linguistic limitations left him no alternative to a return to the east. He had thought that he had done what he could there, but in fact there was one bit of unfinished business, which could serve as a focus for his energies. The need to rush to Corinth in the late summer of AD 55 had interrupted his mission in Illyricum. The church there had not been nurtured to the same degree as his other foundations. The fact that his baby was now seven years old would not have deterred him. His input into its development had been truncated.

This attractive possibility of productive work cheered a defeated Paul as he sailed from Spain to Italy. His pride made a visit to Rome unthinkable. Believers there would not have sympathized with his failure. Unless the ship docked at a port to the south of Ostia, one should rather imagine him swinging around the south of the city to pick up the Via Appia, 'the queen of roads', which would have brought him to Beneventum (modern Benevento). In that oppulent city he had a choice. He could continue on the Via Appia, passing through Venusia and Tarentum (modern Taranto), before cutting across the heel of Italy to the port of Brundisium (modern Brindisi) on the Adriatic Sea. Or from Beneventum he could have gone north-east and then a little south of east through Canusium (modern Canosa) to reach the Adriatic at Barium (modern Bari), whence it followed the coast to Brundisium.[3]

In AD 109 this latter route became the Via Trajana, but its existence at the time of Paul is attested by Horace, who travelled it in the suite of Maecenas in 37 BC. He left a charming record in *Satires* 1. 5, which is summarized thus by Lionel Casson: 'It had taken him about two weeks to do some 375 miles, and he had had his taste of the typical ups and downs of travel: some sunny weather, swift travel on major highways, first-rate accommodations, good company, lots of fun; some rain, slow going over bad roads, primitive hotels, traveller's tummy, nights without sleep, and a rendezvous with a girl who never showed up.'[4] Paul, of course, was not travelling in the company of the richest man in the world. His food and lodgings would have been greatly inferior, and he certainly could not have afforded the carriages which enabled Maecenas and his party to cover 37 miles (59 km) and 39 miles (63 km) on the last two days of the journey.

Brundisium was the principal port for trade between Italy and Greece and further east. Provided that it was not too late in the year, it would have been easy for Paul to find a boat crossing to Dyrrachium (modern Durrës), the eastern terminal of the Via Egnatia, and the doorway to Illyricum. With favourable winds the 30-mile (48-km) crossing took less than a day.

We do not know exactly where Paul had ministered in Illyricum. If it was Dyrrachium, he was already home. If it was Lychnidos, he still had a 90-mile (144-km) walk inland along the Via Egnatia. As Paul approached one or the other, he must have wondered what his reception would be. Would anyone recognize him? After all, it had been seven years almost to the day since he had left. Did anything remain of his foundation? There had been a six-year gap between his visits to the Galatians in AD 46 and 52, and he had found the church alive, if not particularly healthy. However, he had stayed the best part of two years with the Galatians, whereas he had spent barely a couple of months among the Illyrians. Their formation had been the sketchiest of all his churches. Such thoughts would not have depressed Paul. He might have regretted the loss, but he had succeeded here before, and he would succeed again.

If Paul arrived in Dyrrachium or Lychnidos at the end of the summer of AD 62, he probably left at the beginning of the spring of AD 64, when travel in the mountains of northern Greece became feasible. This was about the length of time he had devoted to the evangelization of Corinth, but was shorter than his sojourn at Ephesus. Once satisfied that a church was solidly established, Paul knew that his continued presence would be an impediment to the normal development of the community. As long as he remained, he would automatically be the authority figure in all aspects of its life. Only when freed of the weight of his prestige could the charisms of other members, particularly the gifts of leadership, develop naturally.

Macedonia and Asia

It was a sad moment for Paul when he left Illyricum. He knew in his heart that it was the last time he would work in virgin missionary territory. When he looked around at his familiar world of the eastern Mediterranean, there was no patch that was not someone else's missionary responsibility. He had been so successful that he had worked himself out of a job! Moreover, at 70 he was undoubtedly feeling his age. Retirement, however, was out of the question. Maybe there were some services that he still might render to the churches he had founded in Macedonia and Asia Minor.

Thus, when Paul set off east along the Via Egnatia, his frame of mind was the antithesis of the driving enthusiasm that had animated him as he walked buoyantly west to freedom on that same road some nine years earlier. Perhaps he was cheered by his visits to Thessalonica and Philippi. They had had their teething troubles, but had developed into the churches that gave Paul the greatest pride. They radiated the truth of the gospel (1 Thess. 1: 6–8; Phil. 2: 14). For their part, remembering his pessimism on his previous visit as he travelled to Jerusalem in AD 56, they would have been delighted to see him alive.[5]

How long Paul spent with the Thessalonians and the Philippians is anyone's guess, but it was high summer when he sailed into Troas. He no longer needed his heavy winter cloak. It would have been an intolerable burden as he tramped the 210 miles (350 km) to Ephesus in the intense heat.[6] Thus, he left it with Carpus, no doubt a member of the church, together with his scrolls and the small parchment codices that he used as notebooks (2 Tim. 4: 13).

The 'scrolls' may have contained texts of the Jewish Scriptures, or sayings of Jesus, or archival material, such as the letters that Paul had written to his churches. It was normal practice to retain copies of letters sent. The contents of the 'notebooks' probably varied from the profound to the mundane: ideas for sermons, solutions to pastoral problems, the names of potential leaders, or problematic members, of his communities, directions as to how to find individuals in different cities.

A Problem in Ephesus

As Paul tramped south, did he stop to visit Pergamum and Smyrna, two of the communities founded by the missionary outreach of Ephesus? I suspect that he passed them by. They had been founded by his agents, and he knew few, if any, of their members. Paul, I believe, was looking forward to his return to Ephesus with the keenest pleasure. His two years there had been relatively contented and extremely productive ones. Many churches had been founded from there, and there he had written half the letters that are his legacy to posterity. His anticipation, however, focused principally on being reunited with Timothy, his old companion-in-arms whom he had not seen since he left him there on his way to Jerusalem some eight years earlier.

The joy of the reunion soon faded, as Paul was forced to confront the ineffectiveness of Timothy's performance. A close reading of 2 Timothy reveals that the man who had been a wonderful assistant and advisor proved to be a poor leader. By Paul's high standards, he had let the flame of grace in his heart die down. He was not doing the work of an evangelist; he was not fulfilling his ministry. His failure was not doctrinal but personal. Responsibility frightened him, and he had withdrawn, perhaps with the excuse that he needed to earn his living and not be a burden to the community. In reality he could not endure the pain that leadership entailed. The energetic acceptance and follow-through that Paul demanded were lacking, and the community had suffered. In particular, Timothy had failed to control a group who had turned Ephesus into what Paul considered 'a chattering church'. Foolish and inexpert research fuelled debates that were no more than exchanges of profane and empty words (2 Tim. 2: 14–18).

Paul's response was to remove Timothy from office and to take charge himself. The realization that he had failed Paul reduced Timothy to tears (2 Tim. 1: 4). Paul did not disgrace him publicly. As far as the community at Ephesus knew, Timothy had been sent to discover and report on the state of the churches of the Maeander and Lycus valleys. Perhaps his mandate extended even as far as Galatia. Such a mission made sense, because Paul had been out of touch with these churches for some ten years. Perhaps this was the tricky covert operation to which Onesiphorus made a significant contribution (2 Tim. 1: 18). Only he and his household appear to have been unequivocally on Paul's side (2 Tim. 4: 19).

Paul's assumption of control did not improve conditions in the church. There had always been opposition to him at Ephesus (Phil. 1: 14–18). Moreover, he had no sympathy with the theological aspirations of the debaters or their intellectual pretensions. Without the counsel of Timothy, he repeated the mistakes he had made in dealing with their counterparts in Corinth, the Spirit People. Paul's mentality was such that he simply could not understand or appreciate either one or the other. He was irritated at having to return to the same sort of silliness. Thus, instead of calming the situation, he exacerbated the tensions that wracked the community, in the process alienating the majority of the believers (2 Tim. 1: 15).

Eventually Paul came to the realization that leadership of the church of Ephesus demanded qualities that he lacked. His presence there only made things worse. In a gesture of great humility he withdrew to nearby Miletus. This port city was 50 miles (80 km) from Ephesus, far enough for distance to be a barrier, but not so far that he was completely out of reach, if there were changes in Ephesus.

Paul was not alone. In fact, he moved with a small community (2 Tim. 4: 9–11). Titus was part of his permanent entourage. Luke and Demas had been with him during his captivity in Ephesus in AD 53 (Col. 4: 14). Tychicus had carried the letter from Ephesus to the Colossians (Col. 4: 7). Crescens is otherwise unknown. Erastus was last heard of in Corinth with Paul in the spring of AD 56 (Rom. 16: 23). Perhaps he had gone to Ephesus on business, and met Paul there by sheer coincidence. Trophimus had been one of the group carrying the collection to Jerusalem (Acts 20: 4). In the Holy City he was the Gentile whom the Jews accused Paul of bringing into the sacred precinct of the Temple (Acts 21: 29). After being the unwitting cause of Paul's arrest, he had returned to his native Asia.

A Fateful Journey to Rome

Paul spent the winter of AD 64–5 in Miletus, hoping no doubt that his self-imposed exile would have an impact on the emotions of the Ephesians. He had adopted the same tactic after his unfortunate second visit to Corinth, when he went to Macedonia and later wrote the Severe Letter (2 Cor. 2: 1–4). On this occasion, however, he did not have Timothy to advise him, and did not think of writing a letter to facilitate the process of reconciliation.

Even though it was only a refuge, as Troas had been when Paul was forced to leave Ephesus on another occasion, it is most improbable that Paul bided his time in idleness. The city was big enough to provide him with plenty of work.[7] Miletus was the first city to have been laid out on a grid pattern with long and short blocks. The credit is given to one of its citizens, Hippodamus (*c*. 479 BC), for whom this type of urban development was subsequently named. In Paul's day its four harbours and three markets made it a bustling commercial centre with an estimated population of some 60,000. What was proving to be a fruitful and absorbing ministry came to an abrupt end in the late summer of AD 65.

Nero's Persecution of Christians

In the early hours of 19 June, AD 64, one of the shops near the Circus Maximus in Rome went up in flames. The blaze raced through the valley between the Esquiline and Palatine hills, and raged through the city for nine days. When it was finally brought under control, ten of the city's fourteen regions lay in ruins. The emperor Nero moved quickly to provide shelter for the homeless. Soon, however, he announced that he was going to expropriate 125 acres (50.5 hectares) of private land in central Rome in order to build himself a magnificent new palace, the Golden House, surrounded by a spacious park. Inevitably rumours began to circulate that the one who benefited most might have started the fire. A spontaneous whispering campaign blaming Nero personally gained momentum.[8] Feeling that his position was threatened, the emperor decided (probably in the spring of AD 65) on a drastic method of directing attention away from himself.

To suppress this rumour, Nero fabricated scapegoats, and punished with every refinement the notoriously depraved Christians (as they were popularly called). . . . Their deaths were made farcical. Dressed in wild animals' skins, they were torn to pieces by dogs, or crucified, or made into torches to be ignited after dark as substitutes for daylight. Nero provided his Gardens for the spectacle, and exhibited displays in the Circus, at which he mingled with the crowd, or stood in a chariot, dressed as a charioteer. (Tacitus, *Annals* 15. 44; trans. Grant)

The news of Nero's bestial ferocity spread like wildfire through the empire. At least by the summer of AD 65, it had reached the Pauline churches in Greece and Asia. The believers would have been aghast at the thought of the horrible deaths their fellow believers had suffered. Seeing the impact that such frightfulness made on his own converts, Paul had little difficulty in estimating the consequences for those Christians in Rome who, by chance, had escaped the emperor's drag-net. Brutal reality challenged their idealistic acceptance of martyrdom as a remote future possibility. The vision of an extremely painful, prolonged death was unlikely to have had a favourable effect on morale.

Paul saw clearly that if the Roman community was to survive, its sister churches had to come to its aid. Did he have the right, however, to ask others to uproot themselves from homes and families and thrust themselves into mortal danger? He himself had no such entanglements, and his life did not have long to run in any case. Did he recall what he had once written? 'The love of Christ constrains us, because we are convinced that one has died for all; therefore all have died. And he died that those who live might live no longer for themselves, but for him who for their sake died and was raised' (2 Cor. 5: 14–15)?

His little entourage unanimously decided to go with him. There was still unfinished business at Ephesus, however, and Paul dispatched Tychicus to inform the community there of his plans, and perhaps to take charge (2 Tim. 4: 12).

En Route to Rome

Once the decision was made, Paul wanted to move at once. His temperament dictated immediate action, and the deterioration in the situation of the church in Rome should be stopped as soon as possible. Moreover, he had two seas to cross. It was absolutely imperative that he should be on the Italian mainland before winter interrupted sailing on the Aegean and the Adriatic. It was most unfortunate that Trophimus fell ill at just this crucial moment, but the urgency of the moment was too great. He had to be left behind (2 Tim. 4: 20). He was not in mortal danger, and there were Miletian Christians to look after him.

The fire lit in Erastus by Paul's initial urgency and daring died slowly as the ship made its way to Corinth. The voyage without distractions gave him time to reflect on what it might mean for him to go to Rome where Christians were being tortured for their faith. His imagination gradually eroded his courage. When they finally docked at Cenchreae, the eastern port of Corinth, he dismally told Paul that he did not have the strength to go any further. He and his family would remain faithful to the end if a persecution arose in his own city, but he could not put his head in the lion's mouth by going to Rome (2 Tim. 4: 20).

It was with a much reduced team that Paul crossed the isthmus on foot from Cenchreae to Lychaeum. It took less than a day. Perhaps at Lychaeum he was lucky enough to find a boat going all the way to Italy. If so, he would have interpreted it as a good omen. God approved of his visit to Rome and would aid him there. Otherwise, with increasing frustration, he would have been forced to take a series of coasters. His feeling of desperation would have increased as he inched his way towards the mouth of the Gulf of Corinth. The delay was bad enough, but if it were late in the sailing season, it could mean that he would be stuck in the Peloponnese for the winter.

Back in a Roman Gaol

Somehow Paul and his little group did make it to Rome, probably in the late summer or early autumn of AD 65. At that stage the worst of the persecution was over. It is doubtful that it lasted longer than was necessary to give the citizens of Rome something else to think about. To prolong the hunt for Christians risked directing attention to the motivation of the emperor. Moreover, Nero soon had other matters to occupy him. A group of those who had lost valuable land in the great fire of Rome plotted to assassinate him, and to put Gaius Calpurnius Piso on the throne. The conspiracy was revealed, and the resulting executions gave the citizens plenty to talk about. Thereafter Nero suspected everyone, and heads rolled at a whim.

An Unwelcome Visitor

The victims of the emperor's paranoia belonged to the upper classes, whom he thought had the potential to damage him. He was no threat

228

to the ordinary citizens, who admired him for his generosity and the entertainment he provided. In this milieu Paul was able to adopt the high-profile stance that, in his view, the situation demanded. To have slid cautiously from one refuge to another would have defeated his purpose in coming to Rome. For his absolute temperament, unobtrusiveness was but a first step towards apostasy. Fearlessness in proclaiming the gospel, he believed, was the way to infuse a demoralized community with new courage and hope.

This was not entirely to the liking of the Christians in Rome. The last thing they wanted was to have the imperial spotlight shine in their direction once again. Paul, in their eyes, was an outsider and a trouble-maker. They had experienced his intransigence in the matter of his mission to Spain, and feared that now he would be equally deaf to their remonstrances, even though they had then been right and he had been wrong. Rome was their church. They were the ones who had suffered. It was their responsibility to determine their own road to recovery. His arrogant assumption of leadership carried the wounding implication that they were skulking cowards.

Just how deeply the Roman believers resented Paul became evident when he was eventually arrested. On the occasion of his first appearance before the magistrate, absolutely no one turned up to support him by their presence and prayers (2 Tim. 4: 16).

The purpose of this preliminary examination was to determine the identity of the accused and the general validity of the charges against him. It was held in public, and supporters were permitted to testify, to encourage, and even to advise on points of law. If reputable citizens spoke out forcibly in favour of the accused, he had a very good chance of being discharged, particularly if it appeared that the accusation had been motivated by malice.

The fact that Paul had no relations, friends or even business contacts to identify him naturally made the magistrate very suspicious. As a self-confessed Christian, was Paul perhaps in Rome to take revenge on the emperor for his treatment of other members of his movement? Might he have connections with those members of the nobility who desired nothing more than to get rid of Nero, and who might provide logistical support for a fanatical assassin with his own

229

agenda? These possibilities alone would make any prudent magistrate do two things: first, hold the prisoner until the whole situation was thoroughly clarified; and second, take advice from superiors who knew the thinking of the political echelon before making any decisions.

Chained as an Evildoer

Paul, in consequence, was held 'in chains' as a 'hardened criminal' (2 Tim. 2: 9). This terminology might seem to imply that the conditions of his incarceration were more severe than on previous occasions, but it has to be balanced against the fact that he was able to receive visitors and to write letters, as he had been when he was held in the praetorium at Ephesus.

It is not altogether surprising that no Roman Christians had the charity to visit Paul. Evidently they wished to distance themselves from him; it was certainly safer. This highlights the extraordinary courage of one of his very few visitors, Onesiphorus, who came all the way from Ephesus. The community there had heard of Paul's daring expedition from Tychicus, and later from Trophimus. Only Onesiphorus had the sympathetic imagination to visualize what Paul must be going through, and in a fever of enthusiasm rushed off to join him.

Paul's delight and wonder are vividly conveyed by his words, 'He was not ashamed of my chains, but when he arrived in Rome he searched for me eagerly *and found me*!' (2 Tim. 1: 16–17). The soaring triumph of the last words becomes intelligible only if we recall that Rome had over a million inhabitants, but no street names and no house numbers. Onesiphorus had first to find out where Paul was, and then work out how to get there, both tasks made horrendously difficult if he did not know his way around the city, so could not follow directions specifying prominent landmarks. Success demanded unusual tenacity.

Once having found Paul, Onesiphorus made frequent visits. But then something happened that cost him his life (2 Tim. 1: 18). Perhaps an accident or, more likely, a senseless murder for a few coppers in a back street of Rome. Paul must have been shattered. His sense of isolation increased as those who had come with him from the east drifted away (2 Tim. 4: 9–11). Demas had run to Thessalonica in search of security. The same note of disgust does not appear when Paul mentions the departure of Crescens and Titus. Presumably they went to mission fields in Gaul/Galatia and Dalmatia respectively. The fact that he does not speak warmly of their initiative hints that the self-absorption that Paul showed during a previous imprisonment still lay just beneath the surface. Luke, he informs Timothy pathetically, is the only one to remain with him. The community on which he depended was reduced to just one other person.

A Last Letter

A spell in gaol provides abundant time for writing letters, but if Paul wrote more than one, they have not survived. Fortunately his letter to Timothy has been preserved. It is a rather curious letter for one in his position. Paul does not discourse on weighty matters of life and death, or glorify martyrdom. The letter, in fact, is intensely practical. None the less, it gives us a privileged glimpse into his frame of mind at this climactic moment in his life.

On reflection, Paul realized that it was neither wise nor fair to permit Timothy to float in a limbo somewhere east of Ephesus. He had neither the temperament nor the skill to combat the theological verbalism that had invaded Ephesus, and which could very easily spread to the hinterland. Paul knew that Timothy would be much happier in his erstwhile role of Paul's assistant, and so summoned him to Rome on the pretext that it was for Paul's benefit (2 Tim. 1: 4; 4: 9, 21). His affection was in no way diminished by the failure of his favourite disciple to live up to his expectations.

Since Paul requested Timothy to pick up the cloak, scrolls and notebooks that he had left behind in Troas (2 Tim. 4: 13), he obviously expected him to take the land route to Rome, which involved crossing Macedonia by the Via Egnatia and angling diagonally across Italy by the Via Appia. This was a journey of some

1,200 miles (1,920 km). Paul's messenger would have to travel this route in reverse, which meant that the letter would take the best part of two months to reach Timothy in Asia.⁹ Timothy's concern for Paul would guarantee that he left at once and travelled at his best speed. But even so, it would be the end of the summer before he could reach Rome in response to the letter.

Here we see the optimistic side of Paul's character. Despite his present circumstances, he fully expected to be alive in four or five months from the writing of the letter and, in addition, to be free to work in co-operation with Timothy and Mark. This, after all, was the wisdom of experience. In the past, all his examinations by Roman authorities had ended in his being set free. He could not imagine what new evidence might be produced at his second hearing.

Yet this time, at the back of his mind, Paul is not entirely sure. It would have been kinder, and perhaps more effective, to correct Timothy in person when he arrived in Rome. The fact that Paul goes into detail in the letter regarding the changes he desires in Timothy's life and ministry betrays his unconscious fear that he may not see Timothy again. If Timothy had been in his twenties when he joined Paul's missionary team *en route* to Europe for the first time, he would now be in his mid- to late forties, with many productive years ahead of him, provided that he took himself in hand. Paul could not let the opportunity pass. To wait might be too late.

A clear sense of finality is manifest in the most explicitly self-revelatory words that Paul ever wrote: 'As for me, I am already being poured out as a libation, and the time of my departure has come. I have fought the good fight. I have finished the race. I have kept the faith. From now on there is reserved for me the crown of righteousness, which the Lord, the righteous judge, will give me on that day, and not only to me, but to all who have longed for his appearing' (2 Tim. 4: 6–8). The sense of completion could not be more emphatic. However, it is not the anxious finality experienced by a prisoner on death row whose execution date has arrived, but the complacent recognition of a life well spent.

Paul, who by now was over 70, realized that his best years were behind him. He had given his all in the arena, or battleground, of life.

232

In terms of the normal life span he was living on borrowed time, particularly for one who for so many years had borne in his body the dying of Jesus (2 Cor. 4: 10). Each day was a grace, and he intended to make the best possible use of every moment. He might not live long after his release from prison, but that did not exempt him from the obligations of his ministry. He could plan for the future, and if he was taken, then Timothy and Mark could carry on.

Sentence of Death

Paul's optimism was misplaced. In the last quarter of AD 67, he was again summoned before the magistrate. This time the decision went against him. The mere fact that he admitted to being a Christian was sufficient (2 Tim. 4: 17). Nero had established the sinister precedent that the guilt of Christians could be presumed, and that the appropriate penalty was death.

At this point what happened to Paul depends on how he was assessed by the magistrate. If the magistrate respected Paul's Roman citizenship and applied the law strictly, he would have created a dilemma for Paul that has no parallel in our society. Today in countries that have the death penalty the condemned person is kept under even more rigorous surveillance on Death Row until he or she is executed. Roman law offered the prisoner a choice. Originally the magistrate was obliged to give the condemned the opportunity to escape after the sentence had been passed. The self-imposed penalty of permanent exile was considered an acceptable substitute for the death penalty. It was recognized by a decree of *aqua et igni interdictio* ('refusal of water and fire') pronounced by the court after the prisoner's departure. Its effect was to withdraw all legal protection from him, and to threaten death should he return illegally. In the first century AD this kind of exile was replaced by a formal sentence of deportation to a particular place, e.g. the island of Gyara, which was no more than a rock pyramid with a base of 4×4 kms (2.5×2.5 miles). It was to the Romans what Devil's Island was to nineteenth-century France or Alcatraz to twentieth-century

America. Were Paul in fact confronted with this choice, how would he have acted? I doubt that he would have changed the conclusion he reached some years earlier when he was imprisoned in Ephesus.

For me to live is Christ, and to die is gain. If it is to be life in the flesh, that means fruitful labour for me. Yet which I shall choose I cannot tell. I am hard pressed between the two. My desire is to depart and be with Christ, for that is far better. But to remain in the flesh is more necessary on your account. Convinced of this, I know that I shall remain and continue with you all, for your progress and joy in the faith   (Phil. 1: 21–5).

Death might be Paul's personal preference, because it would mean immediate, permanent union with Christ, but by God's will he was an apostle. He had an obligation, from which no one could release him, to bear the gospel to others. Paul, in consequence, would certainly have chosen life, as he had previously done theoretically in Ephesus. Gyara might not be the ideal place to live, but there were souls there to be saved, and he would meet many others on the long journey to the east. If we accept the witness of Eusebius, 'It is recorded that in Nero's reign Paul was beheaded in Rome' (*History of the Church* 2. 25; cf. 3. 1), we must conclude that Paul was not given the choice that was his right. The magistrate no doubt felt it prudent to follow the example of the emperor in considering it imperative to execute any Christian brought before him. He did not demean himself, however, by ordering the sort of torture that had made Nero a monster of depravity. Paul, as befitted a Roman citizen, should be beheaded. It is unlikely that Paul had to wait long for the sentence to be carried out. In any case he needed little time to prepare his soul. The usual convulsion of the instinct for self-preservation would have been brought under control quickly. For one who had striven throughout his ministry 'to manifest in the body the life of Jesus' (2 Cor. 4: 10–11), it was the supreme grace to have the opportunity to die in witness as Jesus had done. Paul's 'desire to depart and to be with Christ' (Phil. 1: 23) was finally realized under the best possible conditions. As he serenely bared his neck for the sword of the executioner, he knew that his death would be the resonant proclamation that he had kept the faith.

Epilogue

Many rejoiced when the news of Paul's death reached the eastern end of the Mediterranean. He had never been a favourite of those who believed that Christianity should remain profoundly rooted in Judaism. They were scandalized by his refusal to circumcise his pagan converts. His willingness to permit convert Jews to continue their religious practices did nothing to moderate their antagonism. That, after all, was not only their right but a God-given obligation. This situation did not last long. Once Paul became fully conscious of the threat posed by the Law, he forbade Jewish converts to circumcise their children and to observe the dietary laws. This ignited the anger of Jewish Christians who threatened his life on his last visit to Jerusalem. In the second and third centuries Jewish Christian vilification of Paul became systematic. The basic tactic was to contrast him with the orthodox Peter. In the *Epistula Petri*, Peter is made to say, 'Some from among the Gentiles have rejected my lawful preaching and have preferred a lawless and absurd doctrine of the man who is my enemy' (2: 3). The *Kerygmata Petrou* describes Peter's relationship to Paul 'as light upon darkness, as knowledge upon ignorance, as healing upon sickness' (II II. 17: 3). The same document goes on to question Paul's qualifications as an authentic minister of the gospel. The vision at the core of Paul's conversion is dismissed as 'the work of a wicked demon' (H XVII. 16: 6). Even if Paul did have an encounter with Jesus, he falsified what he learned from him Peter says,

But if you were visited by him for the space of an hour and were instructed by him and thereby have become an apostle, then proclaim his words, expound what he has taught, be a friend to his apostles and do not contend with me, who am his confidant; for you have in hostility withstood me, who am a firm rock, the foundation stone of the church. If you were not an enemy, then you would not slander me and revile my preaching in order that I may not be believed when I proclaim what I have heard in my own person from the Lord, as if I were undoubtedly condemned, and you were acknowledged   (H XVII. 19: 4–5).

No one leapt to Paul's defence. This was not because he lacked supporters. It was rather that retort was unnecessary. The slanders emanated from a group within the Church that was rapidly being marginalized. The Judaeo-Christian gospel had no success in Europe, and after the expulsion of Jews from their heartland in AD 135, its supporters drifted north-east and into oblivion.

The communities that Paul founded needed perhaps a generation to shake themselves free of his overwhelming background presence. Then they began to come to a true appreciation of his importance. This showed itself in a renewed appreciation of his letters. Even though these addressed specific problems in different churches, they were recognized as enshrining principles of perennial value. Thus communities carefully conserved what they had received, and requested those that he had sent to other churches.

Partial collections of Paul's letters developed in Macedonia (1 and 2 Thessalonians, and Philippians) and in Achaia (Romans, 1 and 2 Corinthians, and perhaps Galatians). Both had easy and frequent connections with Ephesus, where the partial collections were combined, perhaps by Onesimus, the ex-slave mentioned in the letter to Philemon. He was a native of Colossae, and subsequently bishop of Ephesus.

The collection of the letters, and the fact that they were made easily available throughout the Christian world, clearly betrays the intention of prolonging the influence of Paul. Others animated by the same concern went a step further, and wrote letters in the name of Paul. Believing that he had to be updated in order to confront the changing situations of the Pauline communities, they clothed their views with his authority. Ephesians is by and large a faithful commentary on, and expansion of, the ideas in Colossians. 1 Timothy and Titus, which as personal letters were inspired by 2 Timothy, institutionalize church ministries in a way that would have been alien to Paul. None the less these three letters were accepted into the definitive collection of Pauline letters very early.

These thirteen letters were certainly known and acknowledged as authoritative in the second century. Scholars have detected their literary influence on other works of the New Testament, notably, the Johannine corpus, Hebrews, 1 and 2 Peter (the latter says, 'there are some things in them [Paul's letters] hard to understand, and which the ignorant and unstable twist to their own destruction, as they do the other scriptures' 3: 16), James, and Jude. Other early Christian writers also betray their debt to Paul, for example, Hermas, Barnabas, Clement, Ignatius, Polycarp, and the author of the *Didache*.

On none, however, did the letters make such an impact as on Marcion, who became a dominant figure in the second-century Church. He believed that Paul was the only authentic apostle. He took Paul's refusal to allow the Law any role in the church to imply a radical rejection of the Jewish roots of Christianity. This became the principle that guided his dissection of the New Testament into authentic and inauthentic elements. He looted Paul to create his own vision of revelation.

Paul would have been equally dismayed by his reception among the Valentinian Gnostics. They creatively exploited his obscurity, making particular use of his references to a great 'mystery'. His allusions to 'flesh' and 'spirit' as different facets of the human personality were transformed into a radical dualism. The Gnostics were convinced that they possessed the 'knowledge' (gnosis) which freed their spirits from the fetters of matter. Their illumination brought them into the Kingdom of Light.

As time went on, the church rejected both Marcion and Gnosticism. It would have been understandable had Paul, their claimed source, been tarred with the same brush, and also set aside as unrepresentative of the true gospel. When we couple this with the strident anti-Pauline polemic of the Judaeo-Christians, it is extraordinary that the Pauline letters won a place in the canon of the New Testament.

Certainly by the end of the second century Paul's letters were cherished by too wide an audience to be withdrawn from circulation. In addition their popularity inspired a desire to know more about their author. The hints in the letters, and the stories in the Acts of the Apostles, only stimulated an appetite for graphic, dramatic details. This need was met by a mid-second-century author with a vivid imagination and no historical sources. The *Acts of Paul*, which originally included the *Acts of Paul and Thekla* and the *Martyrdom of Paul*, is a vivid story that both edified and entertained. Not only does it provide the only word-picture of Paul (3: 1), it contains all the classical dramatic ingredients of travel, frustrated love, great danger, and miraculous rescues (e.g. when Paul is condemned to the beasts he is protected by a lion whom he had baptized earlier). Not surprisingly, the *Acts of Paul* attracted readers throughout the ancient world. In places as far apart as Syria and North Africa it was considered canonical scripture. In addition to the story, however, it served a theological agenda that Paul would have repudiated. The heroic figure of the miracle-working apostle is hijacked to proclaim the renunciation of ordinary life and values. To be an authentic Christian demanded life-long celibacy.

The stature of Paul was further enhanced by his endorsement by the first great Christian theologian of the post-apostolic age. Irenaeus (*c.* 130–*c.* 200) was the earliest and strongest bridge between east and west. Born in Smyrna in Asia Minor, where he sat at the feet of Polycarp, he studied in Rome, and ended his career as bishop of Lyons in France. In his great work, *Against All Heresies*, he argues both against those, such as Marcion, who claimed too much for Paul, alleging that 'Paul alone knew the truth' (3. 13. 1), and against those 'who do not recognize Paul as an apostle' (3. 15. 1). The respect that Irenaeus accorded to, and demanded for, Paul is formally articulated in the foundational principle of his work. The test of doctrinal truth for all churches was their agreement with 'that tradition deriving from the apostles, of the very great, very ancient, and universally known Church founded and organized at Rome by the two most glorious apostles, Peter and Paul' (3. 3. 2). It is not surprising, in consequence, that Irenaeus cites or alludes to Paul over 400 times, and evokes every letter with the exception of that to Philemon. What Irenaeus did not do, however, was to take over Paul's theological vision. In the last analysis the letters were merely

238

exploited as a quarry of proof-texts. This was to be Paul's fate throughout all subsequent centuries. An extremely selective approach has been characteristic of the use of his letters in all the great theological debates. If Augustine exaggerated an aspect of Paul's description of unredeemed humanity, the Reformers tore out of its love-filled social context his stress on the importance of faith.

Paul's analysis of the world in which he had to operate is still verified in our contemporary society. Such accuracy and insight should give us confidence in the solutions that he proposed in order to make Christianity an authentic instrument of change. It is not that the Pauline version of Christianity has failed, it has never been seriously tried.

Notes

1 The Early Years

1. Jerome is the only author to assert Paul's Galilean origins (*Commentaria in Epistolam ad Philemon*, on vv. 23–4 and *De viris illustribus* 5). He derived it from a source whose credibility is strengthened by the fact that its creation profited no one.

2. A good summary of the history of Tarsus is to be found in W. Ward Gasque, 'Tarsus', in *The Anchor Bible Dictionary* (New York: Doubleday, 1992), 6. 333–4. On the 'Tarsian Discourses' of Dio Chrysostom (33–4), see C. P. Jones, *The Roman World of Dio Chrysostom* (Cambridge, Mass.: Harvard University Press, 1978), 71–82.

3. See especially Richard B. Hays, *Echoes of Scripture in the Letters of Paul* (New Haven: Yale University Press, 1989).

4. For further details, see Thomas Schmeller, 'Stoics, Stoicism', in *Anchor Bible Dictionary*, 6. 210–14.

5. For the route see the *Barrington Atlas of the Greek and Roman World*, ed. R. Talbert (Princeton: Princeton University Press, 2000), maps 66, 67, 68, 69, 70.

6. For an eyewitness description of first-century Jerusalem, see Josephus, *The Jewish War*, 5. 136–247.

7. For more details on Pharisees and Sadducees in Jerusalem at the time of Paul, see John P. Meier, *A Marginal Jew*, Anchor Bible Reference Library (New York: Doubleday, 2001), 3. 289–487.

8. 'It is typical of Jerusalem that a large section of the population lived chiefly or entirely on charity or relief' (J. Jeremias, *Jerusalem at the Time of Jesus* (London: SCM press, 1969), 111–12).

9. The number of Jews who did not marry could be counted on two hands; see T. Thornton, 'Jewish Batchelors in New Testament Times', *Journal of Theological Studies*, 23 (1972), 444–5.

10. On this crucial insight, which is fundamental to all of Paul's thought, see Terence L. Donaldson, 'Zealot and Convert: The Origin of Paul's Christ–Torah Antithesis', *Catholic Biblical Quarterly*, 51 (1989), 655–82.

Notes

2 Conversion and Its Consequences

1. *Barrington Atlas of the Greek and Roman World*, ed. R. Talbert (Princeton: Princeton University Press, 2000), maps 70, 69.
2. Such reticence contrasts with Luke's vivid account of Paul's collapse on hearing the heavenly voice say, 'Saul, Saul, why do you persecute me?' Luke, however, gives three accounts of Paul's conversion (Acts 9: 3–9; 22: 6–11; 26: 12–18), which differ in significant details. It is probable, therefore, that Luke, who was not an eye-witness, embroidered the essence of the event as revealed by Paul into graphic stories designed to forward his theological agenda.
3. David F. Graf, 'Nabateans' in *The Anchor Bible Dictionary* (New York: Doubleday, 1992), 4. 970–3.
4. For the history and archaeology of Damascus, see Ross Burns, *Monuments of Syria: An Historical Guide* (London/New York: Tauris, 1992), 72–108.
5. For the texts on which this description is based, see my 'Prisca and Aquila: Travelling Tent-Makers and Church-Builders', *Bible Review*, 8/6 (December 1992), 40–51.
6. On Paul's knowledge of the historical Jesus, see especially James Dunn, *The Theology of Paul the Apostle* (Grand Rapids, Mich.: Eerdmans, 1998), 182–206.
7. For a detailed analysis of all the texts, see my ' "Even death on a cross": Crucifixion in the Pauline Letters', in *The Cross in Christian Tradition from Paul to Bonaventure*, ed. E. Dreyer (New York: Paulist Press, 2000), 21–50.

3 Apprenticeship in Antioch

1. For this reconstruction of the beginnings of the church of Antioch, see Justin Taylor, 'Why were the Disciples First Called "Christians" at Antioch?' *Revue Biblique*, 101 (1994), 75–94.
2. For a detailed account of the history and archaeology of Antioch, see Glanville Downey, *A History of Antioch in Syria from Seleucus to the Arab Conquest* (Princeton: Princeton University Press, 1961). A convenient overview is furnished by F. W. Norris, 'Antioch of Syria', in *The Anchor Bible Dictionary* (New York: Doubleday, 1992), 1. 263–9.
3. On the problem of space for first-century Christians, see my *St Paul's Corinth: Texts and Archaeology*, 3rd edn, (Collegeville, Minn.: Liturgical Press, 2002), 178–85.
4. E. P. Sanders, 'Jewish Association with Gentiles and Galatians 2: 11–14' in *The Conversation Continues: Studies in Paul and John in Honour of J. Louis Martyn*, ed. R. T. Fortna and B. Gaventa (Nashville: Abingdon, 1990), 170–88.
5. The complexity of these chapters is well analysed by M.-É. Boismard and A. Lamouille, *Les Actes des deux apôtres*, Études bibliques, nouvelle série 12–14 (Paris: Gabalda, 1990), 2. 229–41, 265–78, 357–60; 3. 179–94, and Justin Taylor, *Les Actes des deux apôtres*, Études bibliques, nouvelle série 23 (Paris: Gabalda, 1994), 5. 127–96.

6. See the *Barrington Atlas of the Greek and Roman World*, ed. R. Talbert (Princeton: Princeton University Press, 2000), map 3.
7. On roads in Asia Minor, see Stephen Mitchell, *Anatolia: Land, Men and Gods in Asia Minor* (Oxford: Clarendon press, 1993), General Index, s.v. 'roads'.
8. The route is traced in great detail in the *Barrington Atlas*, maps 61, 65, 62, 63, 66 successively.
9. The trace of this route is named ibid., maps 65, 62, 65.
10. See ibid., map 66.
11. The best primary source for the conditions under which Paul travelled is Apuleius, *Metamorphoses*, trans. J. A. Hanson, Loeb Classical Library (Cambridge Mass.: Harvard University Press, 1996), with the marvellous synthetic commentary of F. Millar, 'The World of the *Golden Ass*', *Journal of Roman Studies*, 71 (1981) 63–75. A racier translation is given by R. Graves, *Metamorphoses or The Golden Ass*, Penguin Classics (London: Penguin, 1950). For a more general treatment, see L. Casson, *Travel in the Ancient World* (London: Allen & Unwin, 1979), and J.-M André and M.-F. Baslez, *Voyager dans l'Antiquité* (Paris: Fayard, 1993).

4 A Journey into Europe

1. On the complexities of Acts 16–18, see M.-É. Boismard and A. Lamouille, *Les Actes des deux apôtres*, Études bibliques, nouvelle série 12–14 (Paris: Gabalda, 1990), 2. 285–303, 363–6; 3. 207–34, and Justin Taylor, *Les Actes des deux apôtres*, Études bibliques, nouvelle série, (Paris: Gabalda, 1994), 5. 227–335.
2. The best map of the frontiers of the Roman provinces in Paul's time is in the *Tübinger Atlas des Vorderen Orients*, BV7.
3. *Barrington Atlas of the Greek and Roman World*, ed. R. Talbert (Princeton: Princeton University Press, 2000), map 62.
4. For the wide range of suggestions, see Victor Furnish, *II Corinthians*, Anchor Bible 32A (Garden City, NJ: Doubleday, 1984), 547–9, or Ralph Martin, *2 Corinthians*, Word Bible Commentary (Waco, Tex.: Word, 1986), 412–16. The thorn in Paul's flesh in fact was hostility within the communities he had founded.
5. A number of scholars think that the Galatians evangelized by Paul were inhabitants of Antioch, Iconium, Lystra and Derbe, cities in the southern part of the Roman province of Galatia. This can now be absolutely excluded; see my 'Gal 4:13–14 and the Recipients of *Galatians*', *Revue Biblique*, 105 (1998), 202–7. Therefore, the Galatians in question must be the ethnic Galatians of the northern part of the Roman province.
6. On the Celts in Galatia, see in particular Stephen Mitchell, *Anatolia: Land, Men and Gods in Asia Minor* (Oxford: Clarendon Press, 1993), 1. 42–58. For a graphic display of the movement of the Celts into Greece and Asia Minor, see J. Haywood, *The Historical Atlas of the Celtic World* (London: Thames & Hudson, 2001), 38–41.
7. On the topography of Pessinus, see Stephen Mitchell, *Anatolia: Land, Men and Gods in Asia Minor* (Oxford: Clarendon Press, 1993), 1. 105, which deals with its creation and status at 1. 86–9.

8. *Barrington Atlas*, maps 62 and 56.
9. See Edwin Yamauchi, 'Troas', in *The Anchor Bible Dictionary* (New York: Doubleday, 1992), 6. 666–7.
10. See L. Casson, *Travel in the Ancient World* (London: Allen & Unwin, 1979), 149–62.
11. *Barrington Atlas*, maps 56 and 51.
12. A nautical mile is 6,080 feet (1,853.2 m), as opposed to 5,280 feet for a statute mile. A knot is one nautical mile per hour.
13. All that is known about Paul's Philippi is to be found in Peter Pilhofer, *Philippi*, vol. 1: *Die erste christliche Gemeinde Europas*; vol. 2: *Katalog der Inscriften von Philippi*, Wissenschaftliche Untersuchungen zum Neuen Testament 87 and 119 (Tübingen: Mohr Siebeck, 1995 and 2000). An adequate summary can be found in Holland Hendrix, 'Philippi', in *Anchor Bible Dictionary*, 5. 313–17.
14. In the mid-first century AD a woman called Iunia Theodora was the commercial/diplomatic agent in Corinth for the Lycians; see my *St Paul's Corinth: Texts and Archaeology* (Collegeville, Minn.: Liturgical Press, 2002), 82–4.
15. For the complex tradition history of Acts 16: 13–40, see Boismard and Lamouille, *Les Actes des deux apôtres*, 2. 288–93, 3. 214–23; Taylor, *Les Actes des deux apôtres*, 5. 252–64.
16. For the route of the Via Egnatia across northern Greece, see *Barrington Atlas*, maps 49 and 51. There is an informative guide by F. O'Sullivan, *The Egnatian Way* (Newton Abbot: David & Charles, 1972).
17. Despite its importance, we know virtually nothing about first-century Thessalonica: see Christoph vom Brocke, *Thessaloniki—Stadt des Kassander und Gemeinde des Paulus: Eine frühe christliche Gemeinde in ihrer heidnischen Umwelt*, Wissenschaftliche Untersuchungen zum Neuen Testament 2.125 (Tübingen: Mohr Siebeck, 2001).
18. For the working conditions of artisans in Paul's time, see Ronald Hock, *The Social Context of Paul's Ministry: Tentmaking and Apostleship* (Philadelphia: Fortress Press, 1980), and my *St Paul's Corinth*, 192–8.
19. This crucial link between Paul's preaching and the social expectations of his hearers was first worked out by R. Jewett, *The Thessalonian Correspondence: Pauline Rhetoric and Millenarian Piety*. Foundations and Facets (Philadelphia: Fortress Press, 1986), 127–32.
20. The relationships between Thessalonica, Beroea, Methone and Pydna, and the roads linking them, are depicted in the *Barrington Atlas*, map 50.

5 South to Achaia

1. It can be followed easily in the *Barrington Atlas of the Greek and Roman World*, ed. R. Talbert (Princeton: Princeton University Press, 2000), map 57.
2. For Athens in Paul's day, see Hubert Martin, jun., 'Athens', in *The Anchor Bible Dictionary* (New York: Doubleday, 1992), 1. 513–18, and D. J. Geagan, 'Roman Athens: Some Aspects of Life and Culture I: 86 BC–AD 267', in *Aufstieg und Niedergang der römischen Welt*, ed. H. Temporini and W. Haase (Berlin: De Gruyter), II 7.1 (1979), 371–437.

Notes

3. For the justification of dividing 1 Thess. into two originally independent letters and their chronological relationship, see my *Paul: A Critical Life* (Oxford: Clarendon Press, 1996), 104–10.

4. Two ancient descriptions of the road exist. Pausanias (*Description of Greece* 1. 36. 3–44) walked from Athens to Corinth, while Strabo (*Geography* 9. 1. 1–16) travelled the same route in the opposite direction. See *Barrington Atlas*, maps 58 and 59.

5. On the archaeological work done, see N. Verdelis, 'Der Diolkos am Isthmos von Korinth', in *Mitteilungen des deutschen archäologischen Instituts, athenische Abteilung*, 71 (1956), 51–9, and J. Wiseman, *The Land of the Ancient Corinthians* (Göteburg: Aström, 1978), 45–6.

6. The city is described in some detail by Pausanias, *Description of Greece* 2. 1–5. 5, and by Strabo, *Geography* 8. 6. 20–3, both of which are commented on in my *St Paul's Corinth: Texts and Archaeology* (Collegeville, Minn.: Liturgical Press, 2002), 5–39 and 52–66, which in addition deals with all other aspects of the ancient city. Synthetic versions appear in my 'Corinth', in *Anchor Bible Dictionary*, 1. 1134–9, and in my 'The Corinth that Saint Paul Saw', *Biblical Archaeologist*, 47 (1984), 147–59.

7. For AD 41, rather than the conventional AD 49, as the date of the Edict of Claudius, see my *St Paul's Corinth*, 152–60. On Paul's hosts and employers, see my 'Prisca and Aquila: Travelling Tent-Makers and Church-Builders', *Bible Review*, 8/6 (December 1992), 40–51.

8. The authenticity of 2 Thess. and its precise relationship to 1 Thess. 1: 1–2: 12 and 4: 3–5: 28 has been ably demonstrated by R. Jewett, *The Thessalonian Correspondence: Pauline Rhetoric and Millenarian Piety*, Foundations and Facets (Philadelphia: Fortress Press, 1986), 186–92.

9. See E. Richards, *The Secretary in the Letters of Paul*, Wissenschaftliche Untersuchungen zum Neuen Testament 2. 42 (Tübingen: Mohr Siebeck, 1991), and my *St Paul the Letter-Writer* (Collegeville, Minn.: Liturgical Press, 1995).

10. On benefaction and gratitude as essential social virtues by a contemporary of Paul, see Lucius Annaeus Seneca, *De Beneficiis*, in the English translation of John W. Basore, *Seneca: Moral Essays*, Loeb Classical Library (London: Heinemann/Cambridge, Mass.: Harvard University Press, 1958), vol. 3.

11. For Gallio and the date of his sojourn in Corinth, see my *St Paul's Corinth*, 161–9.

6 Antioch and Jerusalem

1. *Barrington Atlas of the Greek and Roman World*, ed. R. Talbert (Princeton: Princeton University Press, 2000), maps 69, 68, 67.

2. On the difficulties of using Acts 15 as a historical account of the meeting between Antioch and Jerusalem, see M.-É. Boismard and A. Lamouille, *Les Actes des deux apôtres*, Études bibliques, nouvelle série 12–14; (Paris: Gabalda, 1990), 2. 279–85, 361–3; 3. 195–205; and Justin Taylor, *Les Actes des deux apôtres*, Études bibliques, nouvelle série 23 (Paris: Gabalda, 1994), 5. 197–225; *idem*, 'The Jerusalem Decrees (Acts 15:20, 29 and 21:25) and the Incident at Antioch (Ga, 2:11–14)', *New Testament Studies*, 47 (2001), 372–80.

3. For documentation of the details that follow, see my 'Nationalism and Church Policy: Reflections on Gal 2:1–14', in *Communion et Réunion: Mélanges Jean-Marie Roger Tillard*, Bibliotheca ephemeridum theologicarum lovaniensium 121, ed. G. R. Evans and M. Gourgues (Leuven: Peeters, 1995), 283–91.

4. See in particular Josephus, *Antiquities of the Jews* 14. 241–61, and C. Saulnier, ' Lois romaines sur les Juifs selon Flavius Josèphe', *Revue Biblique*, 88 (1981), 161–98.

5. See Joachim Jeremias, *Jerusalem in the Time of Jesus: An Investigation into Economic and Social Conditions during the New Testament Period* (London: SCM Press, 1969), 111–19.

6. The concerns of first-century Pharisees are laid out by Jacob Neusner, *The Rabbinic Traditions Concerning the Pharisees before 70*, 3 vols (Leiden: Brill, 1971), and more succinctly by John P. Meier, *A Marginal Jew*, Anchor Bible Reference Library (New York: Doubleday, 2001), 3. 313–30.

7. For more detail, see my 'The Divorced Woman in 1 Cor. 7: 10–11', *Journal of Biblical Literature*, 100 (1981), 901–6.

7 The First Year in Ephesus

1. *Barrington Atlas of the Greek and Roman World*, ed. R. Talbert (Princeton: Princeton University Press, 2000), maps 62, 65, and 61.

2. 'The country around Lyodicea produces sheep that are excellent, not only for the softness of their wool, in which they surpass even the Milesian wool, but also for its raven-black colour, so that the Loadiceans derive splendid revenue from it, as do also the neighbouring Colossians from the colour which bears the same name' (Strabo, *Geography* 12. 8. 6).

3. For Ephesus at the time of Paul, see my *Paul: A Critical Life* (Oxford: Clarendon Press, 1996), 166–71, with the references there given, and Richard Oster, 'Ephesus', in *The Anchor Bible Dictionary* (New York: Doubleday, 1992), 2. 542–9.

4. Our only source for the background and movements of Apollos is Acts 18: 24–8, which survives in two very different versions; see M.-É. Boismard and A. Lamouille, *Les Actes des deux apôtres*, Études bibliques, nouvelle série 12 14 (Paris: Gabalda, 1990), 1. 137–8, 2. 305–6, 3. 237 8; and Justin Taylor, *Les Actes des deux apôtres* Études bibliques, nouvelle série 23 (Paris: Gabalda, 1994), 6. 13 22.

5. As far as I know, I am alone in maintaining this hypothesis; see my 'John the Baptist and Jesus: History and Hypotheses', *New Testament Studies*, 36 (1990), 359–74. A representative selection of other views is provided by M. Wolter, 'Apollos und die ephesinischen Johannesjünger (Act 18: 24–19: 7)', *Zeitschrift für die neutestamentliche Wissenschaft* 78 (1987), 49–73, and Taylor, *Les Actes des deux apôtres*, 6. 13–22.

6. *Barrington Atlas*, maps 56 and 61.

7. Paul's concern in Gal. 1–2 to distance himself from Jerusalem has given rise in some quarters to the belief that his opponents in Galatia and elsewhere came from Jerusalem. It is more probable, however, that his adversaries invoked the authority of Jerusalem, whose perspective on the Law they fully shared,

in much the same way that conservative Catholics today argue on the basis of what the Pope says without any mandate from the Vatican. It is unlikely that Jerusalem had any idea where Paul's churches were located, whereas Antioch had a right to know.

8. The best reconstruction of the way the delegation presented their version of the Gospel is to be found in J. Louis Martyn, *Galatians*, Anchor Bible (New York: Doubleday, 1997), 302–6. I quote a slightly different earlier version in *Paul: A Critical Life*, 196–8.

8 The Second Year in Ephesus

1. T. Mommsen, *Römisches Strafrecht* (Graz: Akademische Druck- und Verlagsanstalt, 1955), 299–305, 945–8.
2. It was long thought that these captivity letters were written during Paul's imprisonment in Rome (Acts 28: 16–20), but this view has now largely been abandoned for very good reasons. See, e.g., *The New Jerome Biblical Commentary*, ed. R. E. Brown *et al.* (Englewood Cliffs, NJ: Prentice-Hall, 1990) 792, 870, 1336; and in more detail my *Paul: A Critical Life* (Oxford: Clarendon Press, 1996), 175–82.
3. The epistle to the Philippians is in fact made up of three originally independent letters written in the following order: *Letter A*, 4: 10–20; *Letter B*, 1: 1–3: 1 and 4: 2–9; *Letter C*, 3: 2–4: 1. For details see my *Paul: A Critical Life*, 215–20.
4. P. Lampe, 'Keine "Sklavenflucht" des Onesimus', *Zeitschrift für die neutestamentliche Wissenschaft*, 76 (1985), 135–7.
5. The most convincing reconstruction of the Colossian 'heresy' is that of T. J. Sappington, *Revelation and Redemption at Colossae*, Journal for the Study of the New Testament sup 53 (Sheffield: Journal for the Study of the Old Testament Press, 1991); note especially the summary on p. 170.

9 Conversations with Corinth

1. The great theoretician of rhetoric, Quintilian, called this arrangement 'Homeric' (*Institutio Oratoria* 5. 12. 14) because of Homer's description of the battle dispositions on the plain before Troy. 'Nestor put his charioteers with their horses and cars in the front, and at the back a mass of first-rate infantry to serve as a rearguard. In between, he stationed his inferior troops, so that even shirkers would be forced to fight' (*Iliad* 4. 299).
2. Good introductions to Philo of Alexandria are to be found in Emile Schürer, *The History of the Jewish People in the Age of Jesus Christ*, rev. and ed. G. Vermes, F. Millar, and M. Goodman (Edinburgh: T.&T. Clark, 1973–87), 3. 809–89, and in Peder Borgen, 'Philo of Alexandria', in *The Anchor Bible Dictionary* (New York: Doubleday, 1992), 5. 333–42.
3. For Apollos as the one who integrated Paul's preaching into a Philonic framework, see the series of articles by Richard A. Horsley, 'Pneumatikos vs. Psychikos: Distinctions of Spiritual Status among the Corinthians', *Harvard Theological Review*, 69 (1976), 269–88; 'Wisdom of Word and Words of Wisdom in Corinth', *Catholic Biblical Quarterly*, 39 (1977), 224–39; ' "How can

some of you say that there is no resurrection from the dead?"': Spiritual Elitism in Corinth', *Novum Testamentum*, 20 (1978), 203–31.

4. This visit is not mentioned in the Acts of the Apostles, but it is a necessary deduction from 2 Cor. 12: 14 and 13: 2; see my *Paul: A Critical Life* (Oxford: Clarendon Press, 1996), 290–1.
5. The arguments that found this reconstruction of what happened at Corinth are to be found in C. K. Barrett, '*Ho adikesas* (2 Cor. 7, 12)', in *Verborum Veritas: Festschrift für Gustav Stälin*, ed. O. Bocher and K. Haacker (Wuppertal: Brochaus, 1970), 149–57.
6. *Barrington Atlas of the Greek and Roman World*, ed. R. Talbert (Princeton: Princeton University Press, 2000), maps 55 and 50.

10 Macedonia and Illyricum

1. *Barrington Atlas of the Greek and Roman World*, ed. R. Talbert (Princeton: Princeton University Press, 2000), maps 56 and 61.
2. See Edwin M. Yamauchi, 'Troas', in *The Anchor Bible Dictionary* (New York: Doubleday, 1992), 6. 666–7.
3. *Barrington Atlas*, maps 51 and 52.
4. Immediately before Paul's departure from Ephesus (Acts 20: 1), Luke narrates the riot of the silversmiths (Acts 19: 23–40). The temptation to relate these two events as cause and effect should be resisted. This narrative is entirely from the hand of Luke (M.-É. Boismard and A. Lamouille, *Les Actes des deux apôtres*, Études bibliques, nouvelle série 13–14 (Paris: Gabalda, 1990), 2. 314 15; 3. 243). Its historicity is bitterly disputed. For E. Haenchen it is so full of unanswered questions and internal contradictions that it is devoid of historical value (*The Acts of the Apostles: A Commentary* (Philadelphia: Westminster, 1971), 569–79). J. Taylor is less negative than Haenchen, but still cannot specify a historical nucleus (*Les Actes des deux apôtres*, Études bibliques, nouvelle série 30 (Paris: Gabalda, 1996), 6. 43–59).
5. *Barrington Atlas*, maps 50 and 51.
6. The division of 2 Cor. into two letters, the first consisting of chs 1–9, the second of chs 10 13, is widely accepted; see e.g. V. P. Furnish, *II Corinthians*, Anchor Bible (Garden City: Doubleday, 1984), 35–41. For the relative dating of the two documents, see my 'The Date of 2 Corinthians 10–13', *Australian Biblical Review*, 39 (1991), 31–43.
7. For details, see my '*Pneumatikoi* and Judaizers in 2 Cor. 2: 14–4: 6', *Australian Biblical Review*, 34 (1986), 42–58.
8. For the trace of the Via Egnatia across Macedonia, see *Barrington Atlas*, map 49.
9. There was no Roman province of Illyricum at the time of Paul. In AD 9 it had been divided into Pannonia and Dalmatia, both of which lay north of the province of Macedonia (see 'Illyricum', in *The Oxford Classical Dictionary*, ed. S. Hornblower and A. Spawforth (Oxford: Oxford University Press, 1996), 747). The western part of Macedonia, however, was inhabited by ethnic Illyrians. According to Strabo (*Geography* 7. 7. 4), their territory extended from the Adriatic coast to Pylon on the Via Egnatia; see *Barrington Atlas*, maps 1 and 49.

With a common sense unusual in those who comment on Rom. 15: 19, W. Sanday and A. C. Headlam say: 'St. Paul would have followed this road [the Via Egnatia] as far as Thessalonica, and if pointing Westward he had asked the names of the mountain region and of the peoples inhabiting it, he would have been told that it was "Illyria" ' (*A Critical and Exegetical Commentary on the Epistle to the Romans*, ICC (Edinburgh: T.&T. Clark, 1902), 407–8).

10. For good surveys of the suggestions (they are nothing more), see Furnish, *II Corinthians*, 547–9, or R. P. Martin, *2 Corinthians*, Word Bible Commentary (Waco, Tex.: Word Books, 1986), 412–16.

11 Farewell to the East

1. *Barrington Atlas of the Greek and Roman World*, ed. R. Talbert (Princeton: Princeton University Press, 2000), maps 49, 54, 55 and 58.
2. See J. G. Harris, 'Old Age', in *The Anchor Bible Dictionary* (New York: Doubleday, 1992), 5. 10–12.
3. The dramatic wedge-shape of Cabo São Vicente (the Sacrum Promunturium in the *Barrington Atlas*, map 26) obviously impressed the ancients more than the Magnum Promunturium (modern Cabo da Roca north of the mouth of the river Tagus), which is in fact some 30 miles (48 km) further out to the west.
4. On the presence of Jews in the Iberian Peninsula, see W. P. Bowers, 'Jewish Communities in Spain in the Time of Paul the Apostle', *Journal of Theological Studies*, 26 (1975), 395–402, and the map in *The Times Atlas of the Bible*, ed. J. B. Pritchard (London: Times Books, 1987), 170–1. The bewildering number of Iberian dialects is graphically illustrated by A. García y Bellido, 'Die Latinisierung Hispaniens', in *Aufstieg und Niedergang der römischen Welt* (Berlin: de Gruyter, 1972), I. 1. 462–91, here 476–7.
5. The verb used by Paul is *propemto*, which is literally 'to help on one's journey', but 'in earliest Christianity it becomes almost a technical term for the provision made by a church for missionary support' (J. D. G. Dunn, *Romans*, Word Bible Commentary 38B (Dallas: Word Books, 1988), 872). The church, of course, would accept such a financial responsibility only if it had commissioned the apostle. In writing the letter, Paul contents himself with a delicate hint. A specific request would come later, when he had established himself in Rome.
6. For accessible approaches to the argument of Romans, see Brendan Byrne, *Reckoning with Romans: A Contemporary Reading of Paul's Gospel* (Wilmington, Del.: Glazier, 1986), and Charles D. Myers, 'Romans, Epistle to the', in *Anchor Bible Dictionary*, 5. 816–30, especially 821–5.
7. With all modern commentators I consider ch. 16 an integral part of Romans; see in particular H. Gamble, *The Textual History of the Letter to the Romans* (Grand Rapids, Mich.: Eerdmans, 1977).
8. *Tous ek tôn Aristoboulou/Narkissou* can only be translated 'the Christians among the slaves of Aristobulus or of Narcissus'; so F. Blass, A. Debrunner and R. W. Funk, *A Greek Grammar of the New Testament and Other Early Christian Literature* (Cambridge: Cambridge University Press/Chicago: University of Chicago Press, 1961), §162(5). Translations such as 'those who belong to the

family of Aristobulus/Narcissus' (Revised Standard Version, New Revised Standard Version) should be corrected.

9. The climax came in AD 66, according to Josephus: 'Eleazar, the son of Ananias the high priest, a very bold youth, who at that time was governor of the Temple persuaded those who officiated in the divine service to receive no gift or sacrifice for any foreigner. This was the true beginning of our war with the Romans' (*Jewish War* 2. 409).

10. *Barrington Atlas*, map 57. We know of Paul's final journey to Jerusalem only from Luke, who takes it from his 'we-source', a schematic travel diary kept by a companion of Paul (see M.-E. Boismard and A. Lamouille, *Les Actes des deux apôtres*, Études bibliques, nouvelle série 13 (Paris: Gabalda, 1990), 2. 215–27). In itself this is sufficient to guarantee that Paul in fact made a circuit of the Aegean. But when? Sometime earlier in his career might appear to be suggested by the fact that the 'we-source' does not explicitly mention the collection, which from Paul's perspective is the motive for the journey. This silence, however, is not absolute. The majority of commentators see a reference to the collection in Acts 24: 17. More importantly, J. Taylor finds a further reference in Acts 21: 19, i.e. within the 'we-source' (*Les Actes des deux apôtres*, Études bibliques, nouvelle série 30 (Paris: Gabalda, 1996), 6. 108). Moreover, a journey from Greece to Jerusalem and then to Rome is precisely what Paul plans in Rom. 15: 23–32. Finally, Paul's fear of what might be awaiting him in Jerusalem (Acts 20: 22) echoes the feeling of Rom. 15: 31.

11. A nautical mile is 6080 feet (1853.2 m) in contrast to the 5280 feet of a statute mile. A knot is one nautical mile per hour.

12. *Barrington Atlas*, maps 56 and 61.

13. On the speed of ancient ships, see L. Casson, *Ships and Seamanship in the Ancient World* (Princeton: Princeton University Press, 1971), 281–91.

14. For the majority of exegetes, Paul's discourse at Miletus was composed by Luke, who inserted it into the 'we-source'. Boismard and Lamouille, however, have shown that Luke merely amplified a brief discourse which was in fact part of the 'we-source' (*Les Actes des deux apôtres*, 2. 222; 3. 247–51).

15. *Barrington Atlas*, maps 61 and 65.

16. Ibid., maps 69 and 70.

17. A table of dates of Jewish feasts for the years AD 52–60 is given by Robert Jewett, *Dating Paul's Life* (London: SCM Press, 1979), 48.

18. The 'we-source' on which Luke has been relying to get Paul to Jerusalem breaks off at Acts 21: 19, and reappears again only at Acts 27: 1. The intervening material has a complex literary history; see Boismard and Lamouille, *Les Actes des deux apôtres*, 2. 254–9, 325–48, 370–81; 3. 257–91; and Taylor, *Les Actes des deux apôtres*, 6. 103–201. Thus, I retain as historical only the broadest outline, and the names of Roman officials.

19. This date is based on what we know of Paul's activities since his confrontation with Gallio in Corinth in the late summer of AD 51 (Acts 18: 12). It is an acceptable date according to E. Schürer, *The History of the Jewish People in the Age of Jesus Christ*, ed. G. Vermes *et al.* (Edinburgh: T. & T. Clark, 1973), 1. 465.

Notes

20. On the legal problems of Paul's 'I appeal to Caesar' (Acts 25: 12), see Taylor, *Les Actes des deux apôtres*, 6. 201–5, and the references there given.

12 The Final Years

1. Paul's journey to Rome is recounted in Acts 27: 1–28: 14. Not only do the Western and Alexandrian texts offer significantly different versions, but both show clear traces of source and editorial manipulation. Hence the generic character of my summary. For details see my *Paul: A Critical Life* (Oxford: Clarendon Press, 1996), 351–4, and Justin Taylor, *Les Actes des deux apôtres*, Études bibliques, nouvelle série 30 (Paris: Gabalda, 1996), 6. 207–66. For the route sailed, see the *Barrington Atlas of the Greek and Roman World*, ed. R. Talbert, (Princeton: Princeton University Press, 2000), map 1.

2. Luke does not tell us how Paul's sojourn in Rome ended, and scholars have debated fiercely whether Luke intended his readers to infer that Paul was executed, or that he was set free. I am convinced that 2 Timothy is authentic, and must be dated after Paul's Roman imprisonment; see my *Paul: A Critical Life*, 356–9, and my review of Howard Marshall and Philip Towner, *A Critical and Exegetical Commentary on the Pastoral Epistles*, ICC (Edinburgh: T.&T. Clark, 1999), in *Revue Biblique*, 108 (2001), 630–2. My reconstruction of what happened after Paul's liberation is an attempt to integrate all the data in 2 Tim.

3. *Barrington Atlas*, maps 44 and 45.

4. L. Casson, *Travel in the Ancient World* (London: Allen & Unwin, 1974), 196.

5. *Barrington Atlas*, maps 49 and 51.

6. *Barrington Atlas*, maps 56 and 61.

7. See John McRay, 'Miletus', in *The Anchor Bible Dictionary* (New York: Doubleday, 1992), 4. 825–6.

8. The report of Suetonius reflects these rumours: 'Once in the course of a general conversation, someone quoted the line, "When I am dead, may fire consume the earth." But Nero said that the first part of the line should read: "While I yet live," and soon converted this fancy into fact. Pretending to be disgusted by the drab old buildings and narrow, winding streets of Rome, he brazenly set fire to the city; and though a group of ex-consuls caught his attendants, armed with tow and blazing torches, trespassing on their property, they dared not interfere. He also coveted the sites of several granaries, solidly built in stone, near the Golden House; having knocked down their walls with siege-engines, he set the interiors ablaze. This terror lasted for six days and seven nights, causing many people to take shelter in monuments and tombs. . . . Nero watched the conflagration from the Tower of Maecenas, enraptured by what he called "the beauty of the flames"; then put on his tragedian's costume and sang *The Sack of Illium* from beginning to end' (*The Twelve Caesars: Nero* §38, trans. R. Graves, Penguin Classics (London: Penguin Books, 1979), 235–6.

9. *Barrington Atlas*, maps 44, 45, 49, 50, 51, 56, 61, 65.

Further Reading

Barclay, W., *The Mind of St Paul*, London: Collins/New York: Harper, 1958.

Barrett, C. K., *Paul: An Introduction to His Thought*, London: Chapman/Louisville: Westminster-Knox, 1994.

Becker, J., *Paul: Apostle to the Gentiles*, Louisville: Westminster, 1993.

Boyarin, S., *A Radical Jew: Paul and the Politics of Identity*, Berkeley: University of California Press, 1994.

Bruce, F. f., *Paul: Apostle of the Free Spirit*, Exeter: Paternoster, 1977 = *Paul: Apostle of the Heart Set Free*, Grand Rapids: Eerdmans, 1977.

Davies, W. D., *Paul and Rabbinic Judaism*, London: SPCK/Philadelphia: Fortress, 4th edn., 1981.

Dunn, J. D. G., *The Theology of Paul the Apostle*, Grand Rapids: Eerdmans, 1998.

Fitzmyer, J. A., *Paul and His Theology: A Brief Sketch*, Englewood Cliffs: Prentice Hall, 1989.

Hays, R. B., *Echoes of Scripture in the Letters of Paul*, New Haven: Yale University Press, 1989.

Hock, R. F., *The Social Context of Paul's Ministry: Tentmaking and Apostleship*, Philadelphia: Fortress, 1980.

Jewett, R., *A Chronology of Paul's Life*, Philadelphia: Fortress, 1979 = *Dating Paul's Life*, London: SCM, 1979.

Knox, J., *Chapters in a Life of Paul*, Macon: Mercer University Press, 2nd edn., 1987.

Lüdemann, G., *Paul, Apostle to the Gentiles: Studies in Chronology*, Minneapolis: Fortress, 1984.

Meeks, W. A., *The First Urban Christians: The Social World of the Apostle Paul*, New Haven: Yale University Press, 1983.

Murphy-O'Connor, J., *Becoming Human Together: The Pastoral Anthropology of St Paul*, Wilmington: Glazier, 1982.

—— *St. Paul's Corinth: Texts and Archaeology*, Collegeville: Liturgical Press, 3rd edn., 2002.

Nerey, J. H., *Paul in Other Words: A Cultural Reading of His Letters*, Louisville: Westminster, 1990.

Roetzel, C. J., *Paul: The Man and the Myth*, Edinburgh: Clark, 1999.

Sanders, E. P., *Paul*, London: Oxford University Press, 1991.

Scroggs, R., *Paul for a New Day*, Philadelphia: Fortress, 1977.

Theissen, G., *The Social Setting of Pauline Christianity*, Philadelphia: Fortress/Edinburgh: Clark, 1982.

Westerholm, S., *Israel's Law and the Church's Faith: Paul and His Recent Interpreters*, Grand Rapids: Eerdmans, 1988.

Index

Index

Index

Index